CONRAN OCTOPUS

DIARMUID GAVIN & TERENCE CONRAN

PLANTING

THE PLANTING DESIGN BOOK FOR THE TWENTY-FIRST CENTURY

conran
OCTOPUS

► The Japanese are renowned for their appreciation and celebration of plant life and nature. In the spectacular azalea gardens of Ome City, Kanto, Japan, the exhilarating summer colours of the azaleas take over from the soft pastel colours of the cherry blossoms, which grace spring.

▶ Found mainly in the remote deserts of Australia, Madagascar and Africa, the imposing baobab tree is one of our planet's oldest living relics. Mature specimens tower over the landscape reaching heights of up to 40m (130ft), creating the most distinctive landscape.

▶ Stunning Japanese simplicity uses a single species to surround this contemporary waterfall. *Rodgersia pinnata* with its richly textured leaves and feathery plumes of flowers creates interest and high impact.

Contents

▶ A picture of serenity: the Patio de Machuca, an historic courtyard that is part of the Alhambra Gardens in Granada, Spain. The ancient yew is clipped to mirror the open canopy, which provides welcome shade from the Mediterranean sun.

▶ Palms and ferns grace the skyline, and tropical climbing plants engulf a pagoda, to create a wash of lush green foliage at the Botanical Garden of Rio de Janeiro in Brazil. The garden is a dense oasis of plant life set against the backdrop of Mount Corcovado.

Influences

I grew up in the world of...

… suburban cherry trees, islands in the centre of square lawns, rockeries flooded with alpines and bedding plants. They were my first introductions to gardens – order, symmetry, colour and a yearning for rural idyll.

We lived in Rathfarnham in suburban Dublin – the purchase of a new semi-detached house was a real achievement, and conformity, in terms of its decoration, the name of the game. The house was on a brand-new road called Fairways, built on land that was once agricultural but more recently a golf course.

As family after family moved into the area, in the days before landscape contractors or garden designers, lawns were laid and trips to garden centres and nurseries arranged. Over the next five years, the winding, sloping road that led from the shopping centre to the village was softened through trees, shrubs and hanging baskets.

Across the river, which once edged the fairway, it was something different, with the remnants of a vast grand garden, Bushy Park, behind tall stone walls starting with spacious woodland of beech, lime and pines. At the bottom of a sylvan hillside, there were large ornamental ponds surrounded by groves of bamboo and mysterious roofless, stone Gothic pavilions, wallpapered with shells on the inside, complete with the carved initials of young lovers. As you climbed the 70 or so wide steps that snaked up the slope, whatever formal or flower gardens there had once been gave way to playing fields.

A grand estate divided up into a park and an education centre, my own garden and my friends' gardens, the banks of the River Dodder and the shady woodland were my playground for 15 years. Neighbours took me on Saturday trips to garden centres, where wise men smoking pipes would deliberate on the perfect plant for a chosen site, and other families would introduce me to fruit and vegetables. A variety of street trees was planted in narrow grass verges framing the road. And in the village every lamppost was adorned with hanging baskets of begonias, pelargoniums, salvias, lobelia and nasturtiums.

Those were my immediate surroundings – there was green everywhere. And everything was framed by hedges. They created lines and made boxes; they framed driveways. In fact, hedges were the big thing – griselinia, fuchsia, privet, thorny berberis, beech, Leyland cypress and rows of thujas. They were the markers of individual space, unique territories. And day after day, year after year, I would walk with my satchel on my back past every territory and gaze, in a world of my own, at the greening of suburbia.

I wasn't born into a gardening family and, although a few generations back on my mum's side a little farming was probably done, our direct predecessors had grown up with small yards to the back of their houses rather than gardens. So there was no tradition there. One may be evolving, though, as I watch my daughter help her granny tend the alpine beds.

Outside of the cosseted life of suburban Rathfarnham, we travelled a lot as a family, right the way round our small island. We climbed mountains through heather beds, walked in countless woodlands and went on coastal treks. And the plant life intrigued me, how it changed from mossy glens to blackberry-laden hedgerows. Most intriguing of all were the mysterious worlds of grasses and sand dunes that held together soft sandy coastlines and created enormous multi-level playgrounds. And, of course, there were grand gardens to be visited, great stately piles, often belonging to the Anglo-Irish or government-funded conservation bodies, with many sold or abandoned through the hard times. These grand

◄ The glass-sided cruciform studio in this garden was designed to merge into its organic surroundings, enabling the user to work and relax in an oasis of calm among plants and trees. Clusters of carex grasses and alliums sweep from front to back, and large, mushroom-shaped buxus punctuate the daisy shapes of the cobbled patio.

gardens for grand houses had less of an effect on me than the natural landscape. I was really intrigued by the beauty and diversity of this small country, from the beautiful wealthy pastureland along the east and south coasts to the rugged, stone-filled fields over to the west and north, from the megalithic tombs on the unique limestone paving of the Burren in County Clare to the miles of stone walls and unforgiving unproductive land divided into ever-decreasing squares by tenant farmers.

Looking at it all made me realize that people have always had an effect on the landscape through farming, whether simple or intensive, through creating memorials, through growing crops and, in the last few hundred years, through bringing in species from other places to create aesthetically pleasing gardens. Ireland has always been a great place to grow plants, with the mild temperatures, high rainfall and the great botanical institutions in Dublin and Belfast.

The influence on me of the Victorian garden, especially enclosed walled gardens and parkland, was very strong, even if I tried to resist it. The Industrial Revolution created a lot

of wealth, and the people who owned the great Irish estates could indulge in the gardening styles of the day. Public parks were full of vast beds of colour, either bright garish bedding plants or more subtle and intricate designs of contrasting colours of sedums and succulents. It was always the combination of structure and plant that appealed to me, so I was fascinated by redbrick walls often with hidden heating pipes and chambers within, against which trained peaches and pear trees were grown.

My first job on leaving school was in a garden shop in the centre of Dublin, which had been trading for well over 200 years. The whole city seemed to buy its supplies there. The farmers from the country would trundle up the wooden stairs to have their vegetable seeds – parsnips, turnips and carrots – carefully weighed out. Every morning, on the busy street outside, a van would pull up and unload another exotic collection of shrubs from the nursery. In season, bedding plants would arrive plucked from their beds in groups of a dozen wrapped in damp newspaper and sold for £1. After three years, I went to study at a great institution – the National Botanic Gardens in Glasnevin, north of Dublin. I wandered there for years in a playground of plants, an arboretum with majestic trees, some of course very memorable – an amazing cedar of Lebanon, a Japanese cherry laden with flowers in late spring and a swamp cypress reflected in the large lily pond.

My true joy as a gardener is that the influences are ongoing – it might be a new book I pick up in a shop or a visit to a flower show, or I may just want to turn away from a style that has consumed me and my practice for a few years. With gardens, change is always good and, of course, most gardens offer different conditions, so I am always challenged to learn. But if you love a subject, learning is easy.

Diarmuid Gavin

Most of us are lost when we have to design...

... a planting plan. This will result in choosing plants we like from a garden or a plant catalogue and putting them together in a bed and hoping they will work well. Sometimes we consider the colour scheme that will result but often we do not properly consider the soil that our selections will be planted in and rarely do we think about their seasonality or light and shade. I have had great pleasure from an acanthus, which has spread so successfully that it has completely obliterated all the other plants that I had hoped would work to create a mixed display for all seasons. Actually, I rather like its energetic rumbustiousness but it is not at all what I had planned.

So, first, know your soil, then know the seasonality of the plants you choose; know how they will balance each other; know what size they will grow to; know what colour they will be through the seasons; know if they like shade or bright sun; know how damp they like to be; know how to plant them and what additives they may like to help them flourish; know if they have to be removed for the winter and when to replant; know if you have to stake them for support against the wind; know how to train them or prune them; and know what to add if you do not have enough ground cover.

Perhaps the most complex planting issue is the living wall and the eco rooftop. I do think there is a huge future for living walls, which bring greenness to unfriendly urban landscapes. I first saw a living wall in the atrium of an office building in Toronto and have closely observed their development around the world ever since. The living wall master appears to be a Frenchman called Patrick Blanc, who has created many schemes, including the wonderful planting at the musée du quai Branly on the Left Bank in Paris.

Obviously the biggest problem in vertical planting is providing an anchor for plants to grow and develop. All sorts of wall pockets have been designed to allow this to happen. The plants also have to be irrigated gently, and thought has to be given to training the plants once they get going. Big

complex problems with new solutions are being invented all the time (*next book, Gavin?*). Living walls and rooftops are part of the future for urban landscapes.

My favourite planting is the vegetable garden. I have a drawing of the various beds and pathways, and decide where the different vegetables will be planted (remember Turnip Townshend's rotation of crops), making sure that the vertical runner beans do not overshadow the peas and that there is enough space between the peas and the broad beans to allow them to be picked easily. I also plan vertical pyramids of sweet peas and clematis so that they can enhance the whole landscape.

The garden looks very neat – rather like a rice paddy field with tiny vegetables popping out of the newly dug and raked soil, with white markers for each row of a different type of vegetable. The greenhouse is filled with trays of shooting green plants ready to be planted out when the chance of frost has abated. I love making little trenches for the first carrots and turnips, also putting small wire netting tunnels over the first shoots to keep the birds at bay.

What a huge pleasure it is when late spring arrives: tiny shoots rapidly develop into fully fledged vegetables, the fruit starts to become edible and you can spot the things that the frost has missed. Yes, we have peaches and greengages this year, plenty of currants, apples, mirabelles and even fraises du bois. But most exciting for me are the first French breakfast radishes and the first asparagus cut and pulled with a background of sweat pea blossoms. What a joy to have a beautiful and productive garden. The rows of terracotta pots for blanching rhubarb and sea kale, I find, add a sculptural seriousness to the vegetable garden.

There is a lot to know about planting, and while we hope this book will help, you should not be afraid to experiment. If you get something wrong, which happens to us all, do not be afraid to remove your wrong decisions and plant them somewhere else. There is always next year.

Terence Conran

◄ Tiered planting, with the different plants contributing at various levels, is the key to any successful border design. Here *Knautia macedonica*, making a bold splash in the foreground, is set off by the spires of the foxtail lily (*Eremurus himalaicus*) behind and the fluffy heads of *Aruncus dioicus* further back still.

▶ Softened uplighting in slowly transforming colours illuminates the daisy parasols and transforms the garden into an exciting night-time destination. A glowing seating area awaits, while a grove of multi-stemmed prunus trees instils a sense of mystery and depth to the scene.

Diarmuid Gavin and Terence Conran in conversation

What prompted you to do a book on planting?

TC We enjoyed writing *Outdoors* together and it has been a great success. We then developed the idea of doing a book on planting, a subject that I know little about but one that is fundamental to a successful garden. In reality, that is where everyone is at when they get their first garden, so it seemed a good place to start.

DG *Planting* is a book to explain and explore in simple ways through looking at the main ideas about planting. As a garden designer, I'm submerged in planting every day. In my garden business we plan and plant up gardens. It is my favourite part of the process of creating a garden. My joy in planting is continuous.

TC And with plants you never quite know what is going to happen. Even when books tell you that this or that plant grows to, say, 1.5m (5ft), it doesn't necessarily do as they say. Yours may reach 1m (3ft) or 2m (6½ft), or it will hardly perform one year and then do extraordinarily well another year, when conditions suit.

DG It's Nature. You observe as it controls. We learn to live with its oddities. Gardening can be about trying to prevent Nature controlling the conditions. The 18th-century designers of formal gardens such as André le Nôtre in France were intent on keeping Nature at bay, and showing that the rulers, the aristocrats, were more powerful. If you have enough money and enough power you can, to a large degree, control the space around you.

What is gardening about today?

DG Most people live in cities or their suburbs so the new reality is gardening in small spaces. We are influenced by beautiful great gardens, and in Ireland, the UK and Europe we have thrilling examples. But suburbia has never been adequately acknowledged for its contribution to gardening. That is one of my fascinations in terms of creating gardens. People are keen to teach kids about gardening, too. They show them how to compost stuff and generally create a more sustainable environment. But they also want all the accessories for the garden, including good furniture. They are wedded to the tradition of gardens but not necessarily to traditional gardens themselves. And they want plants that excite them.

TC People's lifestyles have changed, too, and they are living in their gardens more these days than ever before. In the last two or three years, particularly, there has been a big emphasis on wanting to grow things to eat – vegetables in particular. What they don't want are the run-of-the-mill plants on offer at most garden centre chains, and they certainly don't relish the kind of gardens that we grew up with, such as those with fiddly rockeries…

DG Talking of rockeries, we had one at the back of our garden when I was a kid, under a hawthorn tree. We'd return from every family outing to the countryside with a single stone until gradually a rockery was built in the shade of the tree and planted with alpines. It was my job to weed it.

We also had a lawn with borders all around the edge planted with blue lobelia and white alyssum. Many gardens where I grew up had a cherry tree – First Communion took place in May, when the cherry trees were in blossom, and everything looked beautiful for taking photographs!

TC In those days, I think people were influenced by what their neighbours had, and perhaps now they are becoming more influenced by what they could have, so there is a greater freedom of choice.

DG There was a period of absolute necessity in gardening during the Second World War in the Dig for Victory campaign, when a garden was a place to grow essential vegetables, and definitely a patriotic thing.

TC Of course, before that war people had been influenced by grand gardens and the likes of Gertrude Jekyll, with her famous borders. And then these grand gardens were scaled down by keen gardeners onto smaller plots, to create miniature versions.

DG Scaling down seldom works, though, and can easily result in twee plots – pretty much what happened in recent decades with Mediterranean or Japanese gardens. A lot of these styles originated from Victorian times, when plant hunters and adventurers were coming back from far-flung places or people were climbing the Matterhorn for the first time, bringing back special plants, and the vogue was to create replicas of those habitats.

TC Yes, and there was nearly always a pond in the garden as well. Perhaps that was a scaled-down version of the country-house lake.

DG Now it is much more democratic, and gardeners are not scared to think for themselves.

TC It seems to me because we use our gardens much more for outdoor activities these days and because people like to sunbathe, they prefer to have fences or screens around their gardens. They want privacy at all costs.

DG That tends to take design away from the Modernist principles of community.

TC I agree, but what about that television programme in which they took all the hedges away in the front gardens, and made the space a shared community garden? Brilliant idea, particularly for small terraced houses. It is tremendous when people can work together to create a vision for their street but, unfortunately, cars tend to occupy what used to be the front garden these days.

Why is designing with plants so important?

TC The plants flesh out the bones of the garden. It is so important to remember that the garden changes season by season and to try to create areas of interest throughout the year, rather than having one big splash just once a year. The easiest mistake with planting is to think too small. Go for generous clumps or repeating clumps of the same plants. Keep it simple and elegant as a general rule (like furniture!).

DG When you are designing a garden from scratch, it helps to include a few mature trees and shrubs. They are not cheap, but they do help to

give the garden structure when it is only in its infancy. For the gardens I design, I tend to put in mature trees and shrubs. As a result of being influenced by 'instant' makeovers on television, people don't want to wait years for results.

TC If you already have a garden but want to improve it, then again simplification is often the best solution. And make the beds of plants generous in size if needs be. Nothing looks worse than mean, little borders with too few plants scattered at intervals along them.

DG Yes, and if your garden is a bit on the boring side, you could think about injecting a bit of instant colour in summer while the perennials take time to plump up into more comely plants. But make sure it is big and bold splashes of colour, not tiddly little annuals scattered here and there.

What kinds of planting inspire you personally?

DG I am captivated by sand dunes and flowing grasses, the way they move, the colours, the light, the ripples, the undulations that occur through sand bank movement. These grasses have adventurous root systems that will travel for 20m (65ft) or more, stabilizing the sand. But with gardens and plants there's always something new to inspire. Recently I travelled around London to take photographs of the planting, and the more gaudy it was the more I enjoyed it. I saw one fantastic display with a laminated sign next to it from the owner saying she would be away for two weeks and would passers-by please water the garden for her. And also I love it when people plant in whatever they can find. I remember years ago being on holiday backpacking in Greece and seeing old olive-oil containers being used for bougainvillea. Beautiful and vibrant. And simple.

TC Yes, I enjoy that, too. I pass a pub in Southwark on my way to and from work. It has burgeoning baskets of gold coreopsis, burnt orange nasturtiums, bright blue bacopa and blue and purple petunias. The publicans must love their flowers, and it is a real invitation to drink at their pub. At Barton Court, I have planted up some really big pots with herbs – all those greens and yellows and mauves together. They look just wonderful and, being Mediterranean, they thrive on neglect…

DG … and provide instant gratification, too, as you run your hands through and release the oils and scents. Gardening is about sensual pleasure. Too much looking for the art and craft in gardening can destroy basic enthusiasm. There is too much emphasis on artifice at flower shows.

TC The silly thing about flower shows is that they are just pots of plants. It is flower arranging, not really planting.

DG I am much happier with the idea of communal gardening than competition. And from communal gardening you come to the flower clubs and local organizations with their own brand of exuberance.

TC You get some wonderfully exuberant planting in the Tuileries in Paris, but, sadly, rather less so around the front of Buckingham Palace, although the gardens at the back are fantastic. At the front it is a bit too regimented…

DG Do they take knighthoods away?!

What types of structural planting do you prefer?

TC Structural elements do need to be considered with care. At Barton Court, I planted box topiaries in the borders that flank the terrace I created around the house, to give the beds some form. They have grown far more than I ever anticipated, and I now have to work out what to do with them, as they are threatening to overwhelm the planting! And if I remove them, they will leave an unsightly gap.

DG One solution might be to grow climbers over structural supports of some kind. They look great in English cottage gardens, with clematis or roses. Even the simple slender iron poles that they use in France as supports for vines work well…

TC Everything tend to looks better in France! But they can do 'twee' as well, if you look at the civic planting in any of the tourist towns in France. Gardening is still very polite in France; they haven't gone wild yet.

DG That is true of Switzerland as well. They can have lots of rules on what may be planted, with some communes having particularly strict regulations.

TC In Switzerland, I gather, you have to construct the outline of your new house in bamboo to show that it won't obstruct the view. They tie together bamboo poles to give the height of the outline. They do it, apparently, so the neighbours know what the new structure will be like, but, in fact, you could do something similar with bamboo poles in your own garden when planting a border. You could use different stick lengths to mark the differing heights of the plants in the border…

DG … and put little coloured markers on the tops of the sticks…

◄ One of the most magnificent sights in the natural world, the lotus plant is revered worldwide. Its distinctive circular leaves sway softly in the wind above the water line and its flowers reach for the sky all through the summer months. It has spread across the globe for ornamental reasons as well as being important as a food crop.

TC … apart from a few green shoots of early spring bulbs and hellebores… and we get a lot of January snowdrops at Barton Court and a small field of narcissi in March or perhaps February, if we are lucky…

DG … and then growth starts to pick up in March or April with a host of bulbs like daffodils, tulips and scillas, followed by wallflowers and irises. Summer is obviously the peak time in the garden but the light in September and October is terrific, as the sun is lower in the sky and slants through the soft golden-coloured grasses, for example. I love autumn because this is when you do most of your planting for the following year.

TC That is what designing for planting is all about. Making sure you make the most of the seasons. Even in winter, when there is nothing much in the garden, a single witch hazel will catch your eye as it blooms on bare branches, and you will really notice the scent.

DG I think people are now prepared to create places in their gardens that are a haven for wildlife. Because of intensive farming, the garden is now the last refuge for so much wildlife. An indigenous species will house about 300 other life forms. People now are tending to go more for single flowers than for fancy doubles, which are more insect friendly, and they are trying to achieve a better balance for ecosystems and sustainability. People are beginning to realize that being a gardener is an obligation to others as well as yourself.

TC I have huge patches, almost plantations, of nettles, because I am keen on butterflies and I know that they need nettles. But you don't have to have plantations of nettles or other wild plants in smaller gardens – just a corner will do the trick.

What kinds of textural plants do you like?

TC There are very different kinds of texture. For example, the delicate, toothed leaf structure of nettles is just right in an informal setting, but I also love big leaves, such as those on architectural plants such as banana plants (*Musa*) and huge gunneras – but clumps of slender-leaved bamboos look good too.

DG Beth Chatto's gunneras in her Damp Garden, in Essex, backlit by the sun, look great. London town gardens, though, can even house some big subtropical plants now, and more and more people are able to grow Mediterranean plants these days in cool-temperate climates. Someone was writing last week in a magazine that ten years ago you would never consider growing olive trees in London but you can now.

TC True. I recently bought three old ones for the roof of The Boundary restaurant in London, and these potted trees do overwinter fine, whereas a while back they would not have done.

DG Yes, and if you plant on terraces you do need the right containers. There are some great, really big, round planters, like platters, made of reinforced concrete which are great for plants without deep roots, like little bulbs or saxifrages. I have some big planters that are like shallow bowls, which came from the Festival of Britain in 1951, and I have successfully filled them with lots of scillas. As a student, I used to plant them up with wallflowers…

TC … which smell delicious. But those big planters are ideal for edible gardens on roof terraces, too.

TC … or even coloured balls, like the lollipops you did for your [2003] Chelsea Flower Show garden! I certainly haven't got my planting completely right at Barton Court! But at least enough is right to keep my interest going. In years when we have a lot of rain, it is so exciting as everything becomes a complete jungle.

DG Isn't it just great when the plants aren't under stress? We have had so many water shortages in recent years. I planted 11 huge silver birch trees, really large specimens, in my new garden. They act as a kind of curtain at the front of the house, which you peer through to the hills beyond.

What are the effects of climate and season?

TC Well, the climate obviously influences your planting…

DG … and you see the planting colours differently, as the light changes quite dramatically. The way you respond to a lavender hedge in Provence, for example, is so different from the way it would look in England.

TC *Vive la différence!* We want the seasonal changes; sometimes a quiet period and sometime one of much greater contrast. It's like the seasonality of food. You need the seasonal variation to appreciate what is on offer at different times of the year.

DG As a gardener, the changing seasons affect your emotional state. February is the most miserable time because it's grey and gloomy, and very little appears to be happening outside…

What about family gardens?

DG Isn't it interesting – we missed out teaching a whole generation of children gardening? In the old days, you had kids learning from their grandparents because the parents needed to work – but now kids are at it again. There is a new sense of responsibility because now parents and schools rightly regard it as essential education.

TC The RHS have set up some excellent programmes for children around the UK. Children love it if they can have a tiny patch of their own to grow radishes or anything that grows big, like sunflowers or runner beans.

DG My interest was started off by my Cub-Scout badge, growing cress on cotton wool…

TC … or an old flannel…

DG … and once I had seen seeds germinate in a couple of days, I was hooked.

TC It is certainly a good idea to give children their own special areas, and let them play in sandpits (which you probably need to cover in towns) and in dens under shrubs and trees. And kids love playing with water too, although you have to be so careful, as a small child can drown in even a few centimetres of water.

How can people improve their planting skills?

DG Most gardens contain the same 200 species because the garden centres tend to stock all the same plants, so if you visit only garden centres, it will be hard to develop more interesting planting schemes. But if you go to a plant nursery, it is heaven because there are so many varieties and species to choose from, all exciting in different ways.

TC That is the trouble with most people's planting: they visit a garden centre and pick up one plant of each kind – a geranium or fuchsia or something already in flower – and make their decision there and then about how their border will look. They need to plan a bit more in advance, and think in terms of planting in groups, plus they need to consider the different heights more carefully. But it is hard to work out a border plan with tall plants at the back if you don't know what size the plants will eventually grow to. In this book, we give advice on what to plant, and how to plant.

DG It helps, too, if everyone admits they make mistakes and they are brave enough to move plants if they get it wrong. Beth Chatto is such a wonderful example of someone who experiments continually in finding the right place for the plant as well as the right plant for a particular spot. Her exuberance and her ability to deal with site and soil type, as well as her endless quest to extend her knowledge of plants and planting, are very inspiring.

TC The Elizabeth David of the plant world!

DG Indeed, but she also possesses a humility that a lot of plant people don't have and a really lovely way of going about showing you what should be done.

TC She has never stopped developing her garden. She also makes you realize that it is a growing, evolving process, not a finite solution.

DG Some people become interested in plants because they can't get on with people. They relate to their Latin names, with a lot of showing off and snobbery, but Beth Chatto would personify the opposite to that. Her gardening friend Christopher Lloyd and his head gardener, Fergus

Garrett, were also brilliant, as is Derry Watkins, whose speciality at her nursery is dark foliage and flowers.

TC I think we need to encourage people to go on garden visits. We are awash with great gardens in the British Isles.

DG And abroad – in Italy, you find some fantastic formal gardens that aren't overrun with tourists so that you can have them almost to yourself.

What lessons do you hope people will take from this book?

TC That they have more of an understanding about how to design with plants. I understand about the design of the garden but I still do not yet know enough about the behaviour of plants or indeed the soils that are required.

DG We also want to look at the possibilities around the world. Through the book, I would like to look at beautiful, sumptuous pictures of planting schemes, so readers can realize what the gardener was up to, analyzing very simply what they were trying to achieve, by showing how to work with soil, local conditions, aspect and the raw materials.

TC If you look after the soil, your work is halved. The physical act of planting is so important, making sure that you have given a plant a good start, so that the roots can establish themselves properly. You need to understand how the roots function, so the nutrients and oxygen are available to the plant. Clay, for example, has wonderful nutrients but these are locked away and you have to make them available.

DG Knowing how to dig properly is important.

TC Yes, and the benefits of making compost, like leaf compost…

DG … and teaching people not to cart off waste plant matter to landfill sites, where it makes methane gas. It's also important they learn not to go against the prevailing conditions. If you have gravelly soil, go and look at gardens where they have made a success of gravel gardens for inspiration.

TC You need to understand what your plants require in terms of planting. In the big storms of 1987 in southern England, it was obvious that some plants were not anchored properly and came down as a result.

DG But there was a benefit to the damage of '87, as it gave gardeners a chance to replant and opened up some new vistas.

TC My own trouble was that my house was built in 1772, and a lot of the trees were old and had come to the end of their useful life. It is very sad to see huge beech trees coming down.

DG Gardeners have a duty to look after their trees, as they form such a major element in the landscape and are of such major importance to wildlife, too.

What single piece of wisdom would you pass on to a gardener about to embark on their own planting scheme?

TC Put together a collection of plants you really like. Think about their colour and smell, and the scale of the individual plants. Don't be afraid to root them out and replace them if they don't add up to the display you and the butterflies love. Think in the same way that an artist thinks when painting a still life – balance of form, mass and colour with intriguing detail.

DG Planting is a big learning curve; it never ends. That is why it continues to fascinate. Be bold. Be adventurous. Above all, have fun!

◄ The Echium genus is remarkable for its architectural foliage and incredible for its magnificent blooms. *Echium candicans* is a wonderful feature shrub with a robust, rounded habit. It bears great numbers of dense, spiky blue flower panicles that introduce powerful drama and texture to a garden scheme.

► A meandering river of lawn reflects the snaking grass mounds that are the main feature of this garden. Silver birch trees punctuate the space and form a connection with the surrounding landscape. The planting unrolls in shades of green, changing in form and texture.

Context

|||| The context of your garden is important to consider, whether you have a blank canvas or an existing garden within which you wish to develop new features. In the case of the latter, the rest of the garden and how this new planting will sit within it need consideration. With a blank canvas you can look to the wider context within which your entire garden sits.

Where a garden is set in the natural landscape, you can make use of the 'borrowed landscape', such as opening vistas to view distant trees or rolling hills. In this context, the landscape can be further blended by mirroring some of the neighbouring plants or trees, depending on the scale of your garden. As most people live primarily in urban situations, any opportunity to take advantage of a borrowed landscape is quite rare. However, there may still be views you can adopt, such as a large tree in a neighbour's garden, or a nearby park.

Different localities, too, can have different microclimates, rainfall, flora and fauna. When considering the greater context, think about how your garden will fit into the local environment – is your garden part of a wildlife corridor made up of a number of urban gardens? Ultimately, the context of your garden is important from the perspective of your life, your intended use of the garden and your own taste.

Planting Tactics

Choosing plants for your garden can seem a mammoth task when you look at all the factors that can influence their success and that of your vision for your garden. The key is to plan one step at a time, and the first place to start is with you. Is there a certain plant you always wanted to grow, or an idea you have wanted to try out? Think about your favourite plants, or whether you have a preferred style that you want to come through in the planting. Do you plan to grow some of the plants yourself? If you are a keen gardener and intend to include perennials and annuals, you could grow these from seed. Is your garden to be a useful space, a beautiful space, or both?

When you have made an exhaustive list of your desires, you can then narrow it down based on the reality of your garden. Consider your soil type and acidity, and take clues from your neighbour's garden as to what plants do well in the area. You will need to place plants according to light levels and aspect too. Think about climatic issues that affect your garden such as rainfall, or lack of it.

Initial questions

Picture yourself in the finished garden and consider how much you will use it. Do you intend to eat outside a lot and perhaps entertain friends? Perhaps near this patio is where you should plant scented flowers, especially those that are strongly fragrant in the evening. Are you going to grow your own vegetables? If so, you need to site the plot correctly for sun, shelter and services. If you like to attract birds to your garden, you may want to plant food sources, such as berried plants, close to where you can watch them foraging. To encourage further wildlife, think about plants to entice bees and butterflies, as well as considering a whole area of wildflowers or native plants (see page 50). You may simply want the garden to be your own haven in which to unwind after a long day or week at work. Perhaps create a seating area, or a secluded spot for a hammock, surrounded by plants that will gently sway or create a soothing sound in the wind, such as bamboo.

Another major consideration is children. If you are creating a garden for adults and children, then your planting will be restricted to safe and non-poisonous plants (see page 76).

Flexible approach

As you and your children grow, the garden will mature with you. This is another facet of your planting tactics to think about. A garden is never a finished product. It is constantly growing, changing and evolving. Plant your garden knowing that some borders will take longer than others to mature to eventual height, and that some features will look their best just at the time when the football nets are being put away for good, clearing the view. Also, allow yourself room to manoeuvre. It is easier to change your mind about whether you think a certain shrub is working, or not, if you buy an inexpensive, young specimen as opposed to a very costly, mature one.

◀ Dark evergreen trees and shrubs enclose this garden to produce an invitingly tranquil setting. The areas have been divided to include dining and play areas, but the sprawling blocks of grass and aged wooden sleepers soften the lines of definition. The limited use of materials and colour has produced a harmonious scene.

◄ A raised marble terrace displays an array of bamboos and specimen palms. The bridge over the rectangular pond invites the eye into the space, but the tropical plants – *Trachycarpus fortunei, Phyllostachys vivax* f. *aureocaulis, Yucca rostrata,* agapanthus and *Agave americana* – are what set the exotic scene.

Plant Provenance

Many of us do not realize that the majority of the plants seen in gardens and in garden centres are from far-flung corners of the globe. Plant hunters have been travelling the world taking extraordinary risks for centuries, to bring back new and exotic plants. Initially, of course, the focus of these expeditions was on plants for use as food and medicine. The expeditions were often commissioned by botanic gardens, not least of these the Royal Botanic Gardens at Kew, UK. Soon British nurserymen began to send their own plant hunters to find new plants for garden use or to travel themselves, as did the famous Tradescants – hence the genus name *Tradescantia*.

An important part of the plant hunter's bounty was the information brought with the new plant. Details such as the soil type in which the plant grew and the climatic conditions of the area, as well as altitude and associated species in the wild, were vital. They gave the nurserymen a fighting chance when it came to growing their precious new specimen and propagating it successfully in order to introduce it to the market.

It is no wonder that many plants introduced from the South Island in New Zealand, for example, are so successful in the British Isles, as the climate and topography are quite similar. New Zealand natives such

◀ Naturalistic planting of self-sown annuals – purple cleome, red orach, orange signet marigolds, purple petunias, verbena, *Bassia scoparia* and assorted amaranthus – are rich in depth and colour. They completely engulf the house and meld with the vegetation of the distant hills.

▼ Sumptuous purple lavender and rolling hedges of topiary decorate this coastal garden that gently ebbs out towards the sea. The lines of definition start to blur as the garden gradually merges with its natural surroundings in a seamless finish.

▼ The upright strap leaves of purple iris plants are striking in clumps of single species and create ordered lines in a border that reflects the definition of the building and white stone paving. A white-barked tree further complements the architectural lines and formality of the space.

as *Phormium tenax* are very common garden choices in coastal areas of the British Isles, and one of the most popular suggestions for a seaside hedge or shelter belt is *Olearia traversii*. Common sense must prevail when you choose the plants for your garden. If you are in western Scotland, a Mediterranean garden is not for you, as the drought-loving Mediterranean plants would drown in the high summer rainfall. Similarly, on dry, well-drained soil in the southeast of either England or Ireland, moisture-loving plants from the Himalayas will curl up their toes. Be a nosy neighbour. Look around your area and note what plants are successful. Take inspiration from your

holidays if you are travelling somewhere with a climate similar to your own. And have a look at the native plants of your region – there are probably some beauties that you did not even realize were native. Be sure to source them from a garden centre, and never dig up a plant in the wild – even if it looks like there are hundreds of them.

Choosing native plants or those from comparable climes will increase your chances of growing them successfully. There is a lot of work involved in growing plants in the wrong conditions, as any fan of alpine gardening will tell you. If you choose wisely at the start, you will save yourself time and money.

Rooted in the Landscape

This garden is situated in Sun Valley, Idaho, in the USA, adjacent to a nature reserve that sweeps into the residential site. The restored natural habitat extends the garden far out into the distant landscape. Outdoor living spaces create fascinating transitions between the house and the open space, carving out shape and form within this beautiful ecosystem. In rural settings, it is often the case that the native landscape is appreciated from the house at a distance, but the inspiration of this garden by Ron Lutsko, Jr., was to reach out to the adjacent ecology, blur the property lines and invite it into the residential landscape.

The residence is located in a scenic and rugged valley with a high desert climate and only 38cm (15in) of precipitation annually. The valley is far enough north to receive up to 15 hours of sun in the summer, but it also experiences harsh winters. These conditions have encouraged a unique ecosystem and a diverse array of native wildflowers and perennials that adorn the rolling landscape with colour in summer.

The garden building takes the form of a wall that is folded and wrapped, creating pavilions that open into the surrounding landscape, capturing views of near and distant mountains. There are formalized spaces for gathering and entertaining, a series of smaller building courtyards and an outdoor living space to the rear of the property that faces the hillside.

At the front of the house, shallow-stepped terraces lead to the street. Their steel edges extend as low walls

▲ A series of shallow-stepped stone terraces edged with corten steel leads to the main entrance of the house. The surrounding beds are packed with blocks of single species. These block plantings make strong connections with the larger native landscape and also harmonize with the house.

▶ A section of corten steel wall rises out of the naturalistic planting that engulfs the house. Shrubs are allowed to spill over into the open terraces and trees provide vertical lines that connect the construction with the surrounding trees and hills. Shrubs include *Prunus viginiana*, *Philadelphus lewisii* and *Amelanchier* x *grandiflora*.

▲ The lines blur between the residential and distant landscape due to the selection of a native plant palette. The plants will need no irrigation in order to thrive in their native conditions. Impact in controlled beds has been achieved by concentrating on mass planting.

◄ The garden and its buildings moderate the transitions between the wild and the domestic landscapes. Large mirrored windows and doors reflect the beauty of the surrounding mountain views and enable the building to completely immerse with it. Incredibly, the stark corten steel walls are totally softened by the plants, their now hazy lines gently drawing the eye back to the minimal architecture.

CONTEXT

CASE STUDY #1 CONTINUED

RON LUTSKO GARDEN
IDAHO, USA

DESIGNER
RON LUTSKO, JR.

▼ The corten steel edges of the stepped terraces extend out as low walls that form flower beds. Blocks of native plants include *Geranium caespitosum, Phlox longifolia, Machaeranthera bigelovii* and *Lomatium nudicaule* against a deep green background of *Elymus condensatus* grass clumps.

► The main construction takes the form of a wall that folds and wraps, enclosing spaces to produce a series of smaller courtyards. These partially open spaces create shelter while engaging with the wild landscape through planting and natural light. A warm tranquillity is achieved.

into single-species beds, which establishes a wonderful transition between the hard landscape and its surroundings. The walls also extend beyond the beds into the meadow, maintaining their height as the ground drops away. Two pavilions, paved with stone and enclosing lawn areas with low walls, also reach into the meadows.

The native plant palette, chosen to be in harmony with the surrounding landscape, also serves the garden's dependence on irrigation in summer and increases the biodiversity of the space as a habitat for local wildlife.

The planting has been zoned into controlled beds and open area mixtures of plants, but all reflect and embrace the natural landscape. By selecting indigenous plants, the garden will not need irrigation or feeding, and the plants will naturally look their best. The beds adjacent to the building comprise large blocks of grasses and perennials, which include white *Melampodium leucanthum* daisies, the golden pea-like flowers of *Thermopsis rhombifolia*

var. *montana* and miniature *Delphinium depauperatum* in the deepest blue. The ground is filled with carpet-forming *Geranium caespitosum, Sphaeralcea coccinea* and bright pink *Dodecatheon pulchellum*. Fine purple *Allium brevistylum, Phlox longifolia* and *Thalictrum occidentale* create wonderful vertical accents and colour.

The open areas around the garden are awash in spring with fine white *Galanthus elwesii, Fritillaria purdyi* and many species of crocus and iris. Summer temperatures see the planting transform: blocks of *Elymus condensatus* and *Festuca idahoensis* grasses are joined by deep purple *Salvia azurea*, spires of creamy white *Zigadenus elegans* and fine blue *Camassia quamash*. Shrubs – *Philadelphus lewisii, Prunus virginiana* and flowering species, *Syringa vulgaris* and *Ribes aureum* – are used to soften the hard landscaping. Various varieties of Japanese acer punctuate the garden, while towering poplar trees blend in with the surrounding mountain views.

► The pale yellow flowers of *Lomatium nudicaule* and *Thermopsis rhombifolia* var. *montana* frame the scene of an open courtyard. The rusty brown colour of the corten steel is echoed in the simple furniture and architecture. Huge mirrored windows draw in the landscape so that the building is almost submerged into the distant views and planted flower meadows.

► **Ron Lutsko Garden**

1 Driveway
2 Gravel entry terrace
3 Stepped entry terrace
4 Shade planting beds
5 Garage
6 Residence
7 Chaparral plantings
8 Guest bedroom courtyard
9 Master bathroom terrace

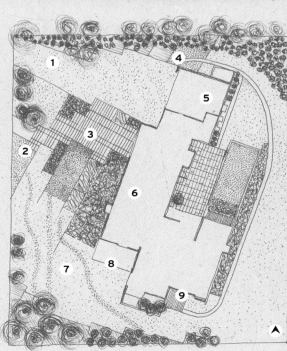

Locality

Put simply, aspect is the direction in which your garden faces, and it is very important when you come to planting. Not only does it determine what plants will succeed in certain parts of the garden but it will also influence the positioning of certain features. One way to determine aspect is by observation, knowing that the sun rises in the east and sets in the west. Or you can simply use a compass. A garden that is south-facing always seems to be the most desired, as it will be filled with sunshine from spring to autumn. Keep in mind that you will still have some shady areas. In fact, you may wish to create some shade if you do not want to sit in full sun all summer. At the other end of the spectrum is the north-facing garden. Well, it is not all bad: if the garden is long enough, the sunny part will simply be at the end, and you can design the seating area here, and choose your plants accordingly. It may mean you cannot grow all those exotic plants you wanted, so be creative with the shade-lovers.

A west-facing and an east-facing garden are similar to each other, with the former getting the morning sun at the end of the garden and the afternoon and evening sun by the house, and the latter vice versa. Spring-flowering shrubs, such as camellias, are best not planted where they will face morning sun, as it can destroy slightly frosted flower buds before they open in spring.

Type of soil

The soil in your garden will also determine what plants will thrive. Different types hold different amounts of nutrients and vary in moisture content (see page 250). Moist but well-drained, fertile soil is the ideal, but you may need to do some work to achieve it. A dark, friable loam

is every gardener's dream: when you roll a damp handful together it will stick and form a ball initially but, when you tap it, falls asunder. A sandy soil is free draining and suitable for plants such as cistus, lavender, some salvias and crambe. You can broaden the spectrum of plants available to you by digging some organic matter into sandy soil, which will help with moisture retention and add the vital nutrients often leached easily from sandy soils. Plants such as lilacs, philadelphus, primulas and ligularias grow well on clay soils. Again, the addition of organic matter will open up the soil a little and help stop it baking in summer, as well as broadening the spectrum of plants you can grow.

The pH of your soil will determine whether you will be able to grow acid-loving plants such as rhododendrons, or if you should stick to the neutral to alkaline end of the spectrum. Use a soil-testing kit to test the pH in your garden (see page 250).

Sun and shade

Choosing the right plants for full sun or for a shady border is also vital. There are a number of sun-lovers that tolerate semi-shade, but a shade-loving plant placed in full sun will soon scorch and often show symptoms similar to nutrient deficiency. This is not because of a lack of food; it is simply that many shade-lovers have less chlorophyll in their leaves and full sun can send them into overdrive, often resulting in photosynthesis simply shutting down. Similarly a plant evolved to grow in full sun needs the high light levels to keep photosynthesis at the level the plant requires. If it cannot make enough food, it cannot thrive, will discolour and eventually die. Take a walk in a forest for some shady inspiration, and make notes on your next sun holiday for plants to place by your south-facing patio.

▲ Great borders brim with hot planting in shades of yellow, orange and red, picking up the colour of the main house and creating a floriferous journey to the upper terraced lawn. Architectural phormiums and mounding grasses ensure a long season of interest in this garden.

◄ An intense planting palette in shades of green has matured so that it almost obscures this large picture window, bringing the outside in and painting the most wonderful picture of nature for this room. The clean white outdoor wall forms a connection with the contemporary decoration inside.

◄ Oleanders, giant ferns, palms and tropical climbing plants define this exotic jungle garden, which is filled with mystery and exuberance. Small garden huts are hidden in the trees, and relaxing day beds are positioned to be in the soft shade of the foliage canopy.

Scale and Climate

When devising your planting plan, always bear in mind the scale of your garden and surrounding features. A small city garden that is overlooked can use clever tricks such as a pergola, trellis or wall with climbers to create a private area, but the remaining planting within the space should be in scale with the space itself. Although borrowed views are useful (see page 27), always be conscious of how much you open up the view according to the size of the garden. The last thing you want to do is make the garden feel like a viewing platform. Some seclusion is needed to establish your garden's own identity.

The sense of proportion in your garden is often created by the hard landscaping features, such as pathways and patios. Plants contribute further to this, especially if you intend to include trees. Research well to ensure the trees you choose will not grow too large. Proportion remains a vital consideration, too, when deciding on the size of drifts or blocks of plants if you are using block planting to create a modern look in the garden.

The topography surrounding your garden will also impact on the decisions you make, as it can affect the localized climate – certainly a factor to keep in mind when planting. A dip or valley may create a sheltered microclimate, whereas an exposed hillside may require the addition of a shelter belt in your garden. Gardens in dips can also be frost pockets, that is, areas of low-lying land where, during freezing weather, cold air will settle

◄ Conspicuous-looking rounded tree forms and mounding shrubs offer contrast to the straight lines of the building. The plants not only soften the architecture but also bring character and drama to a space that may otherwise be quite uneventful.

► A rectangular stretch of a stone pond cools this hot garden as it reaches out to the mountain views in the distance. The still water mirrors the hot and dry planting that fills the foreground, opening the garden to the greater landscape. A specimen cactus creates focus and connects with the lines of the building.

◀ A mixture of native and alien plants has been combined to match the local climate. A border of phormium, lavender, euphorbia, crocosmia, oenothera, curry plant, *Verbena bonariensis*, agapanthus and ozothamnus adorn this attractive garden site. They are all plants that thrive in harsh coastal conditions.

▼ This residential rooftop garden is divided into usable spaces by blocks of evergreen phormium, buxus and rosemary in stainless steel planters that complement the architecture. The garden merges into a cityscape of sports fields and modern buildings, opening the views and enlarging the space.

causing a hard frost. Even on a smaller scale still, an area at the bottom of a slope can attract frost, while the rest of the garden may escape the frost altogether. Due to the saline conditions, planting near the sea will reduce the palette of plants from which you can choose but, again, a shelter belt could help to broaden it a little.

▏▏▏▏ Climatic considerations

Although a couple of wet summers in succession are not a convincing argument, on a large timescale the climate is changing, and with warm, dry summers come water shortages and hosepipe bans. It makes sense, then, to plant some drought-tolerant plants, which will require little or no watering, even in a warm summer. The changing climate also means you can take more risks with plants traditionally not hardy in your garden. You should not, however, throw caution to the wind entirely – you must wrap more tender subjects in fleece, but this is a small price to pay if these are the plants that catch your eye.

▏▏▏▏ Alien plants

It is important to be aware of plants that have become invasive weeds in your area. The classic example is *Rhododendron ponticum*, which is an invasive weed in many parts of the British Isles. Ask at your local garden centre, or a gardening neighbour, for advice. In addition, do some research on plants native to your region. Native plants support more native wildlife, and help to keep a balance of pest and predator. They are sure to grow well in your garden too.

An Affinity with Nature

▲ Although rickety, a simple wooden bridge over a rectangle of still water doubles as a waterside terrace. Hydrangea bushes, weeping tree branches and arching grasses enclose the space to create a tranquil spot for reflection.

▶ A beautiful Japanese acer, in all its autumn glory, illuminates the garden in bright yellow. Its golden light reflected in the water accentuates the yellow pond grasses and water lilies.

◄ The garden appears to melt into the borrowed landscape beyond with no visible boundaries. The mounding grasses that soften the aged cobblestones dissolve into the many levels of the landscape's rolling hills, which are adorned with a forest of deciduous trees.

▼ Purple liatris, verbena and fluffy grass flowerheads of miscanthus dance together in a sunny glade in this sparkling feathery meadow. Golden tufts of *Stipa gigantea* glisten in the sunlight against a green foil of shrubs and trees.

This is a hillside garden with a difficult steep terrain. The objective throughout the site was to create comfortable movement for people, relatively gentle walks and level terraces. The Italians were masters of this for amenity use, stepping landscapes and embracing gravity through gushing water and fountains, and the aristocracy used the levels of a garden as they did the levels of the villa or palace – however far up you were on the social ladder could indicate the level of terrace you were allowed access to. People have often made sloping sites accessible for other reasons – think of the paddy fields in China where water is the great leveller.

But this garden is different. The designers had no such agricultural needs or social requirements. A gentle hand has crafted this garden so it fits into its environment rather than dominates it. A good eye and an innovative use of hard material, as well as water, have laid the foundations for its success. Combining these with unexpected planting has been the key to this gorgeous retreat.

The requirements were to design a series of usable spaces, destinations within the garden, and then – rather than overly manage the area – to work with the site and allow the plants to conjure up or enhance the mood and to make a direct link with the sylvan borrowed landscape.

The overall feel is green. Indeed, almost subtropical. Many of the choices for the planting are brought alive by shafts or speckles of strong sunlight. It is a large area, divided by walkways, but even these are made from green turf carpets. And where intervention with hard materials has been required to provide terraces, pool edges or bridges, these have been dictated by their affinity with nature. Steel has been used, but its rusting colour gives a type of burnt-earth effect. Slabs of granite have been randomly set to form a large space of rectangular paving,

their sombreness wonderfully lifted by invading hairy tufts of deep green grasses. A repeating use of slats of weathered wood creates platforms and an unusual jetty bridge on two levels that becomes a tranquil waterside terrace complete with a weathered wooden chair – the perfect spot for contemplation adjacent to the calming still water. Tall arching grasses and great white hydrangea bushes fill the background, while *Gunnera magellanica* and *Pontaderia cordata* edge the pond.

One area is given over to a very English scene: a meadow of daisies and salmon-coloured foxgloves. But elsewhere in this Spanish garden, bright yellow rudbeckia with their distinctive brown centres stretch up to greet the sun's rays. Edge of woodland planting includes rhododendrons, while further up the ramped grass pathways *Dicksonia antarctica* spreads its fronds like lime-green peacock plumes. White nicotianas grow through wild native grasses on a steep bank, while another meadow unfolds in a mass of verbena, liatris and miscanthus.

Oiartzun is a serene place, and the mix of plants will be familiar to garden owners from many different climatic zones. It feels just perfect.

▼ An exquisite marginal plant, *Equisetum hyemale* in shades of green stands tall against the planting. The outline of the concrete pond is successfully softened by rounded evergreen shrubs, mature trees and large grasses, which fill the scene.

◄ Fluffy tufts of grass bring life to the white granite patio and create an inviting destination point in the soft shade of a weeping tree. Privacy is achieved by tall grasses, ferns and shrubs that enclose the space. A statement oval pond is wonderful as an understated architectural feature.

▼ Soft yellow miscanthus grasses are planted to complement the golden landscaping of the rectangular pond. This natural mirror is painted with the outlines of overhanging tree branches that conjure up beautiful silhouettes in the still water.

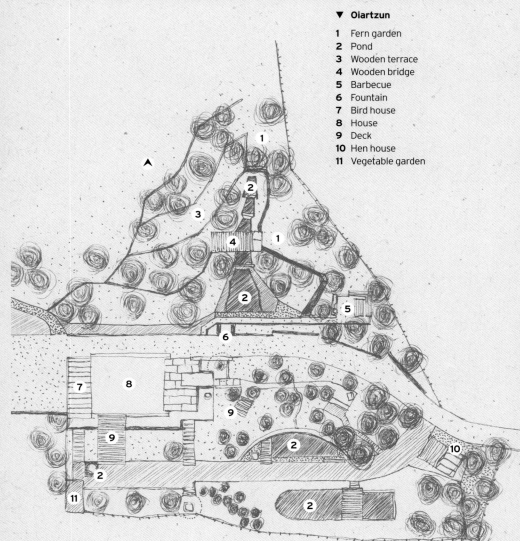

▼ **Oiartzun**

1 Fern garden
2 Pond
3 Wooden terrace
4 Wooden bridge
5 Barbecue
6 Fountain
7 Bird house
8 House
9 Deck
10 Hen house
11 Vegetable garden

► The horizontal line of the main building sets the mood in this stunning modern garden, cutting across the upright trees that form its backdrop. The towering poplar trees dwarf the building, pushing it down into the garden where its proportions are echoed in the grass-covered land forms, terraces and rectangular pool.

► The coneflower (*Echinacea*) is a great perennial, much loved by bees. It looks particularly striking when planted in huge drifts, with its curiously dome-shaped central stamens and slightly reflexed daisy-like petals.

Purpose

|||||| To get the best from your garden, and your planting, it pays to think about both your own needs and your responsibilities to the environment. Everyone has differing requirements and these tend to change over time. Your garden, and the plants you choose, should reflect your lifestyle choices as closely as possible, as well as your dreams and aspirations. The shape and size of your plot have some bearing on what you plant, but even the smallest town patios can offer an area for sitting and relaxing, with a few pots to grow herbs and vegetables, and a few choice small, flowering (and, ideally, scented) shrubs or perennials, and some climbers scrambling up the walls and fences. In suburban or bigger country gardens, the same principles apply but on a grander scale, providing the opportunity to 'compartmentalize' the garden according to the different kinds of activity or need, with perhaps a patio near the house, a kitchen garden at one end, a lawned area with a wildflower meadow beyond, a pond to benefit local wildlife, and various beds and borders filled with shrubs or perennials.

Design Considerations

Anyone planning a garden needs to think, first and foremost, about how they want to use the garden and the particular benefits they hope to gain from it. Those who slavishly copy other designs without much regard to their own requirements will be doomed to disappointment. Another factor to be taken into account is the need to keep some element of flexibility in the overall plan. Needs change with time! Spending a fortune on hard landscaping only to discover a few years later that you require a lawn for young children to play on is frustrating, not to mention expensive. Visual interest at a higher level is also important. A carefully chosen small tree, positioned away from the house, can add a great feature to the garden, offer shade in summer and also a variety of planting conditions in an otherwise unshaded garden, allowing you to include some woodland plants that flourish in semi-shade.

Many good garden plans have designated areas for different activities, linked together by the overall planting scheme. It makes sense for the hard landscaping to be closest to the house, as this is the area where you might choose to relax and possibly eat out of doors, although a lot depends on the aspect of your garden. If the sunny part of the garden is furthest away from the house, then an additional paved area there will make the best use of the available warmth.

In urban areas, where space is in short supply, consider installing some garden lighting, so you can use the garden at night for entertaining. Lighting can play an important part in emphasizing features in your garden such as shapely trees. It also acts to some extent as a safety element because intruders are less keen to cross well-lit areas.

▶ **Great textural contrasts never fail to catch the eye. The delicate arching flowers of _Gaura lindeimeri_ catch the light like dancing butterflies against the uncompromisingly modern decked roof terrace.**

▼ **Even small gardens can offer a little corner for wildlife, ideally by providing some nectar-rich species plants. Here, a traditional beehive nestles among phlomis, with its little yellow flowers, and euphorbias, with their showy greenish bracts.**

Wider considerations

In recent times, almost everyone has become increasingly aware of the pressure on the planet and of the needs of wildlife. Gardeners collectively can play a vital role in improving the chances of wildlife survival: by selecting the best plants for nectar; by trying to ensure that they include plants that offer berries and seeds in autumn and winter; by creating shelter for birds in shrubs and hedges; by including a small pond in the garden; by avoiding the use of chemicals whenever possible; and, perhaps, by giving over a bit more space to plants rather than opting for too much hard surfacing.

Equally, it really can pay dividends to start growing your own produce. You do not need a massive vegetable plot. An impressive range of edible plants can be grown very successfully in pots on a patio with relatively little effort. Even fruit trees these days are bred in more miniature forms so they, too, can be container grown.

Herbs are easy to cultivate, and many of them are good insect magnets, too. Bees love lavender, which makes an excellent low hedge to mark out a small vegetable plot, for example. Pots of herbs cope well with dry conditions, on the whole, and a few pots on the patio, balcony or kitchen windowsill are a huge bonus for any keen cook.

◀ A canopy of purple-flowered wisteria provides welcome shade, as well as some wonderful scent, in an inviting terrace in San Francisco.

▼ In a Suffolk country garden, a woven willow vessel establishes an unusual focal point at the end of a living willow tunnel over a patch of grass.

Importance of Wildlife

Gardens are, increasingly, a refuge for wildlife, as more of our landscape falls to the developers' bulldozers, and gardeners now have an increasing responsibility to play their part in the preservation of species that might otherwise die out. Climate change contributes to the loss of many of them, and an increasingly monocultural agriculture significantly adds to the problem, but you can certainly help in many ways in your garden to lessen the impact by choosing as wide a variety of plants as possible.

It is surprisingly easy to do your bit, and does not involve hard work. Where you can, choose plants that provide winter food for birds as well as summer flowers for nectar for bees and other insects. Many shrubs have attractive and plentiful winter berries. If you plant a hedge – particularly what is known as a tapestry hedge comprising different kinds of shrubs with different flowering and berrying times – you provide a wonderful natural larder for a whole host of insects, butterflies, bees and birds. In addition, the foliage offers nesting and roosting places for birds. Thorny shrubs are particularly useful for providing screening – they not only deter intruders but also benefit wildlife, as they help to protect nesting birds from cats, for example. A blackberry bank will provide an impenetrable boundary in part of a larger garden, for example, as will a rugosa rose hedge, which offers the bonus of terrific winter hips for the birds (and the source of vitamin-C-rich rosehip jelly for you!).

You do not have to make major changes to your garden design; you can adapt it gradually to be more wildlife friendly, perhaps creating a small 'nature reserve' in a corner to begin with, possibly screened off from the principal part of the garden. Every little bit helps.

► This drift of dark-foliaged double dahlias makes a bold splash of colour, especially when planted in front of sedums and *Verbena bonariensis* (both much loved by bees and butterflies). It is further enhanced by impressive stands of grasses in the distance.

◄ A wildflower meadow with a shimmering cloud of dandelion clocks. Even small areas of unmown grass in suburban gardens will help to provide a habitat, and useful nectar, for wildlife.

The organic approach

The use of chemicals in the garden is nearly always to the detriment of wildlife, and there are now many famous and committed proponents of the organic approach to gardening, including the Prince of Wales. As a responsible gardener, you should try at least to strike a balance between your needs and those of the surrounding wildlife. If you poison slugs, which can certainly create havoc with tender young plants, you will as a consequence poison the birds (and other small mammals) that also eat the slugs. Try to find other methods for dealing with them, for example by protecting young plants with plastic cloches or by making slug traps from sunken yogurt pots filled with beer (in which they drown) or from dry cat food (which kills slugs rather disgustingly by drying them out). There is a host of natural, organic substitutes for chemicals, from plant foods to pesticides. Organizations like the Henry Doubleday Research Association (HDRA) offer useful information (www.hdra.org).

Attracting wildlife

Even in a small garden, you can turn over an area to native plants (weeds to some gardeners!), which greatly benefit a wide range of wildlife. Leaving a large nettle patch hidden at the end of your garden behind a hedge screen will give butterflies and bees a much-needed food source. If you are a keen cook, you can benefit from it as well by making nettle soup from the young shoots, which are extremely rich in iron and other beneficial minerals. Italians are rumoured to eat nettles in the spring to get themselves back into shape for the beach in summer.

If you have a lawned area, why not turn over a portion of this to a wildflower meadow, which is cut just twice a year? You can mow a path through it more regularly or simply create wildflower circles in otherwise mown areas. Be aware that if you want wildflowers to survive rather than more thuggish plants like docks and thistles, the soil should not be too fertile, so leave any feeding for a couple of years and, if your soil is heavy clay, add some grit to make it more free-draining. Most of the best wildflower meadows are on chalky uplands where the soil is naturally thin and well drained.

Providing some form of water source for wildlife is another important role for the gardener. The water feature can vary from a tiny sunken pond in a backyard to a lake on a country estate. Any size of pool is welcome! Just make sure that four-legged creatures can make their way to the water's edge to drink – designs that feature a shallow rim on at least one side of the pond are ideal. Changes of level in the pond also provide you with an opportunity to grow different species of water-loving plants, as some of these

◄ Ponds are vital for wildlife, and this natural garden filled with damp-loving *Lythrum salicaria* and the great umbrella heads of giant hogweed (*Heracleum mantegazzianum*) is just right for the purpose.

▶ Insects will relish this late summer feast offered by the burnt orange flowers of crocosmia in the background, achillea in front of them and geraniums in the foreground. Such a planting also provides a wonderful splash of hot colour.

prefer damp ground, others like to dip their feet into the water, while a third group prefers deep water. If you have only a balcony or roof terrace, then provide a small birdbath, which doubles as a drinking bowl in dry weather. Putting out bird food in winter is a good idea, but you need to follow a few basic rules about how to supply it. The Royal Society for the Protection of Birds (RSPB) offers useful guidelines on the different types of bird feeder and the different kinds of bird food. You can also provide useful roosting or nesting boxes for your local bird population. Ducks and geese, in particular, benefit from the safe haven of a lake or pond when seeking to escape predatory foxes. Extreme weather conditions can be just as lethal to birds as predators or a lack of food or water, so ensure you pay special attention to the needs of birds at such times.

Small piles of logs are a great benefit to many small mammals as nesting places, so do not be in too much haste to clear up your garden in autumn. This applies equally to plants with seedheads. Rather than cut these back in early autumn, as many gardening books suggest, it is better to leave them to stand until the first frosts, so that birds can benefit from the seeds.

▥ Plants for bees and beneficial insects

Many insects are particularly attracted to plants with purple colouring and/or strong scent. Certain plants are favoured by certain insects, so it is well worthwhile finding out which plants attract what. From everyday observation, most people are aware that some plants have a magnetic effect on some insects. Every lavender bush hums with bees in summer, and many buddleias are covered in butterflies, but it is worth offering a succession of bee and butterfly plants, so that as one ceases flowering, another begins, providing a constant larder for the visitors. Herbs tend to be a magnet for many different kinds of bee, with borage, thyme, marjoram, lemon balm and rosemary having an especially powerful draw. Wild herbs such as purple loosestrife, motherwort and catnip are very popular with bees, too.

It is also good to encourage other beneficial insects like hoverflies, as the larvae of some species feed on blackfly and greenfly. The trick in an organic garden is to encourage these beneficial insects by giving them the conditions they prefer so that they can do the pest management for you. Firstly, they need dark, damp undisturbed places in which to hide in summer and to shelter during winter: you can grow ground-cover plants or put down tiles in a border. Provide plenty of nectar-rich plants, such as those mentioned above, plus rudbeckia and achillea, as well as members of the carrot family – dill, fennel and parsley – if you have an edible garden. A plentiful supply of these food sources in your garden will encourage beneficial insects to stay put and lay their eggs, and make sure there is some very shallow water in a tray for them, too.

Being nectar feeders, hoverflies help to pollinate the flowers they visit in the same way as bees. There are hundreds of species of hoverfly in Britain alone. They tend to prefer flowers with easy access to the nectar: asters, poached egg flowers (*Limnanthes*), ivy (*Hedera*) and poppies (*Papaver*) fit this particular bill, for example.

It is also a good idea to make sure there are a few bee and butterfly plants in your garden that flower at the beginning and end of the year, which is often when food for these animals is scarce. A rugosa rose hedge, for example, will serve as a good source of nectar, as well as offering wonderful summer scent and a rich supply of food from the hips in autumn. If you plan to harvest your culinary herbs before they flower, then why not plant some extra ones that you allow to flower just for the bees? Recent research into the decline of the bee population says that if the bee population dies off, then we will follow, as plants and trees will not get fertilized or pollinated.

If you want to garden organically, then consider planting a patch of comfrey to make liquid comfrey manure. The flowers will be visited by hoards of bumble- and honey bees, and the leaves will provide you with organic, rich fertilizer (see page 261).

▶ Another banquet: this time the rich bluish purple ball-like flowers of *Echinops ritro* 'Veitch's Blue', mingle with the spires of *Agastache* 'Blue Fortune' in a characteristic Piet Oudolf drift of a single colour.

▼ Even a wild garden can have a formal style, as this wildflower meadow, with its row of regularly spaced trees, at the Château de Pange reveals. The expanse of grass is broken up with formal rows of small trees, and dissected with mown grass paths for access.

▼▼ The ubiquitous cabbage white butterfly, which can be seen flying throughout the summer and whose grubs feast on the leaves of brassicas (to the sorrow of vegetable gardeners), prefers the nectar of white-flowered plants, such as garlic.

PURPOSE

LE MOULIN
NORMANDY, FRANCE

CASE STUDY #3

DESIGNER
CATHERINE WILLIS & ALAIN RICHERT

At One with Nature

With a sculptor and garden designer duo as the creators and custodians of this large country garden, it is not surprising that the garden is not only innovative and poetic but also unorthodox in being so natural in its approach. The result is an amazing haven for wildlife. Catherine Willis is the sculptor half of the team, Alain Richert the garden designer. Richert teaches at the École Nationale Supérieure du Paysage at the Potager du Roi, Versailles, and also travels the length and breadth of France following up many long-term natural gardening projects. Willis exhibits her organically inspired artefacts in Paris.

The gardens at Le Moulin are sited just south of Caen in a fertile plain with a heavy acid soil. Richert was aware from the start that it was essential to garden with the existing conditions and decided to focus on creating natural mixtures of local grasses and wildflowers in the meadows surrounding the mill. William Robinson's founding principle – never go against nature – has been

▲ The deep rich colouring of this mill house roof is wonderfully captured by the eupatorium stems and russet-tinged grasses in the foreground of this view.

▶ An old pump nestles in a sea of lavatera flowers, which provide a summer-long source of nectar for butterflies and bees visiting the garden.

◄ Sitting on the terrace immediately outside the mill, in the heart of the French countryside, you look out across informal groups of perennials and shrubs to the wild meadows beyond, with only the sound of insects or birdsong to disturb the tranquillity.

PURPOSE

LE MOULIN
NORMANDY, FRANCE

CASE STUDY #3 CONTINUED

DESIGNER
CATHERINE WILLIS & ALAIN RICHERT

▼ Nesting boxes, providing sanctuary for birds on the old stone walls of the mill, overlook euphorbias and evening primroses at the foot of the wall. The wall also plays host to a wisteria, which shelters one of the nesting boxes.

▶ The occasional coneflower (*Echinacea*) catches the eye in a sea of bronze-flowered grasses in late summer. Coneflowers are a wonderful magnet for bees and butterflies, and well worth growing in any natural garden. Ideally, plant them in big drifts.

▲ The rich French farmland ensures that grasses such as Yorkshire fog (*Holcus lanatus*) grow luxuriantly in the wild meadows there. As anyone who has created a wildflower meadow knows, it is a long hard slog to prevent the grasses that you want being overtaken by their more thuggish cousins.

▶ An old table makes an excellent home for Catherine Willis's pots of herbs and young plants. Like her art, the garden is constantly renewing itself. Seeds are sown, and weeds dug up, in a constant round of change and improvement, like an agricultural tide that ebbs and flows.

at the heart of the philosophy for this garden. As Richert commented, you adapt your style of garden to your surroundings. Had his garden been in Provence rather than Basse Normandie, his interest and efforts would probably have centred around the dry-loving plants of the maquis rather than on rich meadow grasses. Willis and Richert are also disciples of the late Dame Miriam Rothschild, who did so much to persuade gardeners to create more wildlife friendly gardens.

The bones of the garden are essentially formal, with mown paths that punctuate the meadows, and a great many fruit trees set among them. This, said Willis, makes the windfalls (they have many greengage trees) easy to find and collect, while also giving some vertical structure.

The paths, closely mown several times a year, run up to the mill house and its stream, and are lined on either side with red fescue (*Festuca rubra*) and Yorkshire fog meadow grass (*Holcus lanatus*). Among the grasses grow wildflowers that bees and butterflies depend on, including the magenta tufted topknots of knautia, the ethereal dancing white heads of *Gaura alba* and the mauve plumes of agastache. The garden has a deliberately limited colour palette – mainly mauves, greens, gold and white – which gives it a greater unity and a sense of restfulness. It has taken Willis and Richert more than six years to achieve the balance they were hoping for.

Using the garden's natural resources, Willis has made organic sculptures, perfumes and essences, while actively encouraging interesting plant forms to add to the mix. Once you focus on the natural sweep of the grasses and the almost insignificant wildflowers among them, you see a moving tableau that is part-sculpture and part-painting. Swaying gently in the breeze and in the changing shafts of light, these plants, and the butterflies and bees that feast on them, have an almost magical attraction.

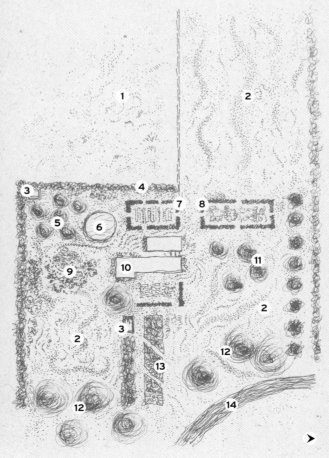

◀ **Le Moulin**

1 Neighbour's field
2 Meadow
3 Compost
4 Hedge
5 Fruit trees
6 Pond
7 Kitchen garden
8 Experimental garden
9 Botanical and old roses
10 Barn
11 Pine trees
12 Oaks
13 Chinese Garden
14 River

▼ Mixing flowers with vegetables can produce some stunning effects, as this walled kitchen garden demonstrates with its massed planting of scarlet-flowered runner beans, red and orange nasturtiums, bright red antirrhinums and neatly clipped balls of santolina.

▶ Neat rows of vegetables, such as different brassicas and leeks, in a formal vegetable garden have a symmetrical beauty of their own. Planting in rows allows you to hoe out the weeds between crops and also allows in the light that the vegetables need to grow well.

Edible Plants

Not much equals the joy of eating the first vegetables, fruit or herbs that you have grown yourself. Nothing tastes quite as good as the tomato you have just plucked from a plant you lovingly tended from its first uncertain beginnings as a seedling. Once you have experienced it, you will rapidly want to grow whole regiments of edible plants with which to delight and astonish your friends and family. Your successes, and your inevitable failures, will make you appreciate fresh produce more, and you will also have the satisfaction of knowing exactly what you are eating, and what your plants have been fed on.

Growing plants successfully for produce demands a fair amount of time and a willingness to pay attention to their needs at times that may not always suit you. The busiest periods are from early spring to summer, and again in the late summer and early autumn, the former when you are planting, and the latter when you are harvesting crops and digging over the soil for the subsequent year. In winter, you can relax.

If you grow your plants from seed, they will need the right soil or compost conditions, plus the appropriate temperature, in order to germinate successfully. Young seedlings are prey to many predators, so you will have to keep a watchful eye on them, too. Once they start to grow away, you will need to support the more vigorous plants, and thin out groups of seedlings to give them room to reach their full potential.

Planning this cornucopia of plenty needs to be done with care. Firstly, it is only too easy to overestimate your needs and plant far too many of one crop. Secondly, it really pays to sow successionally – in other words, to resow the same plant in the week or weeks following the original sowing. Plants do not always grow on demand (particularly if the weather is unseasonally cold or dry) and pest infestations are often short-lived, so a second or third planting may survive whereas the first did not. Successional planting also means that you can harvest over several weeks rather than having a glut of hundreds of lettuces, say, for a week and then no more salads for the rest of the summer.

To prevent pests rampaging through your crops, you should not plant the same vegetable in the same place year after year. Ideally, you need a crop rotation programme, which entails moving families of crops around annually – Charles 'Turnip' Townshend (1675–1738) was among one of the first landowners to introduce crop rotation successfully on his farms. Basically, vegetables divide into four family groups: pods and beans; leaves and shoots; roots; and fruiting vegetables. Plants from these four groups should not be put into the same soil year after year.

▼ Courgettes (long or round) and gourds of all sizes and descriptions are members of the Curcubitae family (which includes cucumbers). They are easy to grow, and extremely fruitful, but vigorous vareties will need strong supports, as pictured here.

What you grow depends on personal preference, the space available and the aspect of your plot. Almost all vegetables, fruit and herbs require plenty of sunlight. A semi-shaded garden will severely limit your choices.

You do not need a lot of space. A plot measuring no more than 5m (16ft) by 8m (25ft) should be sufficient to feed a family of four, if intelligently managed. You should use vertical as well as horizontal space, training climbing vegetables and fruit over the surrounding walls and fences (or your own homemade supports).

Designing vegetable gardens

It is essential that you plan your vegetable garden carefully. Crops need the maximum exposure to sunlight, so you must ensure that your taller plants do not shade the lower-growing ones. That usually means planning the planting so that the rows of vegetables run east to west on the plot, and the taller vegetable are at the north end of the plot. If your plot is poorly drained, it would be a good idea to install some drainage, to improve the water runoff, and on heavy clay you should incorporate a lot of organic matter (such as straw or well-rotted compost) and maybe some sand or grit. Cold, wet soil is the enemy of early crops. The land also has to be level, otherwise one end will drain too fast, the other end not enough.

You can plant crops in traditional rows or in blocks as small as 1m (3ft) square. The latter system works well because you then avoid treading on the surrounding soil when tending the plants. Treading on soil compacts it and removes the oxygen content so vital for root growth. Whether you plant in rows or in squares, you need to create paths so that you can tend the rows easily without treading the soil down too much.

The vegetable garden can be surprisingly beautiful as well as practical, particularly if you give up a little of the available space to growing a few flowers in with your chosen crops. These little areas of mixed vegetable and flower plantings are known as 'potagers' and have a long tradition. Planting flowers alongside the vegetables may have sprung not only from the need to pick flowers for the house – the common practice in large country houses – but also from the abilities of certain flowers to deter pests (many pests are attracted by the smell from vegetables but the scent of these flowers either puts off predators or confuses them). For example, French marigolds, which have an uncommonly powerful scent, are often planted alongside salad vegetables to deter greenfly.

Probably the best-known potager is at the palace of Versailles in France. It was developed by La Quintinie (a lawyer before he became head gardener at Versailles) in the seventeenth century under Louis XIV. La Quintinie's plan was to enrich the soil and develop systems to 'force' early crops, using 'hot' manure or glass bell jars, so that he was able to produce delicious out-of-season surprises for the king, such as strawberries in mid-winter or peas in mid-spring. The wonderful symmetry of these gardens, with their neat box hedges surrounding beds filled with serried ranks of different vegetables and herbs, has been copied the world over, mostly on a miniature scale.

If you are lucky enough to have a sunny wall or fence, in a cool-temperate climate you can use this microclimate to grow more tender fruits such as peaches or nectarines. Training fruit trees against a wall is an excellent way to use limited space, and a well-pruned tree produces much higher yields of crops than normal, while also enabling you to pick the fruit easily without having to climb ladders. There are various forms of training, which include cordons (where the main stem is trained at a 45-degree angle) and espaliers (where the main stem is straight and the side branches are trained horizontally on wires). Training,

◄ Planting in small squares can be preferable to doing so in traditional rows because it is possible to tend the crop without treading on the soil. These decked paths are a neat and easy way to cut down on maintenance, although they can become dangerously slippery in wet weather.

► Exquisitely maintained box-edged beds with clipped box pyramids transform this potager into a work of art. The raised urn with its brilliant splash of deep pink petunias is an eye-catching focal point.

maintaining and pruning exotic fruits is quite specialized, but the resulting crops are certainly worth the effort!

No keen cook should be without a herb garden, no matter how small the space available (see page 64), so ensure you include one in your plans.

Miniature vegetable gardens

With just a patio, a roof terrace or balcony on which to cultivate edible plants, you can grow almost anything you fancy, provided it has good access to sunlight and, for weight reasons, you use multi-purpose (soilless) potting compost instead of a soil-based one

Planting in large deep containers or in raised beds can be highly effective, especially when space is in short supply. When using such deep beds and containers (filled with fresh potting compost), you can plant vegetables much closer together than normally, so a lot of produce can be packed into a limited space. The deep raised bed method is beneficial in many other ways, too: those who are disabled or elderly and with restricted movement can continue to enjoy the benefits of gardening; and it also entails less work, as the deep compost promotes healthy growth and reduces the risk of diseases.

Special developments

In recent years, a wide range of miniature fruit trees has been developed, which are ideal for terraces or patios. You have the choice, too, of family trees, where several varieties are grafted onto one rootstock, so your apple tree, for example, might offer you a cooker and perhaps two eating apple varieties. As apples need to be pollinated, your family tree will include varieties that fruit at the same time to make this more likely.

Containers for strawberries are another space-busting development. You can plant them in hanging baskets (and you can use the little cherry tomato plants this way, too) or in special strawberry planters (which could also be adapted to grow herbs). The disadvantage of these kinds of container are that they demand regular and deep watering if the potting compost is not to dry out.

Vines can be grown on a balcony or roof terrace. Italians are well versed in the art of growing vines in this way, as they are great home winemakers, and can produce as much as 230 litres (50 gallons) of wine from one mature vine on a balcony measuring only 1m (3ft) square.

◄ Mixing herbs and flowering plants with edible ones adds a touch of glamour to the vegetable garden. In a formal potager, low box hedging – neatly clipped to about 30cm (12in) – provides an attractive formal surround to the beds without removing much needed light.

▲ A vast range of containers made from all kinds of material, as well as recycled ones made from old metal watering cans, buckets or washtubs, can be put to good use for growing herbs and other edible crops. Here, a wicker basket provides a home for mixed salad leaves.

◄ Combining flowers with vegetables is popular in many European gardens. Here, dahlias grown for cutting make a welcome splash of colour in a traditional kitchen garden.

▼ Cabbages and black kale jostle for pride of place with flowers such as verbena and nicotianas in this informal mix of vegetables, herbs and flowers.

Fig trees benefit from having their roots restricted by being planted in a container or lined planting pit. They will produce more fruit this way, so there is no reason not to grow figs if you have enough sunshine and the climate is mild enough (Zone 8 or above). A 60cm (2ft) cube will house a mature fig tree up to 2.4m (8ft) high and 5m (15ft) wide. Fig flowers are self-fertile.

Best vegetables to grow

Much depends on your own tastes. There is not much point in growing a vegetable, no matter how easy it may be, if you do not enjoy it that much! You are usually advised to grow vegetables or fruit that are expensive to buy but, today, it makes more sense to grow vegetables that you eat in quantity and would prefer to grow yourself organically – organic crops are expensive anyway, scarce or not. For the best flavour, vegetables are best eaten as soon as possible after they have been picked or dug from the garden.

Within the root vegetable group, potatoes are one of the easiest crops to grow. Opt for some of the more interesting varieties, and choose those that you can harvest at different seasons to make it really worthwhile, even if you plant them in deep containers on a patio. With so many varieties available, you can not only have potatoes for different seasons but also be able to choose between those that are firm and waxy for salads or soft and floury for roasting or mashing.

Of the fruiting vegetables, tomatoes are another crop for which there are a great many varieties, from tiny, intensely flavoured cherry types to massive, juicy Beefeater kinds. What is more, you can now easily find yellow, pink or striped versions as well as the classic red ones. Marrows and squashes are also good news; again, there are loads of varieties now available, from little finger-like courgettes to rampant squashes in many forms. They are usually easy to grow and not prone to many pests or diseases. Globe artichokes are also simple to grow and have beautiful leaves (as well as attractive flowers if you do not pick the heads), while outdoor cucumbers provide you with delicious prickly little fruits that have much more taste than flaccid, shop-bought ones.

▲ Wigwams of brightly flowered runner beans provide vertical interest, and contrast attractively with the deep black leaves of cavolo nero (black kale) and the purple heads of alliums in the foreground.

◀ Salad leaves, dill and onions snake their way around this vegetable garden. Such swirling curved lines of vegetables make an interesting diversion from traditional straight rows.

▶ A formal potager laid out in knot-garden style, with box cut into pompoms as the central feature, and neat gravel paths between the beds. The beds are slightly raised, with a wooden border, making them easier to maintain.

Among the best leaves and shoots to grow are winter leaves, such as cabbages and kale, and summer salad crops, which are a vital element in any vegetable garden. There is a huge range of different salad leaves, with Asian, Italian, American or English varieties, to name but a few. The leaves can be crisp or soft, green or russet coloured, spicy or mild. You can also eat the tops of some young vegetables, such as radishes and turnips. Packeted seed will often offer you 'mixed leaves', which you can harvest on a cut-and-come-again principle, snipping off the leaves you want for each meal while leaving the plant to grow on for a succession of harvesting. The ubiquitous chef's delight, rocket, is one of the easiest plants to sow, germinate and grow, and very fast to mature, too (and, sadly, to bolt into flower in dry weather). Lamb's lettuce is useful as well because it will survive winter temperatures (to just above freezing), whereas other salad vegetables will wilt if the temperature drops that low (although you can protect them to some extent with plastic cloches). Harvest lamb's lettuce using the cut-and-come-again principle to extend its cropping season. Radishes are

good, too: choose between little fiery globes or long elegant French varieties. They are so quick to mature that you can plant them in between rows of vegetables with longer-maturing times.

In the pods and legume vegetable family, runner and french climbing beans are invaluable, providing a plentiful and delicious yield of long-podded vegetables. If twined around a support like a wigwam of sticks, they can create an attractive focal point in the garden, too. They also have pretty flowers – white, scarlet, pink or striped.

One vegetable that does not need rotating is asparagus. It is probably the single most delicious vegetable to grow and well worth the effort because it is expensive to buy. It needs a permanent bed, so prepare this carefully, incorporating plenty of organic matter into the soil and ensuring it is free-draining, adding grit if it is heavy. Asparagus is normally grown from one-year-old crowns, which are ready for planting in spring. The following autumn, cut down all the top-growth. Asparagus must not be harvested for three years, however, to allow the plants time to establish. Thereafter, harvest the spears in spring.

▲ Novel ways to grow herbs were demonstrated at the Gothenberg Festival in Sweden. Containers can assume interesting contemporary forms, like these – an ideal solution on a modern roof terrace.

▶ Pots of herbs like marjoram and thyme can be decorative as well as functional, and are a great draw for bees. Grow them close to the kitchen door so you have them to hand when cooking.

▥ Herbs and herb gardens

Although herbs have been used mainly for medicinal and culinary purposes for centuries, the culinary herb garden has grown hugely in popularity over the last couple of decades as cooks everywhere have realized how essential fresh herbs are to contemporary tastes in food, as well as being increasingly aware of the health benefits that can be gained. As our interest in foods from other cultures increases, so does the range of herbs and spices that can be grown when the climate permits.

The styles of herb garden are as various as their uses, but the traditional knot garden, dating back to medieval times, is perennially popular: low hedges of box, lavender or santolina pruned into neat geometric shapes, contain the beds filled with whichever herbs are required. They can be just as easily organized on an almost miniature scale.

Most herbs are incredibly pungent, so a very small quantity goes a long way. As a result, you can grow probably as many herbs as you are likely to need in just a few containers on your kitchen windowsill or balcony. Favourite herbs for the kitchen that can all be grown in small pots are basil, parsley, thyme, mint, chervil, chives, rosemary and marjoram. Bay leaves are popular, too, and small bay trees, clipped into topiary shapes, planted in handsome big terracotta pots, look wonderful framing a doorway, for example.

Herbs generally thrive in full sun, as most of them originate in lands around the Mediterranean. They also prefer light, free-draining soil. Mint is one of the exceptions, as it will cope with partial shade and has a far greater need of water. Most culinary herbs are herbaceous perennials, grown from seed or semi-ripe cuttings.

Many parts of the herb can be used: leaves, seeds, flowers and roots – fresh or dried. When harvesting herbs for drying, make sure you pick them when they are dry. Hang them in bunches from a drying rack in a well-ventilated room or in a warm cupboard. You can even dry them in the microwave. Small-leaved herbs spread out on a plate should take no more than a minute to dry. Once the herbs are thoroughly dried, store them in airtight jars, label them and keep them out of the light. Some of the finer-leaved herbs do not dry well, but all herbs can be put into small sealed bags and frozen.

One of the major benefits of growing herbs is that it also benefits your local wildlife: insects of all descriptions flock to gather pollen from almost all of the herbs. If your interest in herbs increases, you can create specialized herb gardens related to their different functions – a medicinal area, a dyer's herb garden and, of course, one for the kitchen. Although it is inadvisable to experiment with home remedies, many of the medicinal herbs, such as chamomile, fennel or lemon balm, do make excellent tisanes (herbal teas). Dyer's herbs were once our only source of fabric dyes, and some singularly beautiful colours can be achieved from relatively simple kitchen-sink dyes. Any plant with the Latin species name *tinctoria* was once used for dyestuffs, although, for the dyes to be fast, mordants or natural fixing agents of different kinds are also required. Some of these are poisonous, so using plant dyes is not the kind of hobby to tackle without expert advice.

▲ Fruit is not the only benefit to come from an orchard. The blossom in spring, seen here underplanted with daffodils, is a visual treat as well as a welcome source of nectar for bees and other insects.

Growing fruit

Now that you can buy small, less vigorous fruit trees, even the tiniest garden can find room for at least a couple of fruiting trees, and fruit bushes, too. Fruit has a reputation of being hard to grow, but some fruits are easier than others.

Of the soft fruits, most people love raspberries and strawberries. If you are a novice at fruit growing, strawberries are among the easiest of fruits to cultivate. Simply plant them in a suitable container, in a hanging basket or in a slightly raised bed in the garden and feed and water regularly. Alpine strawberries, in particular, are well worth growing. The biggest enemies of strawberries are slugs, so container growing helps to avoid this problem. If your strawberries are in the ground, surround the plants with straw to help deter slugs and prevent the fruit from rotting where it comes into contact with wet soil.

Raspberries require a bit more attention initially. You normally buy raspberries as bare-root plants in autumn. After planting them in a well-manured bed, cut the plants down to about 15cm (6in) in height, keep well watered; the following year, you will have a smallish crop. The year after that, the raspberry crop will double in size. Remove fruited stems after harvesting has finished. Raspberries spread via runners, so your raspberry bed will quickly re-create itself. Plants do need support with strong poles and wire, as their stems tend to snap when heavily laden, particularly on windy sites.

Other soft fruits such as currants and gooseberries are also fairly undemanding to cultivate, requiring just an

◄ Olive trees, with their gnarled greyish bark and slender grey-green leaves, have become an increasingly popular option in temperate-climate urban areas, where the higher temperatures now allow them to survive the less cold winters.

▼ Strawberries are an ideal candidate for containers, and will grow in special strawberry planters, thereby providing you with a big crop in minimal space. Table-top containers help to avoid slug damage.

addition of general-purpose fertilizer in the growing season, and the annual removal of overcrowded branches to let more air into the centre of the bush.

Blackberries make fantastic hedges, but they are fast-growing and need to be pruned quite drastically and tied back at the end of each growing season to prevent them encroaching on paths and other plants. The fruit will be borne on new stems each growing season, so remove the old fruiting ones in autumn.

Tree fruits such as apples, pears, plums, damsons and cherries do not require much attention apart from pruning, to remove overcrowded branches and to keep the trees under control. Choose varieties, such as the old heritage ones, for flavour, where possible, rather than necessarily for heavy cropping only. In limited space, you can grow fruit trees against a wall or fence, in cordons or espaliers (see page 60), where they particularly benefit from regular pruning, to encourage the production of spur-bearing stems and so increase yields. More exotic fruit, such as peaches or nectarines, are well worth the effort if you have a sunny wall and are prepared to take the time and trouble to look after them.

Birds can demolish an entire crop of fruit in the blink of an eye, so many people grow soft fruit in cages, and net their cherry trees (a particular draw for pigeons). If you do decide to do this, take great care to make sure the nets you use are bird-proof and without holes. It is upsetting to see birds trapped in cages or caught in broken netting.

Floral Food

If you want to grow edible plants but also want to fulfil a romantic dream, look no further than Nancy Heckler's garden at Oyster Point in Seattle, USA. 'Before you decide on what to plant, you need to ask yourself first what your primary purpose is – how much you are trying to grow and why. Don't be afraid to experiment,' she advises. 'The beauty of vegetable gardening is that you are dealing mostly with annuals planted in spring and harvested later in summer and autumn. So there is always next year to try again, unlike perennial borders where your mistakes take years to mature!'

Nancy packs an amazingly varied selection of vegetables and fruit into a plot 18 x 18m (60 x 60ft), with a path down the centre and paths around all the sides, making it easy to access. They are often accompanied by flowers in combinations such as artichokes with cosmos, and purple kale with marigolds and leeks (see plan, page 71). In addition, there are two 9m (30ft) beds full of berrying fruits and six 1.8 x 3.6m (6 x 12ft) raised beds.

An orchard contains both restored old fruit trees and a wealth of new ones. 'I love the old fruit trees in the orchard (even though they do not produce that well) because of their shapes, and the lichen and moss on their gnarled trunks. I planted roses in some of them, and daffodils throughout the grass below,' comments Nancy.

She has always treated vegetables as decorative plants. 'There is nothing more beautiful than a perfectly grown cabbage or cauliflower, or swiss chard, or purple kale, pumpkins or runner beans.' Why not think of these as one would a decorative border? Plan to make the most of their interesting foliage forms, dramatic architectural shapes and unique colour combinations. Nancy even lets some vegetables bolt and bloom: 'Have you ever seen bolted purple lettuce with a cloud of yellow flowers floating above? Exquisite.'

▲ A great decorative yet practical idea for the vegetable garden: grow your runner beans over a rustic arch. The lavender at the foot of the arch is a welcome source of food for bees.

◀ The same arch, seen this time through a tall screen of sunflowers and giant fennel (*Ferula communis* 'Giganteum').

◀ Sunflower, alliums and cosmos all club together to turn the vegetable garden into a visual feast as well as a productive one.

PURPOSE

OYSTER POINT
SEATTLE, USA

CASE STUDY #4 CONTINUED

DESIGNER
NANCY HECKLER

On her plot, Nancy grows many different varieties of each vegetable – there is always something new to try. She might have 12 varieties of potato one year or 25 varieties of squash. (She has built a special pumpkin tower made of sheet metal rounds like a wedding cake to restrain their touring habits, so that the pumpkins and gourds tumble down from the tower.)

Nancy's approach is unequivocally organic, and always has been. 'I don't remember ever using anything in the garden that wasn't organic – even as a child. I recall scattering coffee grounds and eggshells when I was little. Now in my own garden I don't even use anything on my roses. If they don't perform, I replace them with others that do.'

It is well worth taking a leaf from Nancy's book (literally) and keeping a garden notebook of the varieties you grow (along with any pictures you take), as well as the prevailing conditions, as it helps to remind you what you liked and what grew well each year. Armed with this knowledge, Nancy's plot continues to look stunning.

▼ A relatively shady corner of the garden is brought alive with bright pink lilies and deep blue hydrangeas.

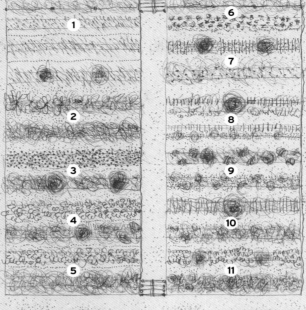

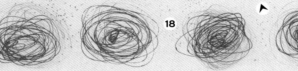

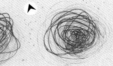

▲ Small, edged beds are much easier to tend than long rows. Edge them with small plants, such as salad leaves, or use marigolds as companion plants to ward off pests.

◄ Another great mix of edible leaves and flowers – Californian poppies in the foreground and dahlias in the background.

► Artichokes, cosmos, love-in-a-mist and teasels are grown together in another of Nancy's rectangular beds.

Family Gardens

Many of you may have a certain kind of garden in mind when thinking of a traditional family garden, and it is usually dominated by a large area of grass, which serves as a lawn in between penalty shoot-outs. Perhaps there is an area where vegetables are grown, or rose beds that are placed off-limits. This describes many a garden that I came across in my youth.

Modern gardens may conjure up a very different picture for you, and may not seem family-friendly, but they can have the same elements as many traditional family gardens. With clever design, an extra element of magic can also be incorporated. Abandon the notion of any area being off-limits. Children thrive in a positive environment, full of exciting things to discover, and this is simply another reason to make the garden safe. Prohibition from certain areas will make them even more curious.

A successful family garden is relevant to all members of the household, including pets. With good planning it is possible to design a garden that evolves with the family. For very young children, an area of open lawn is an aid to their first steps. A patio area can be laid large enough for entertaining, even if it will be covered in toys or trays of mud pies when the children are young. Or you may decide to leave those features until they are a little older. Willow tunnels are marvellous to children at the age when their imaginations run riot. They are very easy to construct from cut willow rods stuck in the ground, where they will root and grow, and they can just as easily be removed once they have served their purpose. Pathways that initially help you to avoid getting muddy on your way to the vegetable patch or compost bin can make effective cycle and scooter pathways later on, so perhaps put in a circular route.

Themed beds are great fun to get into, especially for children. An exotic border, however, must be positioned

in a south-facing part of the garden. A cottage-garden border, though, can introduce a mix of perennials and shrubs that like sun, shade and semi-shade, thereby making use of different aspects.

One of the best ways of addressing environmental concerns with children is through the garden. Children can grow their own vegetables, re-use and recycle items in creating the structure of the garden, and make compost from garden waste. Although an essential part of a family garden, your vegetable plot may eventually evolve into another garden feature, but meanwhile will serve as an educational tool as children grow up. However, if your lifestyle simply does not allow time to grow your own vegetables, it is worth assigning even a very small plot to the children for experimenting. Growing things and getting dirty is such an adventure. Remember to create beds small enough to be manageable, as small arms have a small reach. Use some old paving slabs or stones to make little pathways. If you make the garden magical, the children will want to play in it. A little shed can easily be made from pallets to house their own tools. Suggest easy plants to grow like sunflowers, and let them sow their own carrots and peas. You may have to do some work in the plot yourself from time to time, in order to regain control, but this can be a family affair.

⦀ Low-maintenance

A low-maintenance family garden conjures up different images for various people. The important thing to remember is that unless you want a wilderness some garden maintenance will always be required. However, when you decide on your garden's design, bear in mind the tasks you are making for yourself. With cottage-garden and mixed-border styles, the garden can be a delight, full

▲ Natural pools become part of the garden without taking over. Swimmers can enjoy the water as part of a naturalistic garden design that gradually melds with the environment to become a sanctuary for wildlife. Marginal grasses, reeds and airy perennials thrive all around the pool in a tranquil scene.

◀ Although this small garden includes benches, chairs and open space, there is still lots of room dedicated to plants, and here they make the garden. Large groups of grass, box, ferns and perennials are grown in blocks that reflect the overall garden structure.

◀ A simple family garden can still be inviting. In this magical setting, like a scene from a children's book, an aged wooden bench encircles a tree, where young ones can play, while others can take cover from the sun.

of flowers and colour, but the herbaceous perennials in such gardens often require staking, and they need to be cut back in winter. If this truly is your desired look, you can reduce the workload somewhat by increasing the ratio of shrubs and evergreen grasses to perennials.

The modern look with block planting is often quoted as an example of low-maintenance gardening. Again, using shrubs that do not require much pruning, as well as evergreen grasses, will indeed reduce maintenance. Keep in mind the children, though, and include hidden features for them to discover, otherwise this style of garden may feel a bit sterile to them.

If you live in an area where dry summers force you to water the garden regularly, a gravel garden may be the answer. Maintenance will be reduced because there is no lawn to mow and irrigate. Also, if you spread the rounded pea gravels recommended for children's use, they will love playing on it. A dry garden opens the opportunity to have fun with drought-tolerant, scented plants like lavender and rosemary, which children love. A paved area within it, and perhaps a paved path, will provide both a seating area and a tricycle circuit.

In a larger, low-maintenance family garden there is an opportunity to experiment with naturalistic planting. This could be a mix of perennials and grasses to give a prairie effect in deep borders around a small lawn area. Better still, create a wildflower meadow (see page 193) and mow pathways through it for a magical effect. In such an area, willow tunnels will be right at home (see page 72). The only maintenance will be to cut the new shoots off each year, unless the children are particularly rough with it.

⦚⦚⦚ Practical issues

The paths in your garden will give it structure and also serve practical purposes for the adults as a route to a seating area, a compost bin or a shed perhaps. For children, a path can also be exciting, scary, secluded or simply a great circuit on which to run, scoot or cycle. Keep this in mind in your design. Plant certain areas so that the shrubs will be quite low for the first few years, as you will want small children to be in view for safety reasons. As the shrubs grow bigger and block the view to the path the children will be at the age when they want to feel as if they are in a hidden part of the garden.

The surface that you choose for the path also depends on the children's ages. For very young children, certain types of stone can get quite slippery, and gravel is difficult to negotiate. Look at available paving at your garden centre and consider some of the resin-bonded surfaces that are used in playgrounds. These are very forgiving when fallen on, and some companies use crushed recycled glass to create exciting coloured surfaces.

A lawn area near the house is ideal for young children to play on. It is a soft surface to fall on, and easier for you

◄ Children love to get their hands dirty, and raised beds make plants accessible to them and are easy to maintain. Vegetables such as spinach, lettuce and radish mature fast and are perfect to inspire children to grow their own crops in an organic way, encouraging healthy eating at the same time.

▼ Long upright bamboo canes can be planted to make a perfect wigwam for children to play in, and also be an attractive addition to the garden. A child's imagination is boundless and needs little stimulation. Create a natural den in a secluded shady spot and they will play happily for hours.

to keep an eye on them. You do not need to produce a perfectly manicured lawn. In fact, little fingers love to pick daisies. As they get older, the lawn provides a perfect camping ground or football pitch too.

Tree houses

Tree houses are just the most magical places if you have the right spot for one in your garden. The best trees are hard woods, but if you plant an ash or an oak in your garden for a tree house, your kids will be adults before the tree is big enough. Any existing tree should be checked by a tree surgeon first to ensure it is sound enough to build a tree house in it.

If a tree house is too expensive, or simply impractical for your small garden, you can still create that magic elsewhere. A child's imagination needs only a little secluded spot in order to run riot, so look for nooks in the garden where they could create a den. In a secluded part of the garden, a small willow den or arbour, only big enough for kids, can easily be created, to provide hours of fun. Children's garden sheds and chalets are also available to buy at large garden centres. One of these tucked away – or in full view if they are quite young – can mean that they can play out in the garden on rainy days.

Plant selection for families

Selecting the right plants for your family's garden may seem daunting, but when you have decided on a design this will help you to narrow it down. A good balance of shrubs to perennials will lower the maintenance workload. The age of your children will define to a certain extent what you will plant, initially avoiding poisonous or dangerous plants (see below) as well as rare ones and

► A simple section of basket weave interrupts cow parsley and a grass-mown path to form a natural tunnel for children's play. It invites them to explore the back of the garden and to venture into the flower meadow beyond. The basket becomes a natural sculpture, adding structure and focus to the garden.

▼ Amongst the *Stipa tenuissima* and erysimum, a tree house provides a glorious space to relax amongst the tree branches on a warm sunny day. If you are lucky enough to have a strong mature tree, such a retreat can provide the ultimate destination for a midnight feast.

delicate annuals. If the children are a little older, then they can assist in the plant selection. Bring them along to the garden centre and see what makes their eyes light up. Find out what flowers they like. Is there an easy flower to grow that is their favourite colour?

If you know you have an explorer on your hands, you can include a jungle area somewhere in the garden, using some of the favoured foliage plants of exotic gardeners (see page 204). Fatsias, hostas, bananas, tree ferns and clump-forming bamboos can create a bit of jungle magic for their garden expeditions.

Your chosen style may be a child's dream if, for example, you decide to have a wildflower meadow (see page 193), as children love to run and hide in long grass. A woodland garden (see page 236) is also a place of real intrigue and a perfect place for a den or a fort. If your children are very young, they will grow with the garden, and not disappear into it until they are old enough to do so safely. Use plants such as willow to create living garden features, and grow contorted hazel just for the fun of it. Have a sunflower-growing competition in a sunny spot in the garden.

Dangerous plants

The reason it is important to make the garden safe is that most young children use their mouths to investigate the world around them. Most garden centres will advise on poisonous plants to avoid. The classic example is laburnum, the seeds of which are poisonous if ingested. A fellow member of the pea family, the sweet pea, produces poisonous seeds. If you are a fan of the sweetly scented daphne shrubs, think before planting because these produce poisonous berries. Avoid growing rhubarb, as the leaves are dangerous if eaten, while the leaves of foxgloves cause an irregular heartbeat. Other plants that should certainly not be eaten are hyacinths, daffodils and buttercups. For obvious reasons, avoid plants that are particularly spiny or thorny, or tuck them away safely at the back of a border.

◄ A country cottage-style tree house nestles in what seems like a giant tree. There is something very special about tree houses – they are hidden, secret places that never fail to captivate.

Nocturnal Gardens

As towns and cities continue to engulf vast amounts of land, the area available for gardens and green spaces is ever decreasing. There is, therefore, an overwhelming requirement to make the most of what garden you have so that it becomes an extended living space. To do this, the objective is to stretch the time that can be spent outdoors way into the night. Many aspects come into play here but, in general, any garden design has to produce an inviting and usable space that is ready for occupation at any time. Shade and shelter from all weathers is an immediate need. This can be supplied by a simple good-sized parasol or awning that can be closed after use. For a more contemporary feel, why not invest in a vast cloth canopy or sail held on tall metal supports, which looks very chic? In a more traditional design, plant a spiralling climber over a wooden pergola – and do not underestimate the effectiveness of a dense tree canopy for shelter.

If space is very limited, consider constructing a permanent outdoor canopy in wood or a garden pavilion that becomes the whole outdoor space for use at night and during the day. There is real excitement in creating a new destination point in a garden. A garden building can take the form of a glass cube, a wooden pavilion, a Japanese-style hut or a solid garden shed with extra cladding and lighting; with beautiful planting and some creativity, it can be made to nestle into a space well. Furnish it with appropriate lights, table and chairs, loungers or a

▼ The lighting in these plant borders has been positioned among the hairy grassy leaves of *Stipa tenuissima* and *Gaura lindheimeri*, to produce a soft hazy lighting effect that gently illuminates the rooftop space. Glowing LED squares lead into the space at ground level, and coloured tealights highlight the blue glass gravel and seating area.

◄ Bamboo canes in all their glory. The fine grooves and nodules of these splendid canes are emphasized by white uplights, setting the mood and triggering excitement. The delicate leaves rustle in the wind, to produce changing silhouettes after dark.

▼ Coloured lighting should be low level and sombre for the best effect. Here, it is used to define the amazing twists and turns of this striking tree. The hot colours of the lighting accentuate the deep brown colours of the bark, bringing warmth and atmosphere to the space.

hanging bed and make it as functional and inviting as possible. The outside can be homogenized as an extension of the house by matching the colours and style, but there is also the opportunity to let your imagination run riot in a much more decadent space. Use outdoor heaters and heated walls to take the chill out of the air, but do consider their environmental impact before making a choice. Any planting in the outdoor room, as well as around the garden buildings, will be at close proximity and can therefore be selected to wake up the senses and inspire you to venture outside.

▥ Different approaches

Lighting is not only essential for navigating your garden after dark but it can also be used to create a visual feast for the eyes if planned effectively. The whole character of a garden changes at night, with the main features and focal plants forming outline shapes and texture in shadow. Because there is no visual stimulation, sounds and smells are intensified at night, and a new design approach evolves that incorporates magical aromas, intriguing silhouettes and different lighting for depth. Enclose the garden with trees for privacy and build up a layer of low-lying shrubs that glow in the night. Position a patio under shelter or surround a pavilion with flora. Set each area off with candles for atmosphere, a place where you can relax and unwind with a glass of wine. Imagine yourself star gazing on a summer's evening in a sumptuous lounge chair or catching a nap in a swaying hammock while the leaves rustle in the cool breeze.

▼ Lighting is used to highlight the many layers of this garden. On the main walls, it directs the space, and the fire wall welcomes you to take a seat. The lanterns produce drama, while the tealights suggest intimacy, but it is the illuminated planting that reminds you that it is a garden.

► White lighting enhances the contrasts and definition of the different plant forms in this garden, bringing the space to life. Olive trees are the ultimate garden sculptures, and white bark and flowers are excellent choices for gardens that you particularly want to use at night.

◄ Low-level lamps are set behind arching *Pennisetum alopecuroides* grasses to attract attention to this area of the garden, and, more importantly, to indicate that there are stairs ahead. The lighting is angled to skim the wall, creating moody shadows in subtle tones.

form of outdoor chandeliers, lanterns and candles to reflect the style and ambience you want. Where safety is of paramount importance, use specific lighting by placing simple, white, low-level uplighters along pathways, within an arbour, at any doorways and, most importantly, alongside stairs and changes of level, and around water features. Introduce a softer, illuminating glow to set the mood for an outdoor dining area.

Spotlights create drama by illuminating focal points and should be set against more mottled lighting such as that underneath planting or at the base of walls or raised beds. This softened light creates mood and mystery almost like the effect of dry ice on a stage. Illuminate uprights such as walls, screens or fences with uplighters to wash light across the surface for extra interest in verticals and texture. Lights that shine through particular plants will accentuate their finery so that they can be appreciated in a completely different way.

Advances in technology and the development of plastics have created a huge choice of attractive lighting products that are weather-resistant and durable. Always check they are suitable for your garden. Low-voltage systems are safe to use outdoors as well as within water features, and they radiate a soft ambient quality of light that accentuates feature plants and trees. Select a product range that is in keeping with the rest of the garden and make it simple; do not be tempted to use too many different effects or styles so as to overwhelm the space.

Highlighting trees and shrubs

As you move through a garden, the subtle differences in plant texture, form and shape are at the heart of the excitement; the use of clever lighting effects can transform these subtle differences into spectacular brushstrokes and shadows. Trees are the ultimate garden sculptures, which makes them the most obvious place to start your lighting plan. The focal trees may be obvious or just favoured specimens that can be illuminated with a single spotlight or covered in a series of tiny LED lights for a sparkly effect. A white upward-facing spotlight defines the structure and detail of a tree's branches, creating high drama, so that illuminating just one or two trees will be quite enough in most schemes. Position spotlights behind a central tree for a theatrical silhouetting effect, and secure a set of small lights within the canopy of a tree for a soft downward moonlight effect that is really magical.

Emphasize the contrasts in foliage and form by placing low-level lamps within clumps of plants such as grasses, phormiums and bamboos, and angle soft lights to skim nearby screens and stone walls for patterns and subtle tones. Shine dim spreading lights through plants to set them alight and project them onto smooth walls, producing exhilarating shadows and a constantly changing night-time canvas.

To give a modern feel, incorporate a patio area of smooth natural stone to form clean lines and balance it with strong blocks of planting such as grasses or evergreen shrubs for great impact. Position lights within the plant clumps to produce soft textural effects. Set large contemporary planters nearby and fill them with plants chosen for vertical accent and fragrance; a stronger result will be achieved by planting a single species. Ornamental shrubs and standards create eye-catching shapes and should be illuminated upwards for focus and a sense of drama. Plants such as lavender, sage and thyme will fill the air with spicy scents. Light up any main walls and paths with small halogen lights at ground level. More traditional or exotic designs can include wooden screens, less-controlled planting and ornate pots and statuary.

Lighting moods

Lighting can alter the way you perceive a space by highlighting the unexpected, thereby creating new texture and form – and a new story. Arrange the lighting in the

Lighting in winter

As you set out your lighting requirements, consider what the garden will look like in the winter months. The main pathways and focal points will create direction and drama as usual, but there are other plants that can contribute to the shadows. Solid evergreen hedges and topiary can be illuminated to define the green backbone of the garden all through winter. Interesting effects can be achieved by using modern lighting techniques such as fibre optics or white neon to conjure up a wintry scene. In fibre optics, light is passed through many strands of glass fibre, resulting in hundreds of twinkling dots of light. Pass these microfibres through wintry grass skeletons to create an enchanting frosty border. The cold white light of neon is also stunning on those chilly cloudless nights; place them under modern wooden or stone benches or behind dividing walls to accentuate main garden features that can be seen from the warmth of the house.

Temporary movable lighting

Supplement the light of the moon with flickering candles, tealights and the subdued light of paper lanterns for a warm, romantic ambience where friends and family can gather round a table. The naked flame is the most basic form of light, but it is still one of the most captivating. There is never a shortage of candle-lit garden lamps and Moroccan-style lanterns in the shops that can be brought out for dinner parties and placed around the garden. Fairylights and chains of paper lanterns are particularly

▼ An exotic jungle garden packed with plant divas, all vying for attention. Night-time enables you to illuminate your favourites to indicate a personal journey through the garden. The delicate arching leaves of tree ferns and *Trachycarpus fortunei* glow wonderfully, while the palm trees strike eye-catching silhouettes.

effective, creating a real party atmosphere and adding a splash of colour to the garden on special occasions.

Solar-powered spike lights are extremely versatile. Since they require no wiring, they can be positioned wherever and whenever they are needed. Their soft light is most appropriate around patio areas or plants. The welcoming ambience of soft lighting at the table is enhanced with the muted glow of the garden's structural features and boundaries, allowing the users to gain a rich appreciation of being outdoors.

Night-time plants

You must consider the overall shape and structure of your garden before settling on which plants are to be lit. Plants with strong outline form and robust shapely leaves create fantastic shapes and distinctive silhouettes under the influence of spotlights. White flowers will add to the night-time scene, yet certain blooms have an extra magical effect that can bring the senses to life after dusk.

As the day draws to a close, some plants begin to wake up. Vespertine flowers are those that bloom exclusively at night, emitting powerful scents in a bid to attract night-time pollinating moths and beetles – species that hide away from the bulk of their natural predators during the day. These flowering plants can help to make your garden

◀ The lighting in the multi-stemmed forest establishes an eerie atmosphere, as well as depth and intrigue, within the garden. The pavilion provides a strong contrast, as it is open and welcoming, yet the darkened trees beg you to explore.

▼ This is the same garden as depicted on page 80, but here the white stone finish of the hard landscaping is warmed considerably with soft backlighting and a focal fire wall. The planting serves to soften and enclose the space, which is tasteful and inviting.

into a relaxing refuge after sunset, and so should be introduced in appropriate areas.

One such vespertine-flowering shrub – *Brugmansia* – also brings a taste of the exotic to a garden. Laced with poison and truly mystical, it is the temptress of the plant world, with its elegantly outsized trumpet blooms, up to 25cm (10in) long, which open at night to release a pungent fragrance. *Brugmansia arborea* is a robust shrub with white trumpets, while *B.* x *candida* 'Grand Marnier' produces trumpets in an apricot-yellow. All species are highly toxic, so should be avoided around children, and because they tender, they are best kept in large pots and sheltered over winter. A safer option might be *Zaluzianskaya capensis* 'Night Phlox' (syn. 'Midnight Candy'); its flowers, which are tightly closed during the day, open to release a scent of honey and vanilla that is wonderful at night.

Other plants open during the day but choose to release their scents after dark: *Aquilegia fragrans* emits a rich honeysuckle-like scent from creamy white flowers; and *Nicotiana sylvestris* is valued for its delicate trumpet blooms and pungent evening fragrance.

Night-scented climbers fill the air with sweetness and are fantastic for covering bare walls and fences close to the house or patio area. *Trachelospermum jasminoides* is one of the most beautiful, with their deep green, dense foliage and great numbers of creamy white, star-shaped flowers that have an intense, gardenia-like scent. Position it on a south-facing wall for added protection. Perennial vines that are truly hardy include *Hydrangea anomala* subsp. *petiolaris*, *Lonicera japonica* and *Clematis terniflora*, all of which are evening fragrant and wonderful for scrambling over pergolas and garden buildings.

Plants with white blooms and grey to silver foliage come into their own at night. They reflect the light of the moon and glow in the soft illumination of low-level spotlights, producing eye-catching accents, while the rest of the plants fall into the background. The structural *Astelia chathamica* has stunning sword-like leaves that are coated in a silver foil and contrast strongly with the delicately cut leaves of *Artemisia* 'Powis Castle'. *Dicentra spectabilis* 'Alba' is a small shrub with elegant foliage and white, heart-shaped flowers that drip off long arching branches. Its flowers make wonderful night-time ornaments, and the plant's natural shape also makes interesting shadows. The summer hyacinth *Galtonia candicans* has everything you could want after dark, with its long, white flower spikes and a fine aroma, as does *Salvia argentea*, a variety with compact silver foliage, white blooms and the familiar scent of sage.

▶ Great mushrooms of *Buxus sempervirens* dominate the space in a stunning, rolling display of planting. Early morning frost dusts their surfaces like icing on a cake and gently melts away in the sunshine. Box is elegant, evergreen and amazingly versatile, fitting into any style of garden with ease.

Structure

||||| The structure of your garden is essentially the skeleton. A lack of structure can be difficult to disguise in winter and can lead to a tangled mess in the height of the growing season. The best use will be made of your garden if you have designed it according to your needs and how you intend to use it. When doing this, you can take advantage of existing features and topography: for example, by borrowing an external view or making the best use of a slope.

Although you can express your own personality through the design of your garden, it is important that you distil this down to a unified theme or concept to avoid the garden becoming too fussy or complicated (see page 173). The structure becomes ever more important if the garden is an awkward shape. Using the correct lines and shapes can help to overcome the challenge presented by the most difficult of plots, and will also determine whether your garden has a formal or more naturalistic feel. Patterns and shapes of paths provide definition and features that you can view from a distance when looking at the garden as a whole.

▼ Perennial planting is not all about the summer. Here, perennials have been selected not only to look good in summer but also to carry on providing form and structure through the rest of the year. Grasses, sedums, alliums and agapanthus all make wonderful winter sculptures and shapes.

▼▼ Soft fluffy mondo grass (*Ophiopogon japonicus*) crisscrosses this stone patio to transform the space into something truly stunning. The strong lines of planting in single species reflect those of the building and help to unify the space.

Lines and Shapes

The main structure, or the bones, of your garden are set out using lines and shapes; these essentially determine your garden's style. The features that create the lines are typically those of paths, bed or border edges. Lines can be quite subtle, in the case of bed edges, or stronger and more defining, such as a curved path leading the eye through the garden. Shapes are usually created with paving, decking or a mixture of hard surfaces and lawn areas. They fill the spaces within the overall order, which you created using lines.

An informal design, perhaps with naturalistic planting, can be achieved with sweeping curves and oval shapes. Straight lines and rigid shapes, such as squares and rectangles, add formality and fit better with a more defined planting scheme. Shapes can also be used to create rooms in the garden, but be careful not to overcomplicate the design. If your garden is very large, then you potentially have a number of garden rooms, but be sure to look at the big picture and to provide lines that unify these spaces. The shapes and angles that you use also help to overcome challenging spaces: for example, in a long, narrow garden, you can avoid the tunnel effect by introducing diagonal lines, a series of circles or an S-shape, to draw the eye away from the boundaries. Diagonal lines can also be invaluable in a wide but short garden, to lengthen the perspective; alternatively, attention can be drawn to the centre by an oval placed diagonally, perhaps in the guise of a lawn or a paved area.

The basic lines and shapes are the two-dimensional structure of your garden. In order to make it three-dimensional, you need to look at garden architecture, sculpture, containers and structural plants, which you can then fill in with the rest of your planting. Structural plants can give you more height, screen areas, define some of your garden rooms or just add extra drama. They will be the one part of your structure that potentially changes over the course of the year. If you choose deciduous trees, for example, they will provide a sculptural beauty in winter and a soft green canopy in summer. The rest of your planting can perform different functions throughout the seasons, too. Tall perennials with persistent seedheads can create ghostly brown skeletons in your winter garden or, better still, white skeletons after snow or a hard frost. A spring-flowering cherry tree might mysteriously bloom with purple flowers in late summer, if a cleverly planted clematis such as *C.* 'Etoile Violette' has been planted through it. A hedge of hawthorn will flower in spring, green up for the summer and be a lacy brown screen in winter. Thus, the living structure is the most changeable element, and the easiest to alter from year to year, both in terms of cost and effort.

◀ Wooden decking meanders through a forest of deciduous trees in an enlightening journey that takes in the plant life of this garden. A lush green collection of ornate ferns, grasses and other shade-loving perennials fills the forest floor.

The Framework

This is the key to balancing vertical and horizontal spaces, so it is important to get the proportions of the garden right to create a comfortable balanced space. If a feature in the garden is out of proportion, it will jar with the senses and will not feel restful. Similarly, an unplanned garden with a bed here, a path there and a random specimen tree can feel like a messy room with stuff just thrown around. You sense it when there is no connection, but when garden features follow a line, or create symmetry, the space makes sense and feels comfortable.

You may think this is a very difficult part of your design to get right, but with a bit of experimentation you will find that you have a strong instinct for the right proportions for your space. It will become obvious if tall plants are too close to the house or a path, as they will feel overpowering. Move them back from a path, or further down the garden, where they can be enjoyed with greater ease because the distance and perspective put them in proportion. Laying out a formal garden is a little simpler, as you can use symmetry. In an informal design, try to get the flow right first and then consider the height.

Taking photographs with a person in them for scale really helps the planning process (remember, you are creating a garden for people). You can trace over the images and draw in specimen trees and other features, to help decide what heights you want and where. Think about the purpose of the height that you are adding when planting specimen trees. Trees can provide an accent in a long, sweeping border, to lead the eye through the space. They can be used as a screen, perhaps to give privacy from overlooking windows. A pair of trees can be positioned to frame a view, focal point or other garden feature. In a small garden, it is important not to plant trees that will get too tall or cast too much of a shadow. In such circumstances, you can probably get away with tall, slim trees, which do not cast a great deal of shadow, but they are best planted close to a boundary.

Screens with climbing plants and hedges are other elements that add height to your garden, and it is essential that they, too, are correctly proportioned. If they are being used to hide something unattractive, it is important that

◄ Bright green mosses fill the gaps between elegant, white paving stones, to produce eye-catching ground cover. The green-and-white theme is carried through into the architecture and the focal statue, which marks the end of the space.

◄ In this Japanese-style garden, a beautiful path in white stone snakes through deep green, towering bamboos and spiky mounds of mondo grasses. Pushing through a break in the bamboo, the path emerges in a hidden part of the garden. The planting is minimal and strong in aesthetic.

▶ Banana trees instantly conjure up a feeling of the exotic, with their distinctively smooth, green stems and extremely handsome paddle-shaped leaves that illuminate a garden. A number of varieties, including *Musa basjoo*, that will thrive happily in temperate climates are now readily available.

▼ Tree-lined avenues have graced the gardens of stately homes for centuries, connecting the house and garden to the surrounding landscape, as well as acting as a guided walkway to another part of the garden. Deciduous species create winter structure and also provide fresh green foliage in spring.

▶ A mature cactus specimen has to be one of the most distinctive focal points in the plant world. Thriving in hot, dry climates, spikes replace leaves to conserve water, and pithy stems store any moisture that comes their way. Spiky yuccas complement cacti perfectly for structure at ground level.

the screen or hedge is not too tall, as it will draw attention to that area rather than conceal it discreetly, as intended. By moving it a little away and lowering it a little, you will find that it screens just as effectively but is not so obvious.

▌▌▌ Tall structural plants

Structural plants, such as trees and large shrubs, have been referred to more and more in recent years as architectural plants. This is mainly because they usually have a bold shape or a strong presence, which helps you to create structure in your garden using plants. Place them as natural walls and dividers in the garden space, or as a focal point in a bed. Plant evergreen trees as solid hedges, to enclose an area, and introduce shrubs to provide year-round colour and form in a border. Deciduous trees provide seasonal interest, some giving flowers, berries and autumn leaf colour.

Some plants possess obvious architectural qualities, such as the spiky leaves of an agave, the sword-like leaves of a phormium or the fronds of a tree fern. Others produce glossy leaves (such as *Aucuba japonica*), very large leaves (like those of a stooled paulownia) or lush, green leaves (like those of a banana). All demand attention, so position them with care.

Even in smaller gardens there is often room for a tree. Trees really do add that essential third dimension. Although climbing plants can clothe walls and other structures – adding to the three-dimensional green effect – trees contribute something else: a shady spot to sit in summer, and somewhere for that blackbird to sit while serenading you on spring mornings. They can also serve as a windbreak in exposed gardens, or provide a microclimate under their canopy, which protects plants beneath it from frost. Willow and birch trees are particularly useful, with their beautiful winter stem colour. If you need something smaller, Japanese maples are also wonderfully architectural, with the great winter skeleton that follows their lovely autumn leaf colour.

▲ A pair of beautifully clipped curving beech hedges form the backbone of this garden design. They cut into a well-kept lawn to divide the space, directing the eye towards a shady seat at the end of the garden. The hedges are designed to establish clean lines and a strong architectural composition.

▼ Lush planting illuminates every part of this garden. Trees with an elegant open habit are underplanted with grasses and shady perennials, which are repeated around the pond with a sprinkling of flowering forms. Rounded evergreen shrubs and multi-stemmed deciduous trees provide structure.

◀ This shady garden unfolds gradually as you follow the grass path. Evergreen hedges divide the space, inviting you to explore. The garden is dominated by huge borders of woodland plants. Deeply coloured hostas, tongue-shaped ferns and other shade-loving perennials pack every centimetre at ground level.

▼ Trees and climbing plants spill out of this country-style residence in an exuberant display. Evergreen shrubs, such as low-growing firs, euonymus and *Pyracantha* 'Marcus', glow in glorious colours, framing the gates and creating a sense of excitement at what might lie beyond.

IIIII Mid-height structural plants

Bamboos seem to fall in and out of favour with gardeners. The movement and noise they can bring to a garden is very welcome, as is their evergreen, architectural presence. They are very useful screening plants – they reduce noise from traffic – yet also look good planted as a specimen. Bamboos are invaluable for children's play areas, as they will take the abuse and are not harmful in themselves. Be sure to get a well-behaved, clump-forming species such as the fresh green *Fargesia murielae* or the black-stemmed *Phyllostachys nigra* to maintain the look you desire.

If you wish to create an exotic look, introduce plants with ferny fronds – palms and ferns are ideal. Ferns alone, which are good for shady, damp areas, can also give that woodland-garden feel. Palm trees are excellent eye-catchers, and they really deliver on drama, too, but the fronds get battered in the wind, so be sure to provide some shelter for them.

Spiky plants have a strong shape and bold presence, and succulent ones are good for movable containers, as cold and damp winter weather usually dispenses with them quickly. Be careful if there are children around because these spiky plants also often have little spines along the edges of the leaves. A similar spiky look is created with plants such as cordylines and phormiums, which have sword-like leaves; they are easier to grow, hardy and not nearly as savage as succulents.

IIIII Lower-growing shrubs

Other shrubs that can be useful to create the lower levels of structure in a garden include *Ceanothus* species, with purple to blue flowers and small evergreen leaves. *Skimmia japonica*, also an evergreen shrub, has a very strong leaf shape and wonderful, red berries through autumn and winter. From the delicate, feathery flowers of cotinus to the stout, sulphurous flowerheads of *Euphorbia characias* subsp. *wulfenii*, these accent plants produce a seasonal and magical effect.

◀ A series of pleached trees makes a strong statement in this Mediterranean-style garden, adding another level of planting. They are underplanted with large banks of *Lavandula angustifolia*, which balance them beautifully.

▲ The trees, hedges and grasses have been selected and controlled to perfection in this space. Perfectly clipped hedges divide long banks of miscanthus and pennisetum grasses. Silver birch trees punctuate the design, and taller blocks of planting complete the layering effect.

DIARMUID GAVIN & TERENCE CONRAN

▼ A path of diagonally set white cobblestones gently snakes through distinct lines of diagonal planting. Blocks of box and lavender create structure amid lower grasses and bright yellow foliage shrubs. The diagonals lead the eye to the undulating lawn and grassy mounds for a child's play area.

Spaced to Perfection

Situated on a peninsula overlooking San Francisco Bay, this garden has been designed by Roderick Wyllie and James Lord to instil a grand appreciation of the outdoors. It was inspired by the resident couple's passion for art and their desire to create a wholly enjoyable experience for their children. The Peterson residence incorporates places for reflection and play, as well as acknowledging the regional landscape. Texture and excitement have been integrated into every layer of the design, from the trees and shrubs to the wooden dividing walls through to the mass planting, mound-forming lawns and ground surfaces.

The landscaping has been set out as several distinct areas that embrace the residential buildings and accentuate the spaces around them magnificently. A white path gently meanders around the site, creating a strong sense of connection; it is a feature in itself, as its construction changes into different forms of stonework, all of which produce stunning ground surfaces.

Long elegant white stone rectangles of various widths are laid diagonally across the ground on one side of the house, creating a path and visually expanding the shape

and size of the space; dense clumping mosses fill the gaps in between, while fresh green mounding grasses ebb in and out of the intricate undulations. A pathway of rounded white pebbles runs parallel on one side of the path, adding texture to the composition. Lush groves of bamboos (*Phyllostachys bambusoides* 'Castillonii'), small red Japanese acers, *Cornus* 'Eddies White Wonder' and robust grasses create volume and frame the path's movement.

The path of stone rectangles narrows and arrives at an open space of fine white gravel that is decorated with flush white cobbles in another eye-catching ground surface. Here, the main entrance is heralded with a folding deck made of ipe wood projecting from the house, which doubles up as a climbing wall for the children. It is framed with the most beautiful multi-stemmed *Magnolia* x *loebneri* trees, which are underplanted with masses of *Pennisetum alopecuroides* 'Little Bunny' grass and *Woodwardia fimbriata* ferns.

Diagonal white cobbles form a smaller path that runs on the north side of the house amid a sequence of evergreen hedges and fragrant perennials; lavender, box and

◄ Rectangles of white stone meander through great clumps of bamboo, red Japanese maple trees and ophiopogon grasses, giving this tranquil space a taste of the Orient. On one side rounded white pebbles fill the spaces between the stone rectangles, thus increasing the texture and width of the scene.

▲ A wide folding deck in ipe wood projects from the house and is framed with elegant multi-stemmed trees.

▼ The white cobblestone path stops at a series of hillocks, highlighting the view of the bay beyond and the rolling Californian landscape. A large flat rock provides a wonderful place to sit and enjoy the views.

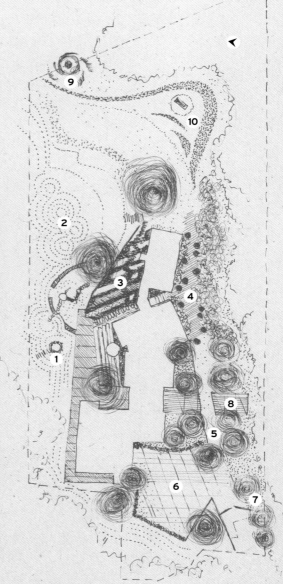

▲ Wide stone steps lead up to a spherical pavilion that nestles among large mounds of grasses. A mature tree canopy creates soft shade in this welcoming play area.

▼ Horizontally laid wooden fences in a rich mahogany colour separate the garden into distinct areas, and also box in luxuriant shrubs and trees. The dark wood contrasts perfectly with the white fine gravel ground surface.

▲ **Peterson Residence**

1	Hobbit house	6	Entrance court
2	Rolling hills	7	Rain garden
3	Zipper garden	8	Folding deck
4	Shifting paths	9	Knot garden
5	Meadow walk	10	Sculpture field

mounding grasses provide remarkable low-level structure. The cobbles stop at a series of hillocks gracing the huge lawn. These hillocks create the foreground for a superb view of the bay and the rolling Californian landscape. A wide flat rock beckons you to rest and take in the view. Meanwhile, the sumptuous lawn embraces children's play areas, including a 'hobbit house' and a 'rabbit hole hill', and pieces of sculpture that have been made by the clients, to offer another dimension to the scheme. The lawn rolls with the natural contours of the land and is punctuated with stout mature trees set within circles of grey gravel.

Dark, solid wood fences in a rich shade of mahogany pick up the deep chestnut tones of the towering Californian redwood trees in the distance. The fences enclose masses of deciduous trees and shrubs, so that they look like huge wooden plant containers packed with lavish foliage plants.

The limited use of colour, gentle blending of hard materials and the structural use of foliage plants at the Peterson residence has produced a charismatic family garden that is truly exhilarating in its use of space.

◄ Multi-stemmed magnolia trees flank both sides of the folding wooden deck, forming a grand main entrance to the house. Masses of pennisetum grasses fill the spaces under the trees, bringing movement and softness to the scene.

Beds and Borders

Subtle lines in the garden can be introduced by varying bed and border shapes. Traditionally, borders were very often rigid and followed the shape of the garden boundary. When garden fashion moved from functional to aesthetic, it became apparent that changing these lines could dramatically alter the experience of the garden space itself. Unified lines that sweep throughout the garden and create the edge of the border can help the garden to flow. The curve or direction of the sweep can lead the eye in an intended direction, to distract from boundaries or mask the overall shape of the space.

The design of your borders and how they connect with the house are important, too, because they can help to make the house look as though it belongs in the landscape. Suddenly starting a bed 3–4m (10–13ft) from the back of the house, which is perhaps where a patio ends, can appear to separate the house from the garden, whereas a border starting by the back of the house,

which sweeps down through the garden creating your sightlines, will connect the house and garden both physically and psychologically.

Less is more, in terms of the number of beds and borders in a garden, as it can be difficult to create a feeling of harmony with too many distinct beds. Choose the plants for your bed or border in the first instance to suit the site of each one and its conditions such as soil and moisture.

Optimum size

If you have the space in the garden, create borders that are deep enough to have a thin path of gravel or bark ribboning through them.

Island beds, on the other hand, can look rather odd if they are not big enough. They work best in a large garden and with naturalistic and woodland garden planting. For me anything that can accommodate a tree and some large shrubs in the centre, and also create a bit more mystery

◄ A sumptuous planting palette in shades of blue and purple fills this hot and sunny garden. Silver-leaved plants such as lavender reflect the sun's rays, protecting them from water loss and enabling them to thrive in dry conditions. Large clumps of *Phlomis russeliana* add a touch of yellow.

► A rich green woodland garden of shade-loving perennials, including white aquilegias and hellebores, sets the scene beautifully for this barn residence. Large clumps of *Euphorbia characias* subsp. *wulfenii* are set against a solid evergreen hedge that defines the boundary of the house.

◀ Keeping the colour palette of a plant border limited to two or three colours produces a strong result with great impact. Here, deep burgundy sedums, the dark brown centres of the echinacea daisies and the blood-red tips of the imperata grass produce depth in colour, while soft pink- and white-flowering perennials provide volume and texture.

▼ This attractive row of fruit trees is given a very modern feel with large blocks of strap-leaved irises in pink, which produce a high-impact underplanting. The zigzag shape of the bed is further defined by a meandering lawn.

and interest, is about right. This may sound large, about 3 x 5–6m (10 x 16–20ft), but if it will not fit in your garden, then this space is too small for an island bed.

▥ Vegetable beds

It can be a challenge to fit vegetable beds into the overall design of the garden because they are usually very rigid rectangles and also because vegetables need a sunny spot in which to grow. Vegetable beds can fit in better by designing an area that is obviously the more functional part of the garden. Once the aspect is right and the beds are not made too wide for access, they can be incorporated seamlessly into the overall plan for your beds and borders without making them appear obvious. I have seen beautiful vegetable beds designed in a fan-like shape with flowers intermingled among them, and it only became obvious on arriving at the beds that they were, in fact, the vegetable patch.

Sightlines

Pergolas and arches, paths and allées fulfil a function in the garden that is common to all four features – they lead you somewhere. Pathways not only guide you physically but also direct your eye through the garden at ground level, creating some of the basic movement in the design.

Although an allée is similar to a path, its function is to provide a much more formal scene. Allées are usually straight and flanked on each side either by a hedge or formally pruned trees. It is these outer edges that define it as an allée rather than as a path; it also has a grass floor, which is not a typical path surface. Although they are usually associated with very large gardens, allées can be used in smaller settings, to create a feeling of a larger garden or to divide a garden.

If a garden has no distinct topography, it can be very useful to use a pergola or archways to create height and a sense of mystery.

IIIII Pergolas

Depending on its length and whether it is straight or curves through the landscape, a pergola will lead you in a certain direction and can be cleverly used to obscure boundaries or belie the proximity to the house, hence making the garden seem larger. It, too, can be used to divide the garden or to create a discreet area in which to sit. The beauty of a seating area beneath a pergola is that in

summer it can be clothed in one or more climbers with scented flowers, offering some protection from the sun. A mix of the evergreen *Clematis* 'Apple Blossom', for its spring flowers, and *Rosa* 'Climbing Lady Hillingdon', for its recurring summer flowers, would ensure a sweet scent from spring until late summer. Another classic plant for a pergola is wisteria, its purple blossoms exuding a heady scent. Walking under the rose pergola at Kew Gardens, in the UK, is magical at the height of summer on a warm day, as the fragrance from the roses wafts down. Such climbers are usually deciduous, so the pergola may also provide a place to sit later in the year, where you can grab a few precious rays of winter or early spring sun.

IIIII Archways

When dividing the garden into distinct areas or different rooms, arches are another useful feature. Whether the garden tapers to an archway, leading you irresistibly to explore further, or nonchalantly offers an archway through a solid hedge to prick your curiosity, most people cannot help but go through an arch to see what there is on the other side.

If you are an avid gardener, you might like the challenge of a laburnum arch. Laburnum can be trained over an archway, creating a beautiful covered walkway that drips with scented yellow flowers in spring. Unfortunately, laburnum seeds are poisonous, so you should avoid the plants if you have children.

▲ An arching pergola planted with rambling roses covers the most stunning walkway and directs the eye down into the next part of the garden. Fragrant rose varieties fill the air with perfume on hot summer days, stimulating the senses and a strong appreciation of the outdoors.

◀ A magnificent meadow of grasses and wildflowers in shades of pink disappears into the distance. Wildflowers thrive on poor thin soils and, once established, are easy to maintain. A simple, curving, mown path adds to the perspective and gives the sense of a journey.

◄ This massive grove of deep green bamboo canes overwhelms the space in a magical way. It forms the structure, texture and atmosphere in a dramatic planting of a single species. Robust upright grasses provide sturdy underplanting, to underpin the composition.

▼ A heavy-looking climber adds to the sombre mood of this garden. Dark evergreen large-leaved species punctuate the beds against dense shady ferns. Climbing plants can be selected to green up walls, mask unsightly buildings or to provide a light covering of colour.

Climbers on Walls and Fences

A climber, in the plant world, is one that twines or otherwise attaches itself to a wall or structure. Fortunately, there is a large palette of these plants, which include not only climbers but also ramblers, ground-cover plants and shrubs, all of which can be trained on various structures in the garden.

Some self-clinging climbers such as ivy, *Hydrangea anomala* subsp. *petiolaris* and campsis produce aerial roots, so will grow unsupervised up a wall or fence; the last two climbers are also great for their dramatic flowers. Virginia creeper, on the other hand, produces special pads that adhere to the wall or structure. These true climbers are of value and, in the past, were very popular grown on buildings, even though they created difficulties by clogging gutters and providing certain wildlife (that is, vermin) with the perfect ladder to climb into a roof space. Therefore, you need to think through the

implications carefully if you wish to grow a climber up a building. Within the garden, however, self-clinging climbers are easier to manage.

Climbers are useful trained on a trellis as a screen for ugly but necessary structures in the garden, such as a shed or an oil tank. They are also invaluable for creating beautiful features. A pergola covering a seating area draped in wisteria is magical not only for its pendulous, purple flowers but also for its heady scent, which can fill a summer evening. If you prefer not to shade the seating area, introduce a green wall using a wooden or metal structure and clothing it in climbing plants.

Scent can be an important factor in your plant choice for a wall or fence. As a result of climate change, climbers such as *Trachelospermum jasminoides* are increasingly hardy in the UK and Ireland, and in places where you cannot get away with growing the common jasmine (*Jasminum*

◄ Stunning purple wisteria enlivens this attractive brick house and heralds the start of the summer months. With careful pruning, wiring and patience, the owner will be rewarded with the ultimate in climbing beauty.

▼ A seemingly endless cascade of plants adorns the face of this building. Such a collection of mixed perennials that are mainly evergreen in nature are excellent for a vertical garden. Vertical walls are becoming increasingly popular in both domestic and architectural settings.

▼ Timeless white *Rosa* 'Iceberg' will scale a wall or cover a pergola with ease – here, it flows from the surface of the house out into the elegant country-style garden. Densely planted borders burst with colour and effervescence.

officinale) outside, plant trachelospermum, whose scent is equally divine. As with certain types of plant, such as roses, many climbers require a little extra work in the guise of pruning, but they will reward you in return.

Climbers can also be grown as specimens in their own right. A beautiful climbing or rambling rose such as *Rosa* 'Paul's Himalayan Musk' can be shown off on an obelisk – probably best in a more formal setting. Another favourite is annual sweat peas growing on a tepee made of bamboo canes or hazel, which will suit a more loosely planted garden, such as a cottage garden, a herbaceous border, or even the vegetable garden. There are other wonderfully colourful annual climbers that can run riot and fill the last few gaps at various levels in your borders throughout the summer, a favourite of mine being the Spanish flag (*Ipomoea lobata*). As the name suggests, the flower is yellow and red.

Host trees and shrubs

As well as running through borders, some climbers look magnificent when grown through a tree or shrub. If you have an early-flowering shrub (such as lilac), which you want to jazz up later in the season, grow a late-flowering clematis (such as *C.* 'Comtesse de Bouchaud') through it. Clematis species are also popular as climbers to grow through trees, along with some rambling roses such as white-flowered *Rosa banksiae* var. *banksiae*. Do be careful to choose plants of matching vigour. If your climber is too vigorous, it could smother the tree or shrub, or cause damage due to its weight. Also, keep in mind the final effect you want and from where you wish to view the flowers, which will always seek the light. There is no point having lovely roses draping the sunny side of a tree and providing a delight for your neighbours but ignoring you who planted them.

▼ Wisteria makes a wonderful dividing hedge or screen because its twisting branches form a rigid, decorative meshwork that is exciting to behold. Drooping flower stems in lilac adorn the natural scaffolding in late spring to early summer. The fresh green leaves emerge later.

▶ Strong lines and division dominate the main gardens at Jardin de la Ballue in Brittany, France. The sense of control is continued in the limited foliage forms that, apart from the hedges, are composed of fine, strap leaves. Slender silver birch trees slice through the layers, to create the perpendiculars.

Hedges and Screens

Not only are the hedgerows in the countryside a great haven for wildlife, so, too, is the hedging in our gardens. Hedges and screens are useful on the outer boundaries of a garden; they can also divide the space into discrete areas or enclose a specific part of the garden. Gardeners like to show off their gardens, but while relaxing in them, they really value their privacy. This may be a wish not to be overlooked by neighbours or simply to have a hidden area to go to away from the house, and everyone in it, for a few minutes each day.

Hedges also provide a physical barrier against the elements. On very exposed sites, they allow you to grow a wider variety of plants in their sheltered, leeward side. In this instance, a hedge is superior to a wall – and even to some fences – because it is a permeable barrier, unlike a wall, and some of the wind will pass through it, reducing its effect. With some walls, the wind flows over them and creates a whirlwind on the other side, which can cause problems with your planting. Hedges are also cheap to create and they are living.

There is something special about a living green wall. It provides the perfect backdrop for a herbaceous border. It can provide symmetry and order in a formal setting or be useful for block planting in a modern design. In a wildlife garden, a hedge of mixed native species offers refuge and food to various animals and birds, as well as

flowers and berries for ornament. I love Piet Oudolf's use of hedges. Within a garden planted with mostly grasses and perennials, this renowned 'naturalistic' plant designer will place hedges of varying lengths and heights, clipped with flowing, wavy tops. Somehow what is often used as a formal feature, to break up the garden space, becomes informal and flowing. Hedges can provide a focal point within a certain area of the garden, or simply screen off the unsightly.

▌ Man-made screens

Other useful screens such as trellis or metal structures can be introduced into the garden. Whether covering them completely with plants or training just a beautiful climbing rose up a lovely frame, screens can hide or highlight different areas of the garden. You can create an area for entertaining, with a wonderful wisteria draped over an open structure, such as a pergola, or provide a more enclosed room, perhaps with a yew hedge, in which to sit and read.

The ultimate living screen, especially if you have insufficient space for a hedge, is a living willow fence. It is easy to make with willow rods, which you can weave and tie together in various shapes; they sprout and grow, so give a living but not very dense screen. After a couple of years, you can take out these movable boundaries and create a different space if you want. Willow screens are particularly good for surrounding children's areas in the garden, and you can vaguely see what is going on through them.

◀ A beech hedge undergoes its autumn colour change from apple green to golden yellow through to the familiar rusty brown of winter. It is a useful species in term of structure and colour as the hedge will retain its brown leaves until new shoots appear in the following spring.

▶ Tightly clipped hedges divide a lawned area from a more sumptuous part of the garden. They allow you see enough to know that you want to take a look. Huge green clumps of miscanthus and flowering trees promise a beautiful garden ahead.

▼ A double wave of lavender transforms a meandering path into a wonderfully fragrant walkway through this woody garden. The sea of purple flowers floods the garden with movement and colour, enlivening an otherwise green space.

Structural Ground Cover

Once you have placed the features and larger structural plants in your garden, look carefully at the rest of your plan. Try to find the spots that you overlooked. They may be obvious places on the edges of other features, such as a lawn, or they might be less evident, perhaps beside a hedge or the shed, which is cleverly hidden by a structure supporting climbing plants. Even though the area may only ever be seen by you as the user, you should plant some ground cover on any bare earth, to prevent the weeds moving in and serving as a seed bank to infest the rest of the garden. Of course, using ground-cover plants is not your only option in such places, but with them you will create a nice balance by filling in these spots with lower, and often verdant, plants.

Challenging sites

Other sites that may be difficult to deal with in your planting plan include awkward features such as a bank or slope, a large old tree whose roots prevent much planting, a rocky area or outcrop, or a particularly marshy or wet area. There was a time when solutions to these situations involved making them suitable for certain planting by, for example, draining a wet site. However, it is much easier to change your plant choice and not the site itself, and in adopting this approach, you get to keep those unique characteristics that make your garden different, quirky or fun. Ground-cover plants are a great ally for these sites,

where it is possible to create a wonderful natural look – or a blocky modern one using mass planting.

If part of the garden is very wet, plant ground cover and erect a raised path through it, transforming the site into an exciting feature. In very dry areas, such as beneath large trees, where the competition for water and light would appear too great, there are always ground-covering options. Hardy geraniums provide excellent weed-excluding cover. In Italy, *Pachysandra terminalis* is planted under street trees; there, it thrives in the shade, likes the dry position and has lovely, scented flowers in spring. With a rocky site or a bank, clump-forming plants can be used to great effect. On such sites, plant in large drifts, to unify the area a little more and help to tie it into the overall design of the garden; avoid planting too many different species, thus making it into a plant menagerie. Similarly, if your garden is quite modern, or symmetrical, just plant in blocks instead of soft drifts.

Some gardeners struggle for years to make a success of a lawn in a damp, shady part of their garden. Had they decided to grow some ground-cover plants instead, they could have popped a bench in and created a lovely, green, secluded spot to sit and think. Ground-hugging ivy with flagstones peeping through as stepping stones can serve a similar purpose to a lawn, but will also give you lush greenery where the lawn failed. You can even naturalize spring bulbs through the ivy, as you can with a lawn.

◀ Epimediums are among the most elegant ground-covering plants, spreading to carpet woodland floors and shady areas of the garden. They are blessed with fine heart-shaped evergreen leaves that slowly bronze as they mature. Tiny star-shaped flowers on long stems come in white, yellow or pink.

▲ This house and garden are situated in rural Virginia on a historic farm along the Rappahannock river. The beds around the mulberry tree are packed with *Aster oblongifolius* 'October Skies'. This photograph was taken on an October morning and showcases the pastel-coloured flowers in all their glory.

▼ An evergreen hedge divides this part of the garden from the drama created by the gunnera and rhododendrons that peep over. It is a strongly contrasting peaceful part of a garden that focuses on a perfectly still pool. A pair of benches looks out over an open space of grasses and evergreen ground cover, to complete the tranquillity.

Lawns

Lawns have been an essential part of English gardens for centuries, providing a space for leisure activities and acting as a foil for planted areas, and they still have a role to play in the modern garden. The kind of lawn you have will depend on your lifestyle, and the role that your garden plays within it.

▥ Function of the grass

What do you want to use your lawn for? Will it be for playing games on or for lounging in the sun? Or will it have a more aesthetic purpose, providing a bold, visual statement. It is important that you are clear on the use of your lawn and the amount of wear it will get, as this will greatly affect the planting material you choose.

Functional lawns for leisure activities need to be planted up with tough hardwearing grasses, such as perennial ryegrass and red fescue, which can stand up to those spur-of-the-moment football matches. It is now easy to get hold of either turf or seed that has been developed for this kind of action, and most hardwearing mixes will contain at least 50 per cent perennial ryegrass.

Purely aesthetic lawns can be made up of any plants that have a very low-growing form. Dwarf forms of *Ophiopogon japonicus* or *O. planiscapus* 'Nigrescens' can be used to create lawns with a strong texture and colour; there are also many ornamental fescues such as *Festuca glauca* 'Elijah Blue' that can be used in a similar way. Moss lawns, which can be planted in shady, damp areas, provide a lush green carpet that resembles those found in Japanese gardens. A plant that gives a similar mossy effect is *Scleranthus biflorus*, and it can be used to create a lush 'lawn' in semi-shaded areas.

A lawn is a fantastic medium to manipulate within the landscape, being fluid and so much less rigid than hard landscaping features, so deciding on the shape of your lawn offers another opportunity for you to be imaginative. Before settling on one of the infinite number of shapes you can cut your lawn into, it is important to consider how you intend to maintain it. As with all lawns, you must mow regularly, while attending to feeding and watering will reward you with a great surface from which to enjoy your garden.

◄ A wildflower meadow will take a couple of years before it flourishes, but rarely is anything more beautiful. Cutting of the grass is reduced as much as possible, and the lawn grasses are starved of nutrients, to allow flowering species to thrive. Once this is achieved, little maintenance will be necessary.

▶ It is useful to think about how you intend to maintain a feature before embarking on its design. Naturally low-growing plants such as armeria can be used within stone features like this one without the need for any trimming. They can be planted to green up delicate patterns in stonework or to fill the crevices between larger square paving stones for a gorgeous effect.

◄ Rectangular paving stones are embedded in the lawn to form a simple, elegant pathway up to the main house. This offers easy lawn maintenance and prevents the lawn from wearing through human traffic. It also avoids having to construct a heavy-looking path that would jar with the design of the space.

▼ The lawn in this garden appears like a lush green carpet that sweeps over the whole space. In a pastry-cutter effect, large sections have been cut out to create rectangular flower beds and a square reflective pond. The long paths of grass are sumptuous and inviting.

Wildflower meadows

The concept of what a lawn is has been increasingly questioned by modern gardeners, many of whom favour a wildflower meadow. This is essentially a lawn that has been allowed to grow wild. In a wildflower meadow, you want less grass and more plants, and this is achieved by cutting the grass less often and starving the area of the nutrients that lawn grasses thrive on. Through a mixture of seed-sowing and planting, you can quickly achieve a wildflower meadow that looks stunning when in full flower, and all for relatively little effort. Meadows also provide food for insects and birds, which are always welcome guests on a summer's day.

▼ Beech hedges are popular in garden design for their unique ability to retain their rusty brown leaves throughout the winter until fresh green growth appears in the spring. They are used in this form to provide structure and colour, and they fit into any style of garden with ease.

Plant forms

Nature has provided an amazing array of plant forms and shapes, which have been made even more diverse by plant breeders. The form of the plant is essentially the way it holds itself in the garden, and this can be either its natural outline or how it is shaped through pruning. It can be very expressive, capturing or enhancing the mood of the garden. Bold, large-leaved and strappy plants such as cannas and agaves give the feeling of an exotic paradise, while a drift of white foxgloves planted through a shady border can provide a sense of otherworldliness, especially on a spring evening. When composing a planting scheme, it is really important to consider these different forms, and how you can manipulate them, because they can greatly affect the final look of your garden.

What does form contribute?

Very upright plants such as the flowing spikes of foxtail lilies (*Eremurus*) give strong vertical lines and can act as punctuation marks or focal points. Such plants should be introduced sparingly, as their overuse can leave a garden looking confused. Those with strong horizontal lines, such as the table dogwood (*Cornus controversa*), give a sense of space, with the open layers allowing dappled light through. Plants with rounded or less angular forms can

be used more extensively because these tend to be more aesthetically pleasing; just think of such plants as spotted laurel (*Aucuba japonica*) or *Hydrangea arborescens*. Some plants provide very little diversity of form in their varieties, while others seem to have an endless range. It is always worth taking trouble to hunt around for a variety that meets your needs.

On a larger scale, tree forms also contribute to the character of the garden. In a small garden, you may be tempted to plant a small weeping tree, for example, when actually something that gets slightly taller but has an upright and airy branching system, and is planted close to a boundary, might be more suitable and provide a sense of freedom and space.

Topiary

Wherever possible, it is best to utilize the natural form of a plant, as this will mean less pruning and training. However, as well as using the forms that nature provides, you can manipulate plants through pruning and training, the most common of these techniques being topiary. The topiary can take the form of just about anything you can imagine, from simple spheres, cones and cubes to cloud-like, amorphous shapes that assume a life of their own.

◄ A sculptural garden of sharp and angular shapes in stainless steel is balanced in drama with stout specimens of *Xanthorrhoea australis*, commonly known as the grass tree. Their dense, brown, hairy trunks are contrasted again with soft green tufts of grass and delicate white colchicums.

▼ A combination of planting has been carefully chosen to ensure that this garden has year-round interest. Evergreen firs and yew provide structure, illuminated with the red and lime-green of the dogwoods in winter; pink blossoming trees herald the dawn of spring, and perennial shrubs promise much for the summer.

Make sure you use the right type of planting material for the finish you require, selecting varieties such as *Ilex crenata* for detailed fiddly shapes, and *Buxus sempervirens* for large, bold pieces.

There has recently been a revival of plant training methods such as pleaching (pruning trees to form a screen) and boxing (pruning standard trees into box shapes). Both methods can be given a contemporary feel by choosing trees such a ginkgo rather than the traditional lime tree.

▥ Evergreen versus deciduous plants

Watching the mood of your garden change throughout the seasons is one of the most satisfying aspects of gardening – from the architectural frameworks of winter that burst into colour in spring and then become dappled shade in summer and may provide another explosion of colour in autumn. It is of great importance that you give this very familiar transition due consideration when planting up a garden. Achieving the correct balance of evergreen and deciduous plants can take some time, but through experimentation you will find what works for your garden.

Initially, look at evergreens and how you can use them. As evergreen trees and shrubs provide the backbone of

▶ Tightly clipped yew forms the most gorgeous towers, punctuating the boundaries of this formal garden. A solid wall of yew surrounds the garden and is adorned with a beautiful twisting wisteria that illuminates the dark green foil.

▲ A specimen of beech has been trimmed into a ring and used in much the same way as topiary, contributing shape and interest to this garden. The beech ring frames masses of irises and other flowering perennials, which are joined with lines of glass cloches.

▼ Formal flower beds brimming with roses and edged with low box hedging are synonymous with traditional topiary gardens. Here, delicate animal topiaries welcome you into the space, and a simple box ball surrounded by colourful perennials provides a central focus.

▶ Elegant green waves of miniature hedging flow across the site like contour lines on a map. Their line and pattern will decorate the garden all year round; in the summer, they will be joined by small herbs and flowering perennials.

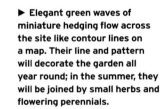

Foliage forms

When you sit back and look at all the different foliage shapes that nature has provided, there seems to be an endless variety. Add to this the work of the plant breeder and you have an almost infinite choice of forms. It is therefore important that you consider the different foliage types and their effect on your overall planting scheme. While it is often the colour of the foliage that first attracts, it is actually its form that will have the greatest effect on your garden.

When leaves are examined closely, there is often amazing variety and detail. Japanese maples possess many different types of foliage, from the feathery, dissected forms to the characteristic, bold, hand-shaped leaves. Equally, hostas provide great diversity, from the large, bold, lustrous leaves of *Hosta sieboldiana* var. *elegans* to the dwarf, glossy varieties. The majority of garden plants have either whole or dissected leaves, and each has its own qualities you can utilize in the garden. Plants such as aloes and New Zealand flax (*Phormium tenax*), with their succulent and strappy leaves, have a whole different group of foliage forms. When used sparingly, these can create stunning effects. Meanwhile, the deeply divided fronds and leaves of tree ferns and cycads offer another type of foliage, which is both bold and translucent – characteristics that are very useful for design purposes. Although many grasses may appear similar in form, there is actually a great deal of diversity for you to experiment with.

In most plants the foliage form is always changing, sometimes subtly, but often dramatically, such as the leaf burst of most deciduous plants. Planting to make the most of these changes will greatly enhance the feel of your garden.

Along with the foliage itself, it is also worth considering how the leaves are attached to the plant. This affects other qualities of the foliage, such as the sound a leaf makes when it moves: listen, for example, to the sound of miscanthus in the wind. Likewise, the leaf stalk will also affect how the leaf moves in the wind, and anyone who has witnessed an aspen tree in a gentle breeze in autumn will appreciate the significance of this. You can use combinations of these diverse foliage forms to create different atmospheres. By mixing large-leaved cannas, hardy gingers (*Hedychium*) with tree ferns and palms, you can create a lush, tropical feel, just by being imaginative with foliage forms. Alternatively you could use aloes, cycads and grass trees (*Xanthorrhoea*) to create a striking arid garden. Remember to introduce foliage forms wisely, and try not to include too many different types at once, as this can look messy and make your garden lack a sense of overall unity.

a garden (see page 86), without them a sense of order can be lost, especially in winter. They give us structure throughout the year, ensuring that our designed features maintain their impact. This structure can be provided either by utilizing the natural forms of plants or by shaping them to fulfil a desired form. The natural forms of evergreen plants vary greatly, from the mounded appearance of rhododendrons and choisya to the vertical profiles of pseudopanax and phyllostachys. These plants can be used to define certain aspects of your garden within the overall design. Shaping evergreen plants in the garden to provide structure has a long history. This has taken the form of the yew or holly hedge, characteristic of English cottage gardens, and the clipped forms of box balls or cylinders in modern gardens. Clipped shrubs are also great for enhancing built features, especially where they are allowed to accentuate or mirror the lines of structures. Since balance is very important, make sure that you plant carefully: too many evergreen plants in your garden can make it too shady and also create a lack of variation throughout the year.

These hedges or blocks of evergreen planting act as the perfect foil for deciduous shrubs and herbaceous perennials, framing their textures and colours. Deciduous and perennial plants provide a wide palette of colours with dramatic contrasts. In spring there are the numerous fresh greens of new foliage and the subtle floral colours of bulbs, perennials and shrubs. Summer delivers an explosion of colours and foliage types such as those of the dramatic cannas and dahlias, while autumn majors on the numerous glowing shades of the turning leaves.

Deciduous trees are generally more desirable than evergreen, as they cast less shade, allowing for a wider variety of plants to be placed underneath. Understanding the seasonal changes, and planting accordingly, ensures there is always something new to see and allows for subtle changes to occur around the core structure of the design.

▼ Long, rustling pennisetum grasses highlight the presence of these stone steps as they proceed down the slope of the garden. The grassy mounds soften the hard landscaping, while the white fluffy flower spikes complement the colour of the stone.

Textures

Breaking down a garden into its different textures or textural combinations may seem like an unnecessary process, but it is one that is well worth pursuing because it will give you a fresh perspective of your garden. Viewing your garden in this rather abstract way can help you refine the planting schemes so that they give maximum impact. Textures can be quite difficult to classify, and gardeners often create their own groups. There is nothing wrong with this, provided that it makes sense to you. The following are a few of the principal textures and how they work in the garden, but take note that this is far from being a comprehensive list.

Textures in the garden are present on many levels, from that of the individual leaf to entire garden features. The rougher types of plant texture, such as holly, fatsias or cordylines, are useful for providing rich backdrops to your planting designs. Feathery types provide a similar function but with a greater degree of translucence; these are typically the grasses, ferns and tree peonies, which help in breaking up lines within a border. Finally, the smooth-textured types; these can be clumps of moss-like scleranthus, *Rhododendron yakushimanum* or a rounded form of *Hosta fortunei*.

▲ Great spiky clumps of pennisetum and stipa grasses sparkle in the golden autumn sunshine. Like fireworks, they set the roof of this den alight, to establish an illuminating garden feature.

▶ Contrasting plant forms dominate this garden. Mounding clumps of sedum fill the square bed, which is enclosed by box hedging, and delicately cut ferns inject contrast and texture into the scheme. Spiky plant species such as *Acanthus mollis* and *Veronicastrum virginicum* create strong accents.

◄ This wonderful form of the asparagus fern, *Asparagus densiflorus*, grows happily in hot climates. Long pointy fingers made up of fine fern bristles stretch out in all directions, each one soft, tactile and elegant. They grow beautifully with other perennials including these small rosettes of sedum.

Plant textures can be either minimalist or diverse in their make-up, and this applies right across the scale. At the lower end of this scale are the localized combinations of foliage textures – a minimalist example is a mixed planting of *Ophiopogon japonicus* and *Liriope muscari*, which presents subtle textural variation. At the other end of the spectrum are diverse combinations, such as a mixed planting of *Alchemilla mollis*, dwarf hostas and acanthus among unfurling fern fronds.

To expand on this and apply it to garden features, it is possible to see how similar principles work on a larger scale. A planted screen of black bamboo (*Phyllostachys nigra*) is an example of how a texturally minimalist planting can work on a large scale. In a less formal garden setting, you could try one of the most texturally diverse garden features there is – that of the wildflower meadow (see page 193). Meadows provide a rich palette of textures to work with, from the many different grasses to the multitude of wildflowers. When combined, they create a sense of harmony that borders on the chaotic.

While you should perhaps not plant out your garden entirely according to how it will work texturally, it is certainly a useful process for helping you to attain the effect you desire.

Leaf and bark textures

When thinking of texture in the garden, different types of leaf and bark immediately come to mind, and they certainly provide an exciting palette with which to work. You would not normally select a plant purely for its leaf or bark texture, though it is always worth giving it due consideration. That said, some plants do deserve selection purely on their bark textures, like the strawberry tree (*Arbutus* x *andrachnoides*), though these tend to be the exception.

On many leaves, the top surface is different from the underside, which can add another level of texture, especially in the wind. The majority of leaves have a smooth surface, which tends to be glossy (as on fatsia and camellia) or to have a lustre appearance (as on many magnolias). Some plants have leaves that are downy or hairy; these span the full spectrum, from the soft down on pulsatilla leaves through to the rough hairy leaves of *Hydrangea aspera* subsp. *sargentiana*. Spiky plants have an even rougher texture, with those such as pseudopanax, hollies and astelias providing an almost industrial texture with their rough edges and sharp points. These different textures are of great use because they are both visual and tactile, which is invaluable in sensory gardens, where people are encouraged to touch the plants.

▲ The spear-shaped leaves of *Yucca filamentosa* are hard and rough in texture, their thorny spikes creating hard lines and shadows. They belong in exotic-style gardens that are rich in lush green foliage and brightly coloured flowers, to balance their strongly architectural forms with ease.

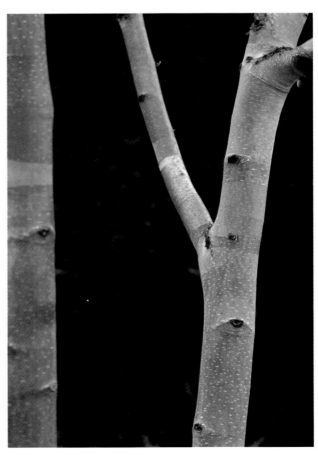

▶ The beautiful bark of a young silver birch tree stands out against a dense green hedge ready to burst into life in spring. As the tree matures, the texture of the bark will change as it begins to peel more and more. The ashen bark gradually breaks up to reveal a chestnut-coloured shiny surface underneath.

◀ A cluster of *Robinia pseudoacacia* 'Rozynskiana' illuminates this woodland scene, with its magnificent apple-green foliage that glows in the soft sunshine. The adjacent lake mirrors the trees, flushing the whole space with light and life. Taller dark green trees accentuate their splendour.

▼ There are many ways of providing texture in a planting scheme, and the aesthetic qualities of bark should not be overlooked. It is visually exciting and provides interest long after the leaves have gone. Cork oak (*Quercus suber*) is prized for its deeply fissured bark, which is spongy to the touch.

Tree and shrubs possess an inspirational variety of bark textures to display in the garden. Trees all over the world have evolved different types of bark to survive a wide variety of environmental conditions. Although bark serves a very practical purpose for the tree, it is its aesthetic, textural qualities that you will wish to exploit in the garden. Many trees have smooth bark, which gives very clean lines to work with – *Betula utilis* var *jacquemontii* 'Silver Shadow' being a fine example or maybe the subtly patterned surface of the snake-bark maple (*Acer pensylvanicum*). Then there are trees with rough-textured bark such as oaks – in particular, *Quercus suber*, which has deeply fissured, spongy bark. Many of the trees that have rough bark are both wonderfully tactile as well as visually stimulating. The most dramatic textures belong to trees that shed their bark – *Acer griseum*, *Betula papyrifera*, *Luma apiculata* and *Stewartia pseudocamellia* all have stunning trunks, which catch the eye. *Eucalyptus* is another exciting genus of trees with bark that peels off, and the snow gum (*E. coccifera*) is by far the most spectacular of these, especially when the bark becomes wet. All these different forms can be used either in group plantings or as focal points. No matter how you choose to use them, remember that sometimes less is more.

◄ The view across the courtyard through delicate stands of golden oat grass is punctuated by the deep rich flowers of irises like 'Supreme Sultan' and makes a great contrast to the darker surfaces of the house beyond.

Textural Feast

Known as the Courtyard, this area of Tom Stuart-Smith's much larger garden in Hertfordshire was the first part of his garden to be designed – more than 20 years ago – and it is also the most recently designed part of the garden. It is quite separate from the rest of the garden, enclosed on four sides, and connects with the house to form an additional outside living space.

According to Stuart-Smith, he re-created it partly as a response to the *Telegraph* Garden that he designed for the 2006 Chelsea Flower Show and also because he felt that it had simply become 'a bit long in the tooth'. The Chelsea garden was based on a minimalist asymmetric plan with an emphasis on texture. In other words, it combined contemporary hard-surface materials, like corten – a pre-rusted steel – with more softly textured planting, and was enclosed on two sides, partly by a hornbeam hedge and partly by a pre-rusted steel panel.

The idea of using rusted weathered materials for the Chelsea garden apparently occurred to Stuart-Smith when he was designing a garden near the sea in Norfolk and saw odd bits of scrap iron – the rusting hulk of an old ship and abandoned machinery – lying abandoned on the shore. In a similar piece of referencing, the barn flanking one side of his Courtyard garden had many years earlier been filled with similarly rusting farm machinery; Stuart-Smith also happened to possess a surplus of the pre-rusted materials post-Chelsea! These have been used in the Courtyard both as panels and for making large tanks of water, and the rusty reddish colour is echoed in the brick-paved sitting area and in the brick-on-edge paths.

◄ A sea of ruby red astrantias and exquisite mahogany and gold irises are among the plants whose reflections are captured in the tranquil water.

▼ This brick-paved patio and its dark patio furniture have been chosen to harmonize with the materials used in the surrounding buildings. To soften these strong lines, feathery Mount Etna broom (*Genista aetnenis*) provides a delicate screen through which to view the informal planting.

STRUCTURE

THE BARN
HERTFORDSHIRE, UK

CASE STUDY #6 CONTINUED

DESIGNER
TOM STUART-SMITH

▲ A similar textural contrast
has been created in this view of
the corten water tanks with the
panelled screens beyond, this
time filtered by the delicate
arching heads of grasses such
as *Stipa gigantea*.

▶ The Barn

1 Meadow
2 Badminton lawn
3 Football lawn
4 Piggery
5 Barn
6 Dairy
7 Seat
8 Rose garden

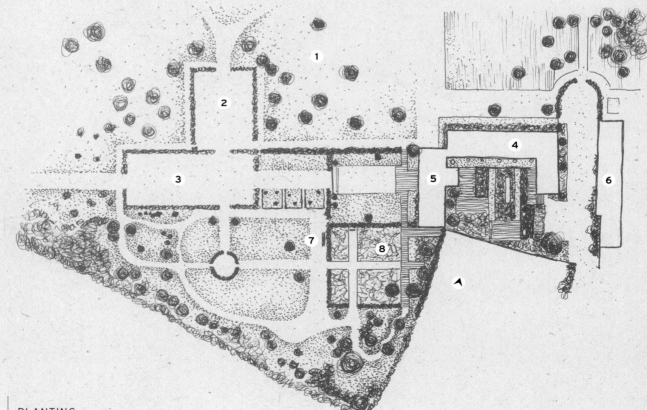

◄ Massed sheets of uncompromising, deliberately rusted steel enclose this courtyard on one side. Stuart-Smith has echoed its russet tones in his plant choices, by using the reddish brown flowers of irises and the deeper reds of massed plantings of astrantias.

The barn is late medieval, and its architecture and that of the surrounding buildings are reflected in the choice of plant colours – rusted metal, warm brick, black tiles and black beams. The planting is simple and softly textural to offset the harder materials and their more uncompromising shapes.

Within the planting, Mount Etna broom (*Genista aetnensis*) creates a useful vertical, Stuart-Smith explains, because it grows to 8m (25ft) without casting much shade. It also has the benefit of producing a shower of fragrant golden flowers in summer on slender arching branches. To balance the lower-level planting, he opted for feathery grasses with more glossy-leaved plants. Among his chosen grasses, Stuart-Smith has included the giant feather grass or golden oats (*Stipa gigantea*), which lives up to its name with its delicate silver-purple stems some 2.5m (8ft) tall and golden arching flowers, and *Carex testacea*, a tufted evergreen grass with stems reaching 1.5m (5ft) in length.

The colour scheme in the Courtyard is a warm but soft palette of rich blues, mauves, yellows and rusty reds, achieved with perennials such as the appropriately named rusty foxglove (*Digitalis ferruginea*), *Salvia nemorosa* 'Ostfriesland' ('East Friesland'), with its bright violet-blue spires, and *Echinacea paradoxa*, which is an unusual yellow coneflower. Also in evidence are *Iris* 'Supreme Sultan', with its gold standards and mahogany falls, and *I.* 'Provençal', with its deep burgundy flowers speckled with yellow. In the shadier parts of the courtyard can be seen drifts of deep rich-red *Astrantia* 'Ruby Wedding'.

◄ The sharp outlines of a brick-on-edge path are softened with the mixed foliage of *Euphorbia seguieriana* and *Alchemilla mollis*, punctuated with the violet spires of *Salvia nemorosa* 'Amethyst'. As in other parts of the garden, the delicate golden heads of *Stipa gigantea* provide a soft filter through which to view the planting.

Flower Power

Although the structure of any garden is largely determined by the hard landscaping as well as the trees and shrubs, the right flowering plants can provide more than just the icing on the cake. It is essential when planning the planting scheme to make sure you create satisfyingly large groups of plants. Each clump should comprise an odd number of the same plant, such as three, five or seven, which is far preferable to having individual specimens scattered around, making the garden look bitty and restless. Gardening novices are always keen to cram in as many different plants as they can, and they tend to run amok in garden centres, like children in a sweet shop. A little restraint, however, pays dividends. Any garden will achieve a much greater sense of harmony if the planting groups are larger and the choice of plants more limited.

Choose your colours carefully so that the different groups of plants blend together seamlessly, unless you are setting out to create a deliberate point of contrast. Working within a colour palette (see page 129) is a key element in creating a sense of harmony and structure in the garden.

▌ Positioning flowers

Flowering plants have varying forms, some of which are very distinctive. Spires, such as those of foxgloves (*Digitalis*), mulleins (*Verbascum*) and veronicastrum, can bring a touch of drama to a border. The big umbelliferous flowering plants such as *Angelica sylvestris* 'Purpurea' and *Anthriscus sylvestris* 'Ravenswing', with their lacy heads of branching flowers rising high above their neighbours, do similar service. A big clump of bronze fennel or brilliant mauve *Verbena bonariensis* are absolute show stealers, particularly when the shafts of a dying sun capture their airy silhouettes.

Some plants with good foliage and brilliant flowers can be placed so they enhance the architectural features of the garden and bring them more into focus. For example, handsome stone or terracotta pots of richly scented exotic lilies, giant alliums or agapanthus look fantastic when used in pairs to flank a doorway or the entrance to an area of a large garden or at the base and top of a big flight of steps. Equally, smaller pots of bright daisies can mark the individual steps, drawing attention to the changes of level.

▲ When massed together, coneflowers (**Echinacea**) are great plants to create a sea of colour in an informal garden. There are many different forms of coneflower, with colours ranging through yellows, pinks and oranges to mauves.

▶ Mixed colours and heights in the border can be just as effective as orchestrated colour combinations. Here splashes of mauve, pink, orange and yellow (verbena, eupatorium, mullein, coreopsis and sedums) jostle together in glorious profusion.

◀ Grasses, such as *Hordeum jubatum* with its starry seedheads, offer a welcome change of key from constant strong colour. Most great garden designers, such as Piet Oudolf, use grasses as punctuation points in hot-coloured borders or to act as a foil for stronger colours.

▼ In this classic example of drift planting, perennials such as *Astilbe chinensis* var. *taquetii* 'Purpurlanze' and *Persicaria amplexicaulis* 'Firedance' make a strong statement, and are interspersed with lighter grasses, such as *Deschampsia* 'Goldschleier'.

Big urns of plants can add a touch of drama to a stone terrace or patio. The planting can be changed seasonally, so the urns are filled with flowering bulbs in spring, deliciously scented, rich-coloured, tender plants such as purple heliotropes or big tobacco plants (*Nicotiana sylvestris*) in summer, and exotic, lily-like, South African *Crinum* x *powellii* in autumn.

Think, too, about using giant perennials, such as *Crambe cordifolia*, that have both architectural leaf shapes and clouds of flowers at high level, so that your eye is lifted to a different plane in the garden. There are some great late-summer giants in the Aster family, including echinaceas and heleniums. A good many of the species in the *Helianthus* and *Rudbeckia* genera can rival any man for height, with the bonus of massed flowers in gold, crimson or mauve. Nothing, of course, can create as much colour impact as some of the big and prolific climbers and wall plants, although these tend to have a comparatively short season of interest.

Foliage and flowers

When buying herbaceous perennials, think as much about the leaf form and its colour as about the flowers themselves because the flowers will be in evidence for a relatively short period of time. Varying the shape and character of the foliage of flowering plants is as important as the actual flower forms and colours. Fortunately, a good few plants offer both interesting foliage and attractive flowers.

The slender, sword-shaped leaves of irises, sisyrinchium and crocosmias provide elegant form in the border long after their flowering display is over. If your garden is backed by evergreen hedges, think primarily in terms of using silver-foliage plants to lighten the overall effect and only secondarily about the flower colour. Bold statements can be made with massive plants such as thistles, which combine eye-catching, handsomely toothed, silvery leaves with arresting flowerheads. What is more, thistles provide a banquet for many different insects.

Informal drifts

Gardeners have become accustomed to concentrating on the individual merits of particularly striking flowering plants, encouraged in part by the great gardening shows where breeders vie with each other to show off ever-more arresting flower forms and colours.

But a garden needs to be seen more like a painter's canvas, in which all the flowering plants play their part. And the form of flowering plants – their general habit and the shape of the clumps that they make – can play as big a part in the structure of the garden as the more widely recognized attributes of purely foliage plants. 'Naturalistic' gardeners such as Piet Oudolf in The Netherlands have designed wonderfully fluid yet structured gardens using repeating soft groups of flowering plants in toning colours, spiced up with occasional spires of contrasting colours or with graceful, airy grasses. This kind of planting can create broad, ribbon-shaped borders, in which the groups of plants blend seamlessly into each other, or much larger drifts can be used, prairie style, over much wider expanses of the garden (see page 196). There is also a hidden bonus.

By concentrating on larger groups of plants, you can provide as much impact with single-flowered species (which benefit wildlife) as you might with the bigger, more highly bred sterile varieties that offer no bonus whatsoever to insects.

When thinking about the structural effects of flowering plants, it is easy to forget the importance of grasses. Although these are primarily grown for their handsome slender foliage, in reality it is often the flowerheads of grasses that make the major impact. Their wonderfully diaphanous form can be introduced to great effect to 'lighten up' denser groups of herbaceous perennials in a flower border or to perform as focal points in their own right. Ornamental grasses have a remarkable propensity for catching the light, as Beth Chatto has demonstrated at her internationally renowned garden in Essex, UK. Her inspired use and precise positioning of different grasses there ensures that their delicate stems catch the first rays of sunshine or the fiery glow of the setting sun. Among the best grasses for this kind of effect are *Stipa gigantea* or *Miscanthus sinensis* 'Morning Light'.

Planting drifts of herbaceous perennials with similar habits and requirements is a great way of providing low-maintenance areas in a big garden, too. Molinia, echinacea, monarda and saponaria combine well in groups with wonderful mauve, silver and pinkish colouring. Running an occasional thread of grasses through such a planting is like putting the fine contrast colour into a tweed fabric – it serves to heighten the overall effect. Equally, introducing a striking colour contrast at certain points can create a focus in the planting.

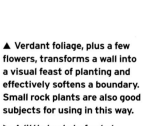

▲ Verdant foliage, plus a few flowers, transforms a wall into a visual feast of planting and effectively softens a boundary. Small rock plants are also good subjects for using in this way.

▶ A little basket of salad leaves, hanging from an old olive tree, maximizes space in a confined area. For additional impact, plant different colours of oak-leaved lettuce, such as red-leaved 'Lollo Rosso'.

IIIII **Containers on walls**

In smaller enclosed gardens, you can make use of walls to create your own flower colour statements. Lower walls, surrounding a terrace or patio, can be used for troughs of container plants. These will have far greater impact if you limit the colour palette to either a single colour or a tonal group of colours. The containers can be replanted each season, so that there is something of interest for spring, summer and autumn, and, if you wish, you can change the colour palette then, too. For an all-white display, go for paperwhite narcissus (*N. papyraceus*) and 'Purissima' tulips in spring, white osteospermum daisies in summer, and white bacopa and little white cyclamen and silver-variegated ivies in autumn. Planting the troughs with two or three small architectural evergreens, such as clipped box (*Buxus sempervirens*), keeps structure throughout the seasons, so you simply replant between these.

Hanging wall pots can give a narrow otherwise unexciting long alleyway a great visual lift. Choose handsome terracotta pots and plant them with some

◄ Masses of pelargoniums and petunias in pots create a floral tapestry in this Spanish courtyard garden. Each season you can experiment with hot contrasts of bright colours, as here, or introduce more subtly toning schemes.

▼ A welcome splash of colour from a basket of petunias (*Petunia* Surfinia 'Pink Vein') gives a visual lift to a shady border. If you feed and water hanging baskets regularly, the plants will reward you with luxuriant growth.

interesting trailing plants, such as the small-flowered but exquisitely foliaged, trailing, ivy-leaved pelargonium or the small-flowered, scented 'Blue Moon' petunias, which flower for months on end. Neither will last the winter in cool-temperate climates. If you have a greenhouse, take cuttings in late summer to replenish next season's planting.

▥ Hanging baskets

Big hanging baskets of flowers cannot fail to make an impact, and some gardeners find them 'vulgar'. They are certainly not suitable for a natural garden, but if planted with enthusiasm and verve, they can bring a real touch of drama to an otherwise boring backyard. Floral hanging baskets look best when seen against hard landscaping, rather than a grassy garden. Plant up great clashing colour contrasts – orange nasturtiums with bright blue daisies and salvias, for example, or bright pink and scarlet geraniums, which will stand out against an area of plain stone. In a more informal setting, go for softer colour combinations, such as silvers, blues and mauves. To achieve harmony in the planting, leave any white flowers out of

the mix unless combined with cool colours or foliage – they tend to diffuse the impact of bright hues.

The most attractive baskets are those made of natural materials, such as filigree metalwork, bamboo or wicker. The less attractive, but inexpensive, hard plastics need to be disguised by an abundance of well-grown trailing plants, otherwise the container becomes more noticeable than the display. The secret of successful hanging baskets lies in choosing plants that have a naturally trailing habit. It also pays to plant the baskets with some attractive foliage plants, such as trailing ivies or scented ivy-leaved pelargoniums, which help to flesh out the display and also disguise and soften the actual basket itself.

To look good, all container plants require regular attention. In hot weather, they need watering as much as twice a day (using gel crystals in the compost helps to retain the moisture better, however) and, to keep the flowering display going, you should deadhead the plants once a week. This cuts off ugly, browning, spent flowers and also tricks the plant into putting its energies into replacing the flowers as you remove the chance for seed to form.

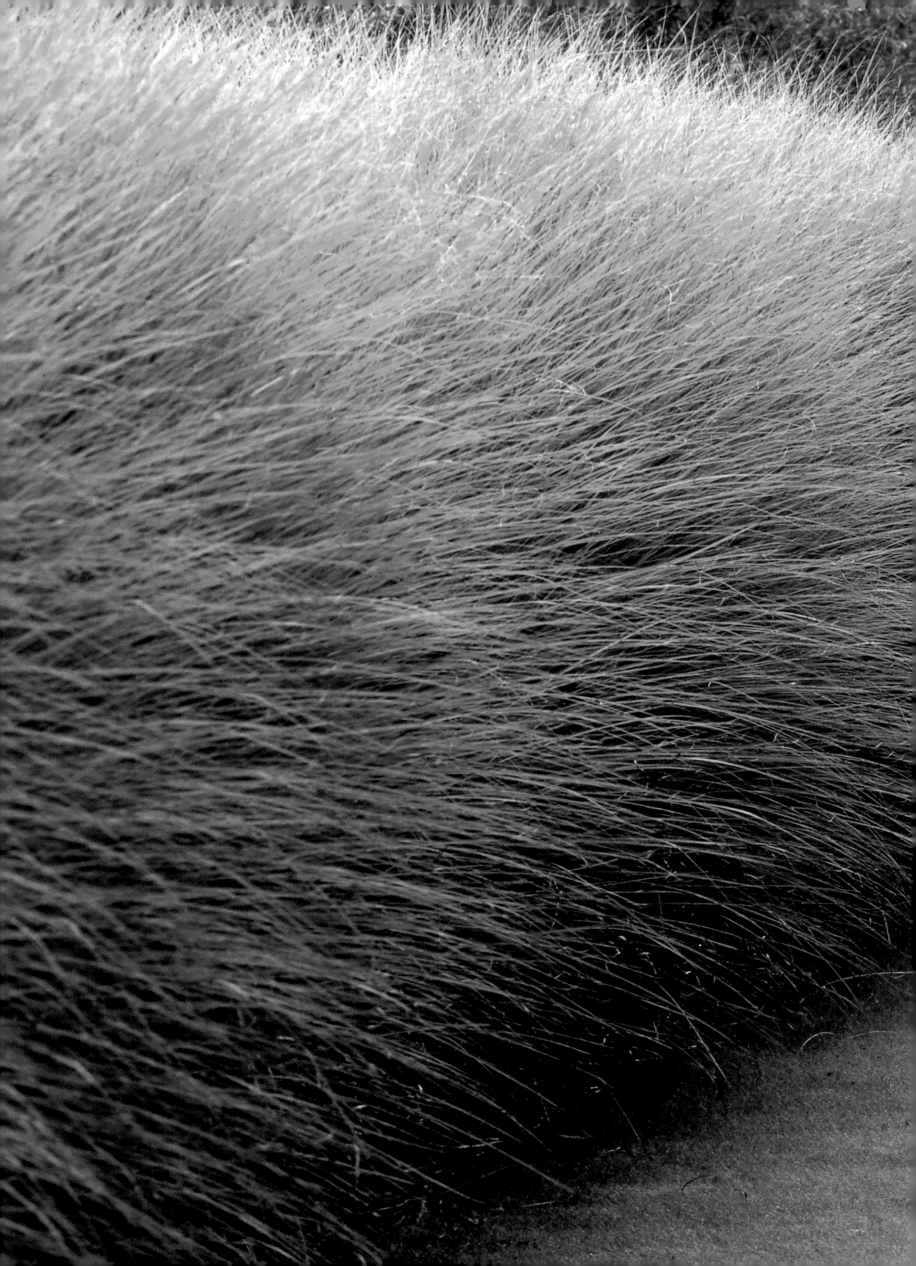

◄ An unusual and handsome screen of tall grasses (*Miscanthus sinensis* 'Gracillimus') creates an exciting green ribbon across this large garden. Later in the year, panicles of flowers will be an added bonus.

▶ The brilliant star-shaped flowers of the azalea *Rhododendron* 'Orange Beauty' offer an explosion in colour, designed to clash with the bright pink wall in the background. Flowers in hot colours conjure up a certain mood and guarantee to fill the garden with brightness and joy.

Colour

Gardeners are like painters in that they create a picture using a certain palette of colours drawn from foliage, flowers, fruit and bark. In using these colours of nature, a gardener creates a scene that is always changing. There is also the opportunity to add to the palette with more permanent garden features such as paving or natural stone, decking, pergolas, painted walls or trellis, and glazed pots. Colour can be used to create areas of light and dark in the garden, to give an impression of distance or proximity and to influence the mood of the visitor.

Not only is the colour in a garden changing through the seasons, but your perception of it also alters throughout the day, and even in different areas of the garden. A south-facing border filled with bright colours might be a bit overpowering on a sunny day, but as the light fades in the evening, the reds, blues and violets become more muted, while the yellows and whites take centre stage. When considering colour in your garden design, decide what mood you wish to create in certain areas, as well as thinking about what colours you like. Do you want a fluid colour masterpiece that Gertrude Jekyll would be proud of, following in her steps of flowing through the colour spectrum, as she did in many gardens, including Munstead Wood, in Surrey? Or will you experiment boldly in true Christopher Lloyd fashion, as he did with his mixes of hot colours in the exotic borders at Great Dixter, in East Sussex?

Flowers and Foliage

Flowers offer a wonderful palette of colours to use in your garden. A flower's intention, of course, is to attract pollinators, but you will benefit from this wonderful side effect. Meanwhile, the foliar foil of green in the form of different leaf shapes and textures means the possible colour combinations are almost infinite. The green base of foliage should not be underestimated. In the garden, green seems to produce a Tardis effect and make a space feel larger. It is also calming and restful, creating a sense of peace and sanctuary. In nature, green is a variable colour; from the lime-green bracts of *Euphorbia amygdaloides* var. *robbiae* to the blue-green hue of *Juniperus squamata*, no two greens are the same, and this variation in colour can also be used to create a rich backdrop for the rest of your flowering plants.

Flower colour evokes different moods and feelings in people, too, and many of these are related to memories. The fleeting pink of cherry blossoms still reminds me of early summer as a child in Dublin, where these trees were widely planted, usually flowering around the time of First Communion. The white nodding heads of snowdrops at winter's end fill me with a sense of optimism that spring is almost here. Many spring-flowering plants bear yellow flowers, which, again, brings a bright positive feeling to the start of the year, while the reds and oranges are usually seen later in summer when things have warmed up a little.

Flowers can add drama with striking upright flower spikes or huge open flowerheads, or can create focal points in a bed. They can create movement physically, like Wordsworth's daffodils 'fluttering and dancing in the breeze', or reflect the movement of light with clever transitions through the colour spectrum in a border. The apparent size of a border can be manipulated using flower colour, employing certain colours to create focal points and attract attention, or others to increase the sense of space by fading into the background. Thus, a feeling of space can be increased in a small garden, or in a large garden a cosy atmosphere can be created.

Foliage, too, can be exploited for its colour, mixing different green tones, adding in red foliage to increase the intensity of a red-flowering plant nearby or introducing variegated foliage to brighten up a shadier part of the border. Leaves with silver or white variegation can be used to separate colours in a border.

To get an idea of the flower and foliage colours that you like, as well as the combinations that will work in your garden, take a camera with you when you next visit the garden centre. Gather some plants on your trolley that you think will be a good combination. Photograph them together, as well as individually. Also take photographs during visits to gardens, or even photograph bouquets outside a flower shop – anytime you see a combination that you like. You will soon have definite ideas about the colours you would like to use. The next step will be to think a little about colour theory so that you can truly produce the effect that you desire.

▼ A graceful border of pastel-coloured flowers instantly produces a restful dreamy garden space where there are no brightly coloured divas to jar the eye or steal the show. The white accents of the variegated foliage are picked up in the fine white flower spikes, and a soft yellow tone attracts the light.

▶ In complete contrast, the deep colours of *Echinacea purpurea* and *Liatris spicata* vie for attention in this eye-catching border. Bright green grassy foliage provides a textural foil that mirrors the upright stems of both flower forms.

◄ In this sumptuous summer garden, the trees and shrubs relax into a beautiful backdrop of many colours, while the ground level is brimming with mottled pinks and mauves and golden grasses. The bronze leaves of *Cotinus* 'Grace' are stunning.

Hot Colours

Whether you are designing a planting scheme for an individual border or one for the garden as a whole, it is important to understand colour theory. The three primary colours are red, yellow and blue, while the three secondary colours – orange, green and violet – are created when two primary colours are mixed. Using this basic colour wheel of red, orange, yellow, green, blue and violet, in that order, helps you to understand complementary colours – those opposite one another on the wheel. Colours are perceived differently because of the length of the light waves reflected by each one. For example, you see green and yellow-green light with most ease because the light waves focus directly on the retina. Red light focuses just behind the retina and, in trying to focus, the eye creates the illusion of anything red being nearer. Conversely, blue light waves focus in front of the retina, and the attempt by the eye to focus on these short waves makes the colour seem more distant.

Red, orange and yellow are considered hot colours. Their bright vivid hues seen in the distance will draw that view closer. Red is the colour sometimes associated with anger, and because it is a stimulating colour, it can bring anger or stress to the surface. This stimulating force, however, brings with it positive energy, alertness, hopefulness and strength. Red provides mental stimulation as well as creating warmth. It is therefore an ideal colour to use near a seating area, or beside an outdoor dining space. In the border, red will jump out at you, so can be introduced to make a wide border seem

◄ Orange is a warm luxurious colour that will entice children out into the garden, and crocosmia is a fantastic garden plant. It quickly multiplies to create large flowing drifts of colour, and its long strap leaves remain tidy and upright, looking great alongside other wide-leaved perennials. The red roses naturally complement the orange tones of the crocosmia.

► The hot-colour, tropical-style border at Great Dixter, East Sussex, is packed with dahlias, salvias, rudbeckias, ensete and ricinus. The reds draw the border closer, while the soft pinks in the distance exaggerate the perspective to make the bed look longer. Yellow tones are found in the flowers and foliage, mediating softly between colours.

◄ Masses of dahlias adorn this traditional garden in an explosion of riotous colour in shades of red and yellow. The rich burgundy blooms add depth and drama to the scheme, and as this fades to pale yellow, the eye picks up on the white details on the bright red varieties in the foreground.

▼ Planting schemes in shades of purple have never been more popular. These colours are excellent for designing exciting and energetic schemes that are also easy and restful on the eye. The purples and whites here are softened by the golden yellow flower tufts of the grasses, to produce a truly beautiful space.

◄ Elegant flowering spikes of *Digitalis ferruginea* are set against deep red Monarda 'Scarlet Garden View'. They are a stunning way of adding texture and vertical accent to a border, either dotted through other perennials or in dramatic clumps. They will flower from late spring through to mid-summer in a shady part of the garden.

cosier – planting red-flowering plants in the centre and the back, perhaps with some red foliage plants to pick out the flowers. In a narrow border, placing reds towards the front and cooler colours to the back will give a sense of a deeper bed. Many reds, such as *Crocosmia* 'Lucifer' with its wonderful flame-coloured flowers, are at their best in mid- to late summer and are a must for those hot late-summer afternoons lounging in the garden. Red foliage is great for picking up the other reds in a border. *Berberis thunbergii* f. *atropurpurea* 'Red Pillar' produces fiery red foliage throughout the season, while *Canna* 'Assaut' bears both red flowers and red- or purple-tinged foliage.

Another warm and sociable colour – orange – is welcoming and luxurious. It is popular with children and is thought to encourage resourcefulness and a sense of fair play. Not only is orange a good colour to accompany red, perhaps near an area for entertaining, but also a hue to consider where the children play most, or perhaps in their wild jungle area. A great orange annual that, once planted, seeds itself each year thereafter is California poppy (*Eschscholzia californica*).

The brightest colour in the spectrum – yellow – is stimulating and inspirational. It is a great colour if you want heated debates in your dining area; perhaps, however, recess the yellow a little because it can be too energetic, even stressful, if it is too close. Many yellow-flowering plants bloom in spring, including daffodils, forsythias and euphorbias, and these lift the spirits as winter is left behind.

Cool Colours

Green, blue and violet are the cool hues on the colour wheel, and they create a sense of space and distance. The predominant cool colour in the landscape is green, forming the backdrop for all other colours. For this reason, green is the most important colour in the garden. It is a restful colour and creates feelings of safety and sanctuary. It is also a hopeful colour, symbolic of new life. The different tones of green produce different feelings, too: for example, the optimistic yellow-green of buds opening in spring or the tired brownish greens of autumn. Dark green leaves are a good foil for bright colours such as reds and yellows, while blue-greens contrast well with pale yellows and pinks. Have a look around your garden centre for different shades of green and different foliage shapes and textures. Pretend that you are planting a green-only garden, and you will be amazed with the variety that you find.

Blue is a calm and relaxing colour. It encourages contemplation and healing. In colour therapy, blue is thought to have a cooling, cleansing, quietening effect. Blue creates a feeling of spaciousness and, because of how the eye perceives it, tends to recede into the distance. Use it to conjure a sense of space in a small garden. However,

if blue is right beside your dining area, too much of it may be excessively calming. It is a great colour for a meditation area, or around a thinking seat. One of my favourite blue-flowering plants is sea holly (*Eryngium* species), and it has numerous cultivars, from almost silver to intense blues. Another great strong blue, *Geranium* 'Johnson's Blue', flowers throughout summer. Try growing some of your blues from seed: I love blue cornflowers and love-in-a-mist (*Nigella damascena*). Blue is useful as a static colour as well, and is often painted on glazed pots.

Violet is an inspiring and insightful colour, equally invaluable for an area in which peace and meditation are sought. In colour therapy, it is believed to ease emotional upsets and to help induce sleep. Why not cluster this colour near your hammock? Violets have a very short light wave just like the blues, and so can be used to create distance in a similar way. Be careful not to plant too many violets together, however, as they can dilute their colour's intensity. They work well interplanted with reddish purple tones, such as *Phormium tenax* Purpureum Group or *Heuchera villosa* 'Palace Purple'. If you wish to make your flower border seem deeper than it really is, plant the hot colours (see page 132) to the front and place your violets and blues to the back. You could also include some blue foliage plants, such as glaucous-leaved hostas, in the border itself, or in the backdrop plant blue-green-leaved shrubs or trees such as *Eucalyptus gunnii*.

▲ A beautiful sweeping border of pastel tones and fresh foliage gently spills out onto the lawn in this garden. Lilac lythrums and white nicotiana clumps create elegant verticals that connect with the taller trees in the background.

◀ In this detailed cross-section through an intricately constructed border of flowers, the colours of *Persicaria microcephala* 'Red Dragon', *Stipa tenuissima*, *Salvia x sylvestris* 'Mainacht' and *Heuchera* 'Obsidian' were chosen to offer contrast and look unusual in a garden designed to excite children.

◄ This fresh and exhilarating planting scheme is set in gorgeous colour tones. Lilac allium globes jump out from apple-green grasses, which could not be in contrast more than they are with the deep maroon berberis cones. Masses of *Phlomis russeliana* disappear into the distance.

▼ The planting here is based primarily on flowers in shades of yellow that harmonize with the foliage in tones of silvery grey. The effect is restful and monochromatic. In the distant landscape, variegated grasses are picked up in the sunlight, contributing soft sound and movement.

Using Tonal Colours

Colours that lie alongside one another on the colour wheel or are varying shades of the same colour are known as tonal colours and, because of their proximity on the wheel, such colours possess some tones in common with their neighbours. These colours or tones create harmonizing combinations.

The use of consecutive colours on the colour wheel, such as blue, violet and red, can gently ease the eye along a border as it makes the transition through the colour spectrum. Soft blues giving way to intense blues, followed by violets, crimson and red, will progress the visitor along the border in a visually calm manner. This style is sometimes called analogous planting, and was very much favoured by the English garden designer Gertrude Jekyll, who used it to great effect in her gardens in the early twentieth century. In the average-sized suburban garden, overuse of this technique can detract from the peaceful intent, however, and the constant variation of colour can become a little demanding visually. This is especially true of gardens where all borders can be seen at one time. The fact that there are a number of modulating colour schemes all vying for attention can detract from the restful effect. In such a situation, it is best to have one large border planted in this style.

Using many tints and tones within one colour can also produce a harmonious design. This is a good way to start experimenting with harmonious or tonal colour schemes, as you will avoid the discord of a multi-coloured design that has gone wrong. There is an art to getting the harmony right, even within one colour, but the subtlety of such a border means you will get away with more if it is not quite right the first time around. A monochromatic border, for example a blue border (see page 144), can always be added to with violets and reds in later seasons in order to create a border of consecutive colours.

Texture, too, is important to consider when choosing a planting list; select flowers of different shapes and sizes to punctuate here and there. Foliage can also be used to good effect, and blue-greens or sage-greens can help the blue flow in a blue border, and with most monochromatic borders the best foliage colour to set off all colours is a silver-green or grey-green. Static colour – for example on a painted wall in the background – can be introduced to bolster the monotone, but the tone used should not be too overpowering. It is also important to balance the floral interest in the border according to the season so that it remains attractive.

▲ In a garden with planting by Piet Oudolf, prairie-style borders are dominated by grasses and spiky flowering forms. The definite lines of *Angelica gigas* are carved out against masses of *Deschampsia cespitosa*. Bright red flowers excite the background, which explodes into arching clumps of miscanthus grasses.

◄ The various garden areas at Sticky Wicket in Dorset are designed with plant combinations in gentle harmonies, with a focus on attracting wildlife and seasonal interest. The similar tones of the main planting in pinks and lilacs complement the elegant shapes of the beds, to produce a harmonious space.

▼ Delicate changes in the tones of burgundy and pink establish an attractive and eye-catching collection of plants. The purple matchsticks of persicaria are strong and distinctive and echo the allium lollipops that are just about to pop open. Cushions of white and pink flowers bolster the planting scheme.

◄ A long, decked boardwalk in the Hakansson garden, designed by Ulf Nordfjell in Sweden, leads out across the water over a miniature pebble beach to another part of the garden. Perennials and grasses are planted in repeated blocks, resulting in a certain naturalistic effect and creating a tranquil place.

▲ Tonal planting of *Lythrum salicaria* and *Galega officinalis* in shades of pink are attractively set against a background of mixed foliage and golden flowers.

Unusual Contrasts

For anyone who wants to create interesting colour combinations, allied with a strong sense of form and texture, there is no better guide than Piet Oudolf, the Dutch master plantsman. His creative and dynamic use of native perennials, with a particular interest in their seasonal changes from the full glory of high summer to the delicate skeletons and seedheads of winter, has had an enormous influence on garden designers of today.

Oudolf's planting style often focuses on creating large loose drifts of perennials, contained by a formal structure. His early work was influenced by that other great Dutch garden designer, Mien Ruys, whose strong sense of form, combined with experimental use of perennials, took shape at her gardens at Dedemsvaart over several decades, until her death in 1998.

At Oudolf's garden in Hummelo, Ruys's influence is present in the way he has compartmentalized the garden. Within this structure, Oudolf has increasingly turned his attention from the overall scale and shape of the garden to concentrating on the delicate tapestry of flower colour,

▲ Neatly clipped yew hedges provide the perfect foil for a wonderful planting colour palette of mauves and silvers. Spires of verbascums provide textural contrast with the softer mounds of perennials.

▶ Strong bright yellows make eye-catching splashes of colour. Good perennials with daisy-like flowers that serve this purpose well are *Inula magnifica* 'Sonnenstrahl' (shown here), as well as coreopsis, helianthus and heleniums.

◄ The ball-like heads of globe thistle (*Echinops bannaticus*) are a great magnet for bees and butterflies, while offering useful verticals to punctuate more low-growing mounds of perennials and grasses such as *Eragrostis curvula*.

COLOUR
CASE STUDY #7 CONTINUED

PIET OUDOLF GARDEN
HUMMELO, NETHERLANDS

DESIGNER
PIET OUDOLF

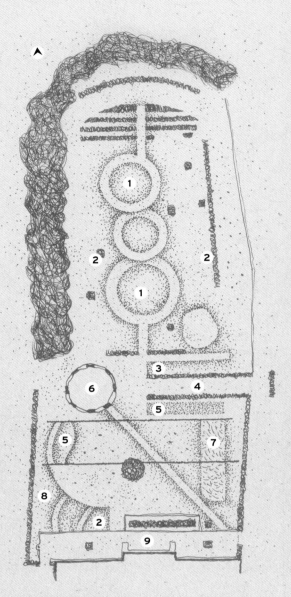

▶ **Piet Oudolf garden**

1 *Stachys* 'Big Ears'
2 Perennials
3 Perennial border
4 Tunnel of beech
5 Shrubs
6 Ornamental grasses
7 Grasses and perennials
8 Spring planting

▼ Sentinels of *Astilbe chinensis* var. *taquetii* 'Purpurlanze' seedheads make a strong colour statement in this garden during autumn. Seedheads of most late-flowering perennials are best left to provide structure in the autumn months rather than being cut down.

texture and form in the perennials he has chosen. His plant preferences are for the taller perennials, many of them flowering in late summer, which he fell in love with when he first saw them in their native American habitat.

The conditions in the North American prairies – with the combination of high heat and heavy rainfall – encourage some really statuesque plants. Among them are the echinaceas, veronicastrums, sanguisorbas. monardas and heleniums. Hummelo shows these simple but distinctive plants off to perfection. Early autumn is the best month to see the garden, when everything in it is at its full height, full growth and flowering more than at any other time of the year.

Oudolf's chosen colour schemes often have unusual colour contrasts: tall mauve spires punctuate a sea of gold in one planting scheme; pinks, scarlets and mauves jostle with each other in another. One reason why his colour combinations work so well – even when they often involve quite surprising contrasts – is that they are softened by the inclusion of grasses. These are threaded through the overall planting design, connecting colours and forms, and blending them seamlessly. The result is an organic flowing sea of colour and texture.

▲ Flowers spires of mixed perennials in soft mauves, blues, pinks and silvers (veratrum, filipendula, veronicastrum, stachys and scabious) combine to conjure up a dreamy colour mix, with an emphasis on form and texture.

◄ Bright yellow *Helenium* 'Die Blonde' makes a stand-out colour splash against the quieter tones of mauves and pinks, which in their turn are set off by dark, contoured yew hedges in the background.

► Harmonizing colours in tones of reds, pinks, gold and silver have been offset by dark foliage. This planting includes the red spires of *Persicaria amplexicaulis* 'Firedance', which contrast with the rounded, pinkish mauve heads of *Eupatorium maculatum* 'Atropurpureum', starry little white aster flowers and the golden umbels of *Foeniculum vulgare* 'Giant Bronze'. The planting is effectively punctuated with grasses like miscanthus and calamagrostis.

Colour Combinations

Colours are perceived slightly differently when viewed in combination. This alteration of perception is subtle yet effective, as it often leads to colours seeming even more vibrant. Colours are seen at their truest beside white or grey. For this reason, it is helpful to use a white-flowered plant to separate colours in a mixed border, while grey-green foliage is a good backdrop for a monochromatic border. In Mediterranean gardens where walls are painted white, colours always look particularly vivid against such a background. When planting different colours alongside one another, a very effective contrast is achieved by putting complementary colours together.

Complementary colours are essentially the six colours of the basic colour wheel paired as follows: red–green, yellow–violet and blue–orange. Each primary colour is paired with a secondary colour with which it has no pigment in common. This creates maximum contrast and intensifies each colour. It is important to balance the colours so that they are not demanding equal attention, and a split of about 70:30 will create a sea of one colour, with drifts or focal points of the other. Use texture and flower form for further variety and richness in the planting scheme. The intense effect produced by planting complementary colours together is quite exciting, so bear this in mind when placing such a design in the garden: for example, if you had a blue-orange mix near your quiet seating area, you may wish to change the colour ratio to tone down the orange a little.

A thoroughly eye-catching colour combination is a design using all six colours of the colour wheel, including variations within them. This can create a bright happy, energetic feeling in the garden. The riot of colour will show forth its stars at different times of the day, too, depending on light levels. Blues, yellows and whites will have a little more magic in the evenings, while the bright, hot oranges and reds will become more muted. Of course, this does not mean that you throw colours in anywhere and hope it works. It takes some experimenting to get it right. The principles of analogous planting or the use of complementary colours will come in handy, but your greatest ally here will be the colour white. As well as showing off true colours well, white is the great palette cleanser in the garden and helps the transition from one colour to another. It separates and bolsters colours, and does not have to be limited to white-flowering plants, but can be in the form of white variegation on leaves or a silver-leaved plant.

If you want to experiment with complementary colours, write down the three colour combinations and bring them with you to the garden centre. Pick out plants of these flower colours and pair them, then photograph them. Look out for these combinations in gardens and even in hanging baskets and window boxes. Once you start to notice the use of complementary colours, you will suddenly see them everywhere, and will soon know what combinations you like.

◀ The planting in the sunken garden at the Great Dixter gardens in East Sussex is by the renowned plantsman Christopher Lloyd. His gardens are famous for the sheer mass of colour and exuberance, where plants fill the senses with energy and excitement. Here, alliums and latycodon are in full bloom in early summer. The primary colour of the yellow erysimums pierces through the scene.

▶ The use of two primary colours is sure to produce a striking flower border. The blooms of *Dahlia* 'Bishop of Llandaff' glow brilliant red in the sun, but the deep blue hues of *Salvia guaranitica* 'Blue Enigma' are enough to match them in beauty and colour tone, and usually steal the show.

▲ Outstanding *Rudbeckia occidentalis* 'Green Wizard' is wonderful for its brown to black cones that are surrounded by short green bracts. Here, Piet Oudolf uses them to create the structure and focus of the planting; they illuminate the scene against a hazy sea of lilac flower spikes.

Colour-themed Gardens

Sometimes when you use colour in the garden, less can be more. Designing a monochrome garden that exaggerates your favourite colour may seem a little over-indulgent, but it can certainly make a bold statement.

There is a history of gardeners planting up single-colour gardens, the most famous probably being Vita Sackville-West's white border at Sissinghurst, or, more recently, Helen Dillon's red border and blue border at her garden in Dublin, Ireland. Monochromatic planting looks lovely as the light falls in the evening, and you may like to try it by the patio, where you watch the sun go down, or near a contemplative spot where you recharge at the end of your day.

A monochrome theme can run through particular borders or an entire garden, though whether or not it works is often a question of scale. Certain colours such as whites or reds lend themselves to entire gardens, whereas colours such as blue work better in an isolated border. Linked to this question of scale is whether the garden is an open or a closed space. Open gardens use elements from the surrounding landscape such as trees or buildings, and these will influence the colour scheme chosen. Closed gardens are designed to be viewed in an enclosed space from which the outside world is excluded; such spaces allow for greater control of the chosen colour.

When selecting the colour theme for your garden, it is first worth investigating the variety of different plants available in each colour, bearing in mind that you can use foliage as well as flowers. You will find that some colours, such as white and red, offer a wide variety of different options, while the choices for blue are much more limited.

▲ A rustic scene with large clumps of *Tagetes erecta*, a member of the marigold family, that collapse onto the path under the weight of the burnt-orange flowers. Fine white flower clusters of *Nicotiana sylvestris* contrast with them in every way.

◄ This spectacular monochrome garden of cow parsley fizzes with excitement and life. The cow parsley has been left to take over the garden in an exhilarating break away from the delicately planned mixed planting schemes that are so familiar. A mown path leads to a hole in the hedge and beautiful views beyond.

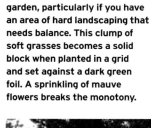

◄ A limited colour palette can produce a bold statement in a garden, particularly if you have an area of hard landscaping that needs balance. This clump of soft grasses becomes a solid block when planted in a grid and set against a dark green foil. A sprinkling of mauve flowers breaks the monotony.

Having an extensive range of plants to select from helps to ensure that you can maintain your scheme throughout the year, though you should not let this stop you from being adventurous.

In reality it is uncommon to have an entirely monochrome garden, as most plants provide contrast against green leaves, but this fact can be used to great effect. Dark green foliage can really enhance whites, making them radiant, especially in the early evening light. There is a huge selection of white flowers and an equally wide variety of flower forms. Blues also work well against green foliage, with hydrangeas being a prime example with their vivid blue flowers. While reds do contrast well with green, being complementary colours, it is possible to find plants that have reddish foliage and these can add further depth to the design. Red gardens work best during the summer months when the higher light levels really help to bring them to life.

In contrast to all these brightly coloured gardens, you could have a purely green garden, which emphasizes texture. Such green gardens can be very rich in texture, contrasting all the different shades of green and mixing these with the wide variety of interesting foliage types. The Victorian fernery is a fine, classic example of how an entirely green garden can work perfectly and create its own atmosphere.

▲ An extraordinary garden of white cliff terraces steps down steeply towards the coast. Tonal planting in shades of pink and lilac, including eupatoria, lavender and bergenias, thrive in the rock-face beds to create a warm and inviting place.

◄ Flushed pink *Aster lateriflorus* var. *horizontalis* flanks a stone pathway of York stone that leads down into the peacock topiary garden at Great Dixter. This historic part of the estate houses 18 birds fashioned out of yew and are joined only by tall green *Stipa gigantea* grasses in a unifying wash of green. The garden is timeless, classy and powerful in its appreciation of topiary art.

Inspiring Innovation

Sir Thomas More was described as a 'man for all seasons'. Helen Dillon is definitely a 'woman for all seasons'. Her gardens at Sandford Road, Dublin, are justly famous, from her books and broadcasting. They are a *tour de force*, put together by a gardener with a wonderfully exuberant eye for shape and colour. In a few pages it would be hard to do more than capture the flavour of this very remarkable garden, and gardener, but concentrating on her eye for colour combinations makes a good start. As Dillon herself says, visiting gardens is an essential way to learn about what works, what you like and what you might grow. Therefore, if you are seeking to discover how colours can be put together, there is no better place to start than with her own garden.

Dillon has achieved soft subtle tonal combinations that are extraordinarily graceful but, unlike many other designers, she also has great fun with whizzy colour contrasts, orchestrating a fascinating array of unusual or otherwise fascinating plants in the process.

In the two long borders that form the backbone of her garden, you can take your pick from two equally matched contestants: dreamy and delicate, or hot and handsome. In the cool corner, alias the delicate blue border, you will find common or garden cornflowers and love-in-a-mist rubbing shoulders with spires of delphiniums

◄ The beautiful distinctive, long, purplish pink spires and typically spotted strap-like leaves of the handsome orchid *Dactylorhiza* x *braunii* make a truly striking statement. Most orchids do best in moist woodland or meadows.

▲ On the terrace, there is a hot mix of colours, from orange and pink dahlias and bright red *Perovskia* 'Firetail' to pink *Eupatorium purpureum*. These are set off by the foliage of big-leaved cannas at the back and the variegated grass (*Miscanthus sinensis*) on the right.

▼ The hot border, with its backdrop of *Acer griseum*, eucalyptus, apple trees and brilliant shrubs, features bright pink cosmos, red roses, pink *Lythrum salicaria*, rusty red *Helenium* 'Moerheim Beauty', bright red *Dahlia* 'Bishop of Llandaff' and deep magenta *Knautia macedonica*.

◀ The blue border lies under the canopy of an olive tree, and there are geometric blocks of box nearby. The principle players here are *Galega officinalis*, aconitum, *Penstemon* 'Sour Grapes', eryngium, campanula, shrubby clematis, catmint, perovskia and delphiniums.

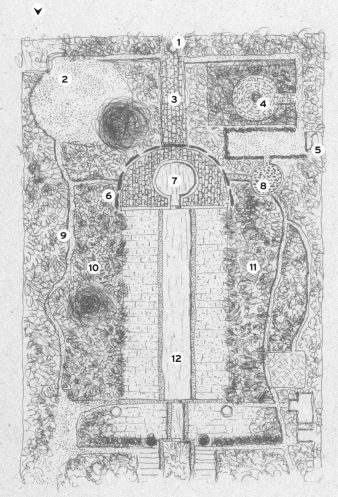

◀ **Sandford Road**

1 Statue
2 Gravel garden
3 Arched walkway
4 Sundial
5 Hen house
6 Ivy-covered arches
7 Circular shallow pool
8 Cobbled circle
9 Winding path
10 Red border
11 Blue border
12 Canal

◀ Lining the path on the left-hand side are stately delphiniums, vying for height with *Eryngium* x *oliverianium*. On the right are white and pink clouds of valerian, with the abundant pale pink flowers of *Rosa* 'Paul's Himalayan Musk' towering above them.

▼ Stonecrops (*Sedum*) and echeverias relish very dry conditions and thrive in containers. They are grown primarily for their handsome foliage, in this case attractive, rose-tinted rosettes.

◀ The water rill divides the hot border on its left with the cool one on the right. It directs the eye to the series of arches clad in variegated ivy and deep purple clematis. The colour of the latter helps to link this area with the planting in the adjacent blue border, which features pale purple clematis, buddleja, perovskia, aconitum, catmint and *Abutilon* x *suntense*.

▶ This pretty, little, starry pink-flowered plant is excellent for containers, flowering in autumn and winter. It hails from South Africa and has the less-than-attractive Latin name of *Rhodohypoxis baurii*.

and spiky eryngiums, skirted by blowsy catmints and brilliant blue salvias. Not only does Dillon mix the types of flower but she mixes textures, too, which gives the borders their sense of movement and a natural liveliness. In the hot corner, the red border dazzles with scarlets, purples, sizzling oranges and deep velvety wine colours: flame-coloured exotic cannas stand out against the delicate lacy umbels of *Angelica sylvestris*, dahlias contrast with dark *Scabiosa atropurpurea* 'Chile Black'.

But, as good as it gets, it is never going to satisfy Dillon for too long. She is at heart an innovator, keen to try out new ideas, new plants, new designs. She moves plants around whenever she feels they, or the garden, demand it. As she points out, you need to be on your toes. Nature has a way of making sure your best-laid plans 'gang agley' – her allium collection was laid waste by onion neck rot, and her numerous cultivars of *Iris reticulata* fell prey to inkspot disease.

Not so long ago, Dillon dug up her exquisite traditional lawn and replaced it with a very contemporary limestone canal, establishing a very strong sense of theatre. As Dillon comments, she is torn between her eye for design and her need as a plantswoman to find space for her new acquisitions. It is this on-going battle between colour, shape, form and texture that is at the heart of this dynamic and exciting garden.

◄ These undulating bougainvillea hedges in full bloom are a most spectacular sight. Careful nurture and clipping of this climbing plant has produced a solid mounding hedge. Tiny white flowers are housed within the brightly coloured flower bracts that are characteristic of bougainvilleas.

► Japanese acers display their magnificent autumn colours at the Westonbirt Arboretum in Gloucestershire, UK. In ancient Japan, villagers walked miles to view the brilliance of these trees, brought home their favourites, and cultivation produced the wonderful specimens that grace gardens across the world.

Seasons

One of the great joys of gardening is its seasonal nature. Depending on where you live, the differences in daylight hours and climate can have a vast effect on your garden in so many ways – on how you use it, on when you do so and on what happens in it. Of course, these variations will be reflected in the landscape at large. Having relatively defined seasons is what makes gardening in the northern hemisphere so exciting. Most people have their favourite season. In my tradition, spring is all about renewal and regrowth; summer – especially early summer – deals in colour; autumn revolves around harvest; and winter is about decay and rest. Many of these sentiments, however, are generalizations. But the fact that you are anticipating changes, and you are working with so many different elements, explains why gardening is such a favourite pastime. With a selection of so many different climates, gardeners are tricked into trying a wide range of species, some of which would not be natural bedfellows throughout the whole of the year but will bask in their favourite three or four months.

Things are always on the move, never static, and the more time you spend in your garden, the more you will become aware of the subtle changes between the seasons. The plants in your garden act as a kind of calendar, reminding you of the time of year and providing an insight into what is to come. So when you plant out your garden, try to get the most out of what every season has to offer. In the well-planted garden, there are always things of interest, so plan to cover all the seasons and celebrate the different charms that they have to offer.

Spring and Summer

Spring is a time of hope. It is about the anticipation of the season as much as the reality because, of course, the seasons work in contrast to each other. So even in the depths of winter, you are egging on spring, waiting for those first bulbs. And when it does arrive, it goes much too fast. You cannot keep up with all the changes in your garden – sap is rising, the air is full of optimism, and colour is everywhere, whether from shrubs or from bulbs that have been imported from many different lands over the centuries. New lime-green leaves are appearing from buds like fragile, tiny silk handkerchiefs. You may wait until the ground is warm to sow the lettuce and tomatoes, peas and courgettes (see page 252), or you may try and cheat spring by starting them off inside or in polytunnels, sometimes with added heat.

Spring starts gradually and ends with an explosion of foliage and flowers. The first green shoots of snowdrops pushing their way up through the frozen ground of winter are a welcome harbinger of the new season. A kaleidoscope of colours is possible with bulbs alone: white and blue anemones, yellow and blue crocuses, tulips in just about every hue imaginable, the vibrant yellows of the many *Narcissus* species, gentian-blue chionodoxa, chequered fritillarias, as well as irises in purples and blues. Many trees and shrubs also come to life at this time of year: *Osmanthus delavayi*, *Choisya ternata* and *Viburnum carlesii* all burst onto the scene exuding heavy fragrance. Pre-empting these are the magnolias and early-flowering cherries, which on a clear day shine white and pink against a blue sky. Later on will be a profusion of scents and blossoms as the rest of the cherry, apple and pear trees burst into bloom.

When summer marches in, initially it is all about colour: the erect white or pink plumes of a horse chestnut, white cow parsley, the amazing yellow of oil-seed rape in fields, the red of poppies and the joy of the herbaceous border. It can be a competition to keep the symphony going – in early summer, everything vies to be in flower at the same time, each plant wants to show off. For the gardener, the trick is to maintain the drama till the third act.

The explosion of colour and scents can be overpowering during summer but, with careful planning, it is possible to create memorable combinations. The smell of wisteria mixing with philadelphus on an early summer's evening is as unforgettable as that of old-fashioned roses and sweet peas. As you will be spending more time in the garden in summer, it is worth thinking about your favourite fragrances and making sure they are in plentiful supply. Equally, you should plan for exciting colour combinations, such as yellow tiger lilies with the tall dark spires of *Buddleja* 'Dartmoor', which make a dramatic display in any garden.

▶ Irises are delicate and understated, yet make a strong statement when planted in solid blocks. This beautifully established border stands tall in a proud display of straight-lined stems and strap leaves in all their splendour. The soft pastel shade of lilac is the icing on the cake.

▼ Spring is a wondrous time in the garden when the cool sunshine gently warms the soil and sleeping bulbs and perennial plants burst into life. The early doronicum daisies wash the ground in a golden yellow as flushed pink tulips dance in the sun.

▶ A topiary garden is enlivened with the colours of summer. Clusters of pink bush roses and lavender flank a gravel path, creating a wonderfully fragrant walkway that leads through the garden towards a topiary arch and a beautiful vista. These plants are a timeless combination, with strongly contrasting habits and flowers.

◀ There is something enchanting about the blossoms of spring. They fill the landscape with colour and life, but, more importantly, herald the end of the winter and the dawn of warmer, longer days in a spectacular celebration.

Autumn and Winter

Although autumn arrives with a very definite change in the weather, it is accompanied by beautiful golden light. It need not be a sombre time of year; there can still be plenty of drama in the garden. Gardeners who are reluctant to give up the summers colours can fill out their borders with late-flowering dahlias, sedums and asters. Yet, eventually, they will grudgingly yield to the pleasures of autumn as they discover new joys when harvesting fruit and watching the sugars in broadleaved tree foliage turning greens to rich reds, pinks and yellows. There can be a crispness in the air, and – with your memory always recalling the best autumn you have had – the leaves are dry to kick on the pavement and conkers are abundant.

By choosing plants that give good autumn colour or have colourful fruits, you really can extend the drama in your garden until late autumn. There is a wide palette of yellows, oranges and reds to work with, and some like the katsura tree (*Cercidiphyllum japonicum*) have the bonus of giving off the smell of burnt toffee. Trees that reliably produce a wonderful display include *Liquidambar styraciflua*, *Nyssa sylvatica*, most of the acers and many of the oaks. Later on is the time for shutting up the garden and retreating indoors, letting your borders disappear into the ground.

Winter divides into pre- and post-Christmas. It is manageable up until mid-winter – the glow of autumnal colour still feels good. After Christmas is when nature does its job: snow can carpet the garden and, in its

▼ Grasses are fantastic garden plants for texture, volume and colour. Here, fluffy mounds of miscanthus are adorned with the magnificent tassel-like flowers that appear in summer and last right through to autumn. In winter, they remain standing, to form rusty coloured winter sculptures.

illusionary way, make all seem perfect, united, balanced and bright. It creates a landscape over which you have no control. Frost attacks on the soil can be helpful, but they play havoc with any imported exotics, such as tender dicksonias and hebes.

This is a great time of year for berries: the soft fruits that grow brilliantly in a cool-temperate climate; the brightly coloured fruits that adorn many shrubs and trees following their blooms; and the fruits that nourish local birds and animals on the hunt. Berries bring colour, shape and a richness to a planting scheme, and are another reason to choose plants that will add another dimension to your garden's seasons of interest and extend the life of your plot well into autumn and beyond. Rowan trees produce great clusters – *Sorbus aucuparia* has dark orange berries, while *S. hupehensis* bears wonderful pinkish red ones. For a more unusual-coloured berry, try the shrub *Cotoneaster* 'Rothschildianus', with its delicate light yellow fruits. Being evergreen, it is useful for all-year foliage, too. Or for something really special, plant *Callicarpa bodinieri*, which will reward with iridescent mauve berries in the depths of winter.

Winter can also provide some subtle flowers and scents to tide you over through the coldest months. Of these, winter sweet (*Chimonanthus praecox*), winter box (*Sarcococca*) and witch hazel all contribute a flash of colour and scent at some point throughout winter; likewise, a swathe of snowdrops lets you know that spring is not too far away.

Fantastical Greens

The most successful year-round gardens are usually dominated by the colour green. And 19km (12 miles) east of Oeuf in France, there is a good example – Les Jardins de Séricourt. Designed by Yves Gosse de Gorre in 1985, it has matured beautifully and covers an area of 4 hectares (10 acres). It is a poetic garden, a plot divided into a series of rooms, designed to surprise, delight and appeal to children of all ages, including adults. This garden reminds the visitor of fairy stories – gothic, dark and slightly sinister in some places, and light, airy and colourful in others. It is a true fantasy.

If you are not dealing in the formal idiom, it can be difficult to create gardens that work throughout the seasons. What de Gorre has done so successfully is to embrace different themes – a garden drama, if you like, that builds up act after act to a beautiful climax.

While there is a predominance of green in the form of trees, lawn and topiary, the garden sings with colour throughout the year. The wonderful rose arbour is cathedral-like in its broad reach. Garden archways rarely achieve this breadth. The sheer width allows for a cacophony of dripping plants, and the overall impression

◄ An imaginative topiary set – an outdoor room made from clipped box, complete with sofa, chair and table – opens the mind to the many and varied possibilities of topiary.

▲ Evergreen topiary shapes with a light dusting of frost create a mysterious and atmospheric winter scene, heightened by the white-painted tree trunks.

◄ The Rose Cathedral is a hymn to roses in summer. Graceful wide-span arbours provide magnificent frames for a host of climbing plants in this majestic space.

SEASONS

LES JARDINS DE SERICOURT
PAS-DE-CALAIS, FRANCE

| CASE STUDY #9 CONTINUED

DESIGNER
YVES GOSSE DE GORRE

▼ When deciduous trees are bare, the green topiary shapes beneath provide sculptural interest and invite the visitor to wonder and explore.

▼ **Les Jardins de Séricourt**

1 Yellow room
2 Geometric garden
3 Rose cathedral
4 Circle of willows
5 Topiary garden

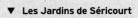

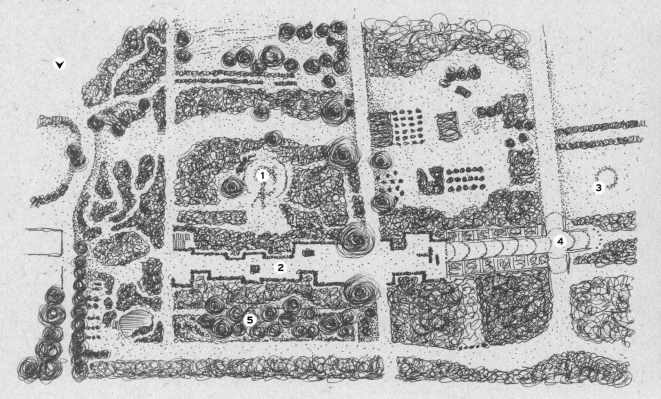

◀ The yellow room's central feature is box (*Buxus sempervirens* 'Rotundifolia') carved into a serpent shape, winding in and around the gravel enclosure. The use of other plants such as gleditsia, golden yews and maples will brighten this area even on overcast days.

is one of wonder. A succession of seasonal colour has been achieved by planting climbers that really shine at the different times of the year: for example, clematis during the spring months, an explosion of roses in summer, and a multi-colour display of vines in autumn.

The outdoor topiary room is pure fun and escapism – reminiscent of some of the extraordinary fantasy gardens of the Italian Renaissance. A series of everyday shapes, such as couches and coffee tables, complete with wine bottle and glasses, has been lovingly tended to form evergreen outdoor rooms. The very mundaneness of the shapes, clipped and trimmed over the years to resemble domestic items that we all have in our homes, adds to the Alice-in-Wonderland feel.

This garden does change throughout the year, but the differences are even apparent in a single day, with strong sunlight and shadow. In winter, dustings of frost or snow add to a Narnia effect. Les Jardins de Séricourt is a dramatic place, packed with symbolism – original, contemporary, imaginative and humorous – and will delight the visitor on any day of the year.

▲ A strong rhythmic, geometric pattern is built up with tightly clipped box, establishing strong lines and definition throughout winter. In summer, these beds contain a profusion of delightful and colourful herbaceous plants such as phlox, hemerocallis and asters.

◀ The trunks of lime trees painted with whitewash stand like ghostly sentries, sparking intrigue and curiosity, and creating a surreal impression.

▼ Well-planned planting ensures that this garden is still filled with colour as autumn moves in. Late-flowering dahlias and hebes provide invaluable late-season nectar, vital for pollinating insects. Bees and hoverflies will be useful for the kitchen garden of sweetcorn and runner beans, which grow nearby.

▶ A tight colour palette of purples, pinks and whites produce a serene and relaxing atmosphere that invites you to slow down and stroll among the flower blooms. Larger shrubs and tall, arching grasses stand out as puntuation marks leading the eye down the path.

Year-round Interest

As a young gardening student, the request from clients that demented above all was for a garden with year-round colour but little maintenance. It does not exist. To create a symphony, you need to work very hard. Knowledge is king – to be able to appreciate what the seasons have to offer, what plant looks good when and why. A garden that relies exclusively on seasonal colour, on the show-offs popping up to display their newest, freshest colour and then retreating, can be just too much work for many people. If you rely only on those showstoppers, you ignore the vast quantity of plants that offer much more subtle interest. It is true that the previous generations embraced colour like never before. But now there is an equally appreciative audience for more subtlety. Greens in their many shades, as well as silvers and bronzes – all have their fan clubs. Often the delicate difference in shade and texture, provided by plants that do not feel the need to shout for attention, can be an emotional and sophisticated.

Evergreens that will form a hard-working backbone to your garden include yew, box, cypress, holly, pittosporum, skimmia, viburnums, *Garrya elliptica* and *Prunus lusitanica*. Many of these can be clipped to create distinctive shapes and lines that will keep the eye entertained all year round. Add to these the 'ever-silvers', such as the wonderful *Astelia chathamica*, *Festuca glauca* and lavenders, some 'ever-bronze' grasses (for example, *Anemanthele lessoniana*) and you will have an understated but satisfying picture in all seasons. As well as interspersing spring and summer bulbs such as narcissus and allium for extra seasonal punctuation, the addition of ferns will provide texture and interest. Many ferns are evergreen, while the deciduous ones provide interesting shades of bronze and rust.

There are certain plants that give something in every season: for example, *Amelanchier lamarckii* – a specimen that is stunning in multi-stemmed form. A fragrant and fine creamy white blossom in spring is followed by ovate apple-green leaves in summer, which then develop luminous autumn colours. The bare stems are covered in shiny black berries for winter decoration. Strawberry tree (*Arbutus unedo*) is another gorgeous plant that performs throughout the seasons; it is an evergreen, covered in shiny dark green leaves, and has tiny white bell-like flowers that are joined by strawberry-like fruits in autumn. It is known for its deep reddish brown bark that slowly peels to reveal new layers in different hues. Finally, do not dismiss the most common tree, the humble birch (*Betula*), which is native to so many places and offers an abundance of interest all year round.

▲ A magnificent Japanese acer begins to undertake its autumn colour change. Acers are perfect trees that will suit any size of garden, as they are extremely slow growing. Their trunks can be trained to stay short so that the beauty of their finely cut leaves can be closely appreciated.

▼ A serene and inviting garden composed almost entirely from plant life. A meandering path leads through clusters of perennials that will see the garden through all four seasons. Colourful shrubs and grasses create highlights on the way down to a handsome focal tree.

◄ A magnificent wisteria tree takes over this garden in a spectacular summer display of lilac flowers. It awakens an otherwise sombre garden of pond reeds and boggy plant species.

▲ Frost softly coats the evergreen backbone of this garden, which is composed of box and yew, in a twinkling winter scene. The rest of the garden sleeps and conserves its energy after the energetic summer just past.

Seasonal Plants for Cutting

▲ Plants that produce brightly coloured flowers create impact in the garden, but bringing them inside as cut flowers highlights their intensity and beauty even more. The burnt orange blooms of *Lilium* 'Fire King' and deep purple flower spikes of *Penstemon* 'Midnight' would make a stunning statement as the centrepiece of a room.

▶ Hot-coloured flowers offer drama and energy and an instant feeling of the exotic. These blood-red cannas make fantastic cut flowers that will need to be balanced with other high-impact blooms such as strelitzias and zantedeschias; the glossy leaves of *Fatsia japonica* will finish the arrangement beautifully.

There really is no comparison between air fresheners and fresh flowers, so it is well worth designing your planting scheme to include plants that you can use in the house. Growing plants that are good for cut flowers throughout the year adds another dimension to your garden, while also building a connection between your inside and outside spaces. If you are looking for ideas of what to use for cut flowers, it is well worth visiting your local florist for inspiration. While you might not be able to grow some of the exotics that modern florists stock, you certainly get a good idea of the different types of flowers and foliage available. Do not be afraid to experiment and create your own statements or combinations. Let your imagination run away with you.

Spring provides a number of options for cut flowers. Early in the season there are various bulbs such as tulips and daffodils, along with certain shrubs such as magnolias. If you choose the correct varieties of both daffodils and magnolias, they can provide excellent fragrance in the house. Late spring offers the Lenten rose (*Helleborus orientalis*), early alliums or maybe a branch of a heavily scented purple lilac.

When summer explodes onto the scene, there is a whole host of cut-flower options. Many of these plants have stunning form, such as foxtail lilies (*Eremurus*), cactus dahlias or the fabulous *Gladiolus murielae*, which is also heavily scented. This time of year also provides some of the most dramatic scents: for example, the powerful Asiatic lilies and subtle iceberg roses, which both mix beautifully with the sweet fragrance of sweet peas. Other plants work well on their own, such as a vase of sunflowers or white echinacea, which brighten up the dullest of days. Although flowers tend to illuminate the centre of any arrangement, there is always space to add interesting foliage from plants that you may have in the garden – for example, eucalyptus branches.

Autumn can be a difficult time to find flowers for cutting, but if you plan carefully, you can extend your season well into mid-autumn. A number of plants such as *Anemone hupehensis* 'Honorine Jobert' or the numerous hydrangeas will faithfully provide you with cutting material over a long period, and if you dry hydrangea flowers, they will last even longer.

Finally, you may think that winter has nothing to offer in the way of floral decoration for the house, yet there are a few plants that can tide you over. A branch of winter sweet or winter box will provide delicious fragrances that come to life when brought into the house, while hollies can also cheer up any festive winter table, with their many different-coloured berries and types of foliage.

◀ Box ball topiary forms a rich, mounding backbone that is sumptuous and tactile. Alliums punch their way out and bloom as fine natural sculptures, making a powerful statement in outline and colour. Alliums are becoming an essential part of beautiful summer gardens and will grace a vase of flowers like nothing else.

SEASONS

BROUGHTON GRANGE
OXFORDSHIRE, UK

CASE STUDY #10

DESIGNER
TOM STUART-SMITH

▼ Fabulous tones of green, brown and golden yellow in the mass planting march summer on into autumn. Upright clumps of calamagrostis glow in the sunlight, being the highlights in a sea of persicaria, hakonechloa and eupatoriums.

Seasonal Moods

The garden at Broughton Grange is a walled one in its most modern form, built with square sections that echo the traditional kitchen garden but which are filled with the most sumptuous collection of horticultural plant species. These change the emphasis within the garden depending on the season. The space is quite separate from the main house and is laid out in definite lines and terraces, creating a sense of order that contrasts beautifully with the colourful undulations of the flora.

The terraces that step gently down into the landscape open out onto the most wonderful views of the surrounding countryside, over rolling hills and farmland and a river. The eye is pulled back into the garden through the order that is achieved by the hard landscaping within the space. Fine gravel paths allow passage through the terraced beds that are boundless in pattern and form, texture and colour, and dotted with structural topiary

shapes. A straight rill runs through the terraces and ends in a large square pool over which floating stepping stones traverse. These features and the abundant flower beds are all fashioned in smooth golden yellow York stone in a harmonious and sophisticated look.

The reflective pool creates a tranquil setting for a table and chairs; the area is softened with fine gravel and provides a perfect place to stop and take in the views. This space is largely adorned with sun-loving Mediterranean plants and highlighted with towers of yew (*Taxus baccata*) in deep green vertical accents. Drought-tolerant silver foliage plants such as stachys and artemisia intermingle with deep purple spikes of sage and lavender; silver towers of *Verbascum olympicum* pierce through the composition, and the succulent sedums form fantastic mounding forms.

The main beds here are packed with some of the most glorious plant combinations that are synonymous with

▼ The vast flower beds in all their glory – a wonderful combination of purple, white and yellow with tiny hints of pink. The great swathes of perennials at Broughton Grange are profuse in texture, form and colour. Broad bands of lavender run along the pea gravel paths, adding drama and a sense of the Mediterranean.

◄ A straight rill splices the main flower beds in a dramatic contrast with the free-flowing perennial planting. The yellow stone edges complement the soft yellow flowers of *Phlomis russeliana* and golden foxgloves.

SEASONS

BROUGHTON GRANGE,
OXFORDSHIRE, UK

CASE STUDY #10 CONTINUED

DESIGNER
TOM STUART-SMITH

▼ Drifts of persicaria, eupatoriums and phlox create a scheme in colour tones from light pink through to a deep crimson in autumn. Masses of grass species and their fluffy flower spikes bring softness and movement to the composition.

▶ Golden stepping stones traverse the square reflective pool and also define the large flower beds in a wonderful contrast of structure and naturalistic planting. The rusty beech topiary is starkly illuminated against the fresh green growth of spring.

Tom Stuart-Smith. Grasses, salvias and euphorbias ebb in and out of soft yellow phlomis, santolinas and foxgloves; soft white poppies, silver eryngiums and stachys glisten as highlights in the sun; alliums and yews punctuate the space and reach for the sky. The planting flows towards the horizon and finishes in a series of great mounds of yew against a final canopy of mature deciduous trees. Sections of pleached beech trees decorate the stone walls and indicate separate sections of the garden. Clipped beech topiary appears throughout the scheme and is particularly striking among great plantings of persicaria, eupatoriums, calamagrostis and low mounding grasses.

What is so amazing about this largely herbaceous composition at Broughton Grange is its long season of interest. It is the rusty beech towers and square blocks of calamagrostis grass that become the most striking features in the winter months. Frosty mounds of grass and persicaria carpet the ground, while the spent flower baubles of *Phlomis russeliana*, alliums and sedums etch wonderful shapes against the grey skies.

▼ **Broughton Grange**

1 Glasshouse
2 Fruit cage
3 Beech tunnel
4 Upper terrace
5 Espalier boxes
6 Terrace and pool
7 Middle terrace
8 Parterre
9 Topiary lawn

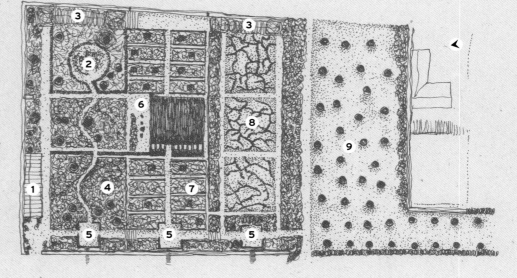

▶ In the small Italian village of Bomarzo is the most extraordinary garden containing outlandish statuary and a precariously leaning tower. Known as the Park of Monsters, the garden was devised by Pirro Ligorio on commission of Prince Orsini, to vent his grief at the death of his wife Giulia.

Styles

||||| Many different classic garden styles have evolved in a variety of places around the globe for innumerable reasons. Humans started off as hunter-gatherers but it was not long before an innate sense encouraged them to grow for pleasure. They appreciated pretty things. And they seemed to have a natural inclination to create order around them. The more sophisticated humans have become, the more extreme this trend has manifested itself in gardens.

Over hundreds of years, when travel was very hard and influences were, therefore, not spread or diluted, many different garden styles evolved – formal, informal, exotic – and were perfected through reasons of power, religion and social evolution. These days, of course, influence is immediate. If there is a new style in vogue, it soon makes its way onto television, the pages of magazines and the catwalks that are the annual flower shows. And it is digested, and regurgitated, often without recourse to its origins or philosophy. But can you imagine a time when this did not happen – when there was real excitement at the discovery of a different way of doing things; when intrepid travellers returned with sketchbooks and specimens; and when rumours would spread about the cultural and artistic achievements of a king in a neighbouring land who had commissioned the best garden to perfect the style of the day?

Although gardening has always been about fashion, the wonderful thing is that the best styles tend to last. Over the years, those that can be replicated as both grand gardens and as smaller showpieces are the ones that usually become popular.

Which Style?

Although the various garden styles that have emerged over time have left templates for your own garden, you also have the freedom and ability, depending on your circumstances, to go it alone and develop your own style. There are a number of factors, however, that contribute to your decision – your local environment being the most important one. What will grow, and does the climate or microclimate suit your own desires and ambitions? When you are creating a garden, you must be careful not to fight against the prevailing conditions.

Plants are the most important element in your design – they will give you the most joy, and if you work with the conditions and tailor your style to those conditions, you are a long way towards creating a successful garden.

You also need to think about what you like. What is your personality? People find it very easy to reflect their own styles with their clothes and interiors in their homes, but do not always do this in their gardens. Style is often about what could be considered superficial choices. Are you very flowery? Do you like the idea of lots of colour? Or is it a restrained palette that you have chosen for your outfits and your wallpaper? Is there a particular place in the world that leaves you with a warm and exotic feeling? Do you love all things Japanese, or is elegance in a French romantic garden what you would love to reproduce?

Of course, the other big factor when considering a style for your garden is practicality. Do you have enough knowledge, time and money not only to create your favourite verdant vision but also to look after it? Will it work for you? And will it work for everybody who lives with you?

▲ The water that forms a natural part of this garden lends itself to the Japanese style, which has been chosen for the aesthetic. It is important to embrace the virtues of your site to obtain a much more unified final result. Water-loving carex grasses, shady hostas, azaleas and a central acer set the scene.

◄ Shaped topiary gardens grace grand houses and castles throughout the world in a show of affluence and wealth. They create permanent structure and shape. Yew hedges suit hot, dry conditions, being highly drought-tolerant; elegant drifts of lavender lead up to a cooling water fountain.

Do the aesthetics match the practical requirements of the plot? What background does the garden have, and is what you would love to create going to match or distract from the landscape wallpaper? If you have rolling lush hills in the background, how is an Arizona-inspired arid cactus garden going to look? Not well. Also, do you want to fit in or do you want to stand out? Is gardening a passion or is the space – the garden – just a something that has to be looked after? There are lots of questions – but also lots of styles and opportunities.

Even having a basic understanding of the evolution of garden styles helps – you do not have to be a scholar. Some great garden writers have illuminated my knowledge and painted wonderful pictures and displayed great understanding of how, for example, the Persian garden, in what is now Iran, originated, or how some of the Renaissance gardens of Italy developed. There are always stories, often power struggles and occasional ritual behind the perfecting of styles. And there are always a few prominent people, the names of whom are sometimes passed down through the centuries, whose work in those styles is regarded as seminal. Recent examples would be Gertrude Jekyll, Capability Brown and André Le Nôtre, but there were also Zen monks who were very influential in passing on the rules and laws of the oriental edifice but it is not known who they were.

Capturing an essence of a true style is what really matters. Understanding why or how it evolved will result in much greater appreciation, while knowledge about its origin enhances the success and contemplation of your vision of paradise. It also helps if these old notions can engage with intellectual or romantic minds of today, so that styles are allowed to be reinterpreted and advanced. With a spark of contemporary input, you can reinvent and add new life and vitality to your garden knowledge.

▲ Carved out in definite dividing rooms and complementary open spaces, this garden displays a strong sense of taste and style. A beautiful water feature sweeps through the site, cooling the atmosphere and inviting you in. A limited planting palette brings the garden together in sumptuous shades of purple and green.

▼ The unmistakable grandeur of a Persian-style garden is the ultimate display of opulence. This magnificent residence displays its privileged water supplies, and the flowers in hot garish colours include varieties from all over the world.

Historical Context

Deeply held principles, practical considerations, passion or massive egos combined with climate, soil and available vegetation have been the main influences behind the successful styles that are familiar today. So, despite many old ideas of garden creation not surviving, those that remain influential to this day have lasted because they are valid, they have a coherency and they satisfy. What time has provided is endless refinement, and also space to define the rules.

The Islamic garden is steeped in religious ideals and the perception of the garden as an oasis. The word for paradise in Arabic is *Jannah*, which also translates as 'garden'. If a man has led a good life, his eternal reward will be in that garden of plenty – shade and sustenance through date palms, fruit trees, canals of water and milk and honey, and sweetly scented and colourful flowers to delight and entertain the senses. Add symmetry and enclose it all in a courtyard. This style is timeless, has spread throughout the world and has been reinterpreted in many different cultures.

French formality is about controlling on a vast scale. Symmetrical patterns are interpreted through acres of parterres, clipped shrubs in baroque forms with Mediterranean fruit trees in urns and containers wheeled in and out as seasonal accents. Combined with carpet bedding or coloured gravel, it revolves around making a bold statement.

The English parkland was perfected in the eighteenth century by William Kent and Capability Brown as a new style that did away with ostentatious European formality. It sought to improve on the natural landscape, using what appeared to be simple ideals: lawns that rolled out from the main house and, with the introduction of the ha-ha, cattle, sheep and horses seeming to graze within the garden itself; majestic trees that framed views; and water that mirrored the sky. Such simple elements aimed to enhance natural beauty, while often allowing the landowner to farm profitably.

Since the grand garden and since the development of these styles, populations have changed, and there has been a greater spread of wealth since the late nineteenth century. With vast, new middle classes emerging around the world, most recently in India and China, many of these people enjoy suburban homes with gardens attached. Along with this, the modernist architects of Europe from the 1920s on were convinced of the benefits of outdoor space to the health of the population.

And so, the classical styles have been embraced and adapted to suit. They have become the dictionary for garden planning, and sometimes they have been the pattern to rebel against. Most importantly, these various styles of planting have morphed into popular culture. They have become stereotypes – they are, for many, what gardens are all about. Sometimes their contemporary interpretation can bring a tear to the eye, so having a modicum of understanding of why and where these styles have evolved, for whom and for what sort of lifestyle, can really help you to reinvent the old in a valid way.

▼ This extraordinary walled garden was built for the house of the princes of Savoy and is situated in Pérouges, France. It is a re-creation of a thirteenth-century garden, constructed from delicate topiary parterres and Mediterranean herbs and flowers. The garden hangs above beautiful cobbled streets and old stone houses of the ancient town.

▶ A grand central avenue of water is flanked with gracefully stepped terraced lawns and flower beds packed with brightly coloured blooms – a worthy setting for this magnificent palace. The majestic topiary trees echo the shape of the central turret.

◀ The garden that surrounds this Mediterranean castle is styled completely with plants that thrive in hot, dry conditions. The front courtyard houses a dense tree, offering refuge from the sun, and a grove of olives that soaks it up. A towering Italian cypress connects the garden with the architecture.

Formal Gardens

Humans sometimes yearn for order in what appears to be an extremely disordered natural world by levelling, terracing, shaping and squaring. In gardens, they often seek clarity before they can proceed but they also look to impose their will on people, space and plants. Therefore, over the centuries, a highly stylized picture of gardening has emerged. Through many different embodiments, and of many varied requirements, people have begun to marvel at formality in itself or the contrast between this and wilderness. Imposing their will on space and plants has resulted in the formal garden in many of its incarnations becoming probably the most revered style. If you examine the work of Le Nôtre at Vaux-le-Vicomte and Versailles, you will see that formality is an expression of power and dominance over the landscape, an idea designed to humble the visitor.

The formal style is the manipulation of plants and space in a quest to attain order. It is also often a search for symmetry. You can have a simple or an elaborate formal garden, and in its most common form it is manifest with symmetrical arrangements of clipped common shrubs such as bay (*Laurus nobilis*) or box (*Buxus sempervirens*), cut into balls, cones or manipulated into lollipops and positioned in a small space as a symmetrical design. Even two bay trees acting as sentries on either side of a prominent doorway, most often the entrance to a house or hotel, can achieve this. Frequently, this formality can be contrasted against wild or softer foliage – the clipped shrubs retaining their shape or stature through summer and winter as their seasonal attendants come and go. And formality is often a way of heightening drama – plants are often used as an architectural framework.

One of the most marked transformations in gardens since the early twentieth century has been the adaptation of these grand schemes and their manipulation, squeezing them into first of all the villa gardens and then the city plots. Such formal gardens acted as a display of wealth, and were viewed as a barometer of taste. And many cities, such as London and Paris, and some on the east coast of the United States, such as Boston, still rely on this slightly

▲ Brilliant white stone forms a trickling rill of water that makes a real statement against a backdrop of desert plants and cacti. The stark contrast between the hard landscaping, its control over the water and the relaxed planting serve to heighten the drama of the formality.

◄ This has to be one of the most handsome reflective gardens for its sculpture, definition and for the strength of its simplicity. The golden leaf sculptures pierce the surface of the water, to dominate the deep green tranquillity of the space. The temptation to add more plants, which may weaken the aesthetic, has been resisted.

▼ An extremely modern courtyard garden has been constructed to be an extension of the living space. Walking out on the same level ensures a seamless progression from the house and a much stronger connection to the garden room. A row of standard trees and matching pots decorate the scene.

◄ Formal gardens are relaxing spaces because of the element of control over nature where nothing grows wild and nothing jars the eye. This contemporary design displays total control in its clipped blocks of box, hedges and lawn. A row of identical trees is attractive for its repetition and encloses the space.

▲ In this elegant formal garden in shades of green, clipped hedges step down from a lawn area out onto open land, which is adorned with intricate topiary squares and flower beds. Rows of irises and bulbs promise summer colour, yet the beauty of the garden relies on its structure.

▼ A traditional topiary garden divides the large outdoor space surrounding this elegant residence. The ordered geometric shapes accentuate the size of the space and create a garden that is pleasing to look at.

lazy style to tell a story. When done beautifully, these formal gardens can be amazing, but there is often a marked lack of understanding of proportion and a paucity of imagination. These gardens are often very easy to plant up. Trips by the designer or contractor to the nursery enable the purchase of instant formality, yet frequently with these gardens it is how they are maintained over a period of time that determines their true success. They can be the perfect solution when you want order and seek to balance the architecture of your house with a feeling of stateliness, but it is when such formal gardens become pretentious that the style is overbearing.

On a smaller scale, formal gardens such as the National Trust garden at Sissinghurst, in the UK, have had a big influence. Thousands of visitors bring home ideas from them and try to mimic them to within an inch of their lives, so you will often get the formal style in just white flowers, or formality with ferns, or formality with grasses. It is nice to pay homage to great gardens, but it may be better if there were more exploration of the style itself. Some designers have done this very successfully – and indeed somewhat subverted the style – like the Wirtz family in Belgium.

Geometric elements

Steps, paths, water features and grass areas are generally considered to be the very making of a formal garden – its geometric elements. Presumably based on the notion of repeating pattern, used liberally as a decorative form inside the house, as an architectural feature and in so many other crafts such as dressmaking and joinery, these elements were transferred to the garden for a number of reasons.

Humans love order and repetition. There is symmetry to it. They like the illusion of reflection – whether it is in mirrors or still ponds. And they have an abiding desire to control outdoor space – to clean it, and to level and decorate it with familiar lines and shapes.

Perspective, trickery and illusion, using not only line and shape but also, most importantly, form and proportion, are the building blocks to successful geometric designs. As with baroque frescos, many formal gardens are designed to be seen from a distance, such as from the terraces outside the state rooms of a palace or villa. They are intended to create majesty and to heighten the notion of grandeur. Using geometric shapes – squares, rectangles and circles – is a brilliant device.

However, land attached to dwellings, whether palatial or suburban, often does not come in such neatly ordered packages. But you can create your own sense of drama and theatre within the boundaries of the plot by laying out grids using evergreen shrubs. This involves first leading the eye and then possibly enticing the visitor to explore. In a church or cathedral, the baroque may encourage

◀ Wild clover has been left to thrive and take over this lawn with a soft sea of white flowers. A rectangular rill of water slices through the space and changes your perception of the garden completely. Do not be fooled – everything is considered in this ordered place, even the clover.

▼ Formal spheres of box topiary are arranged in a tumbling, random way as they pack the ground beneath this multi-stemmed tree. Box is fantastic when used underneath trees and tall shrubs to fill the ground level as a kind of border, but here it has become the main attraction.

◀ Mounding hills in large garden spaces and parks make striking sculptural landscape features, which can be viewed for miles as well as from up above. They also provide fabulous fun for children, encouraging them to run and jump and to appreciate the outdoors and the beauty of nature. A soft covering of perennials defines the pathway and helps to retain the soil.

your eyes and your thoughts up and up to a magnificent skylight and heavenwards; in a garden, it will generally direct you across a landscape, potentially framing Arcadian views beyond.

In gardens, the reasons that symmetry has evolved as a device is that plants lend themselves so easily to manipulation. Over many years, gardeners have learnt how certain species react to being told what to do and to being unmercifully clipped, year after year, into rigid symmetrical shapes. So the plants that never complain are the ones you will see repeatedly in formal gardens – box, yew (*Taxus baccata*), privet (*Ligustrum lucidum*), juniper, holly (*Ilex*), even berberis. In contemporary times, it has been known for other species such as bamboo to do this job as well. You can easily make little formal hedges that may be no more than 20cm (8in) high or you can clip hornbeam (*Carpinus betulus*) or species of lime (*Tilia*) into very unnatural but pillar- or column-like structures. Identical rows of 'pleached' trees make an impressive statement, perhaps as a central avenue in a large space or as a grand walkway to an important area of the house or garden. Other deciduous broad-leaved species suitable for pleaching – their standard trained trunks remain as structural features over winter – include beech, ash and plane, as well as fruit trees such as pear and apple. Such trees also provide autumn interest. Living archways of floriferous tree species create glorious passageways

▼ Tall modern-style containers are used here as architectural elements that define a decked patio space. Box ball topiary provides evergreen colour and a crisp contemporary planting that is appropriate for the design. The repetition and alignment of the pots lend themselves to a formal setting.

▶ The contemporary style of the square white stone pots is softened by the white-flowering bulbs and annuals that surround robust evergreen shrubs. The line and form of the containers are used here to bring structure to a softer tree-filled garden in a strengthening of its design.

filled with fragrance and colour, the most striking being made up of bright yellow-flowering laburnum trees and twisting varieties of lilac wisteria.

Gardens originating from medieval times have featured tightly clipped parterres combined with herbs such as thyme and sage and also with fragrant mounds of santolina. These and knot gardens take the idea of dominion over nature to the extreme, but balance is achieved when they are contrasted with more relaxed, soft plants such as *Gaura lindheimeri* and *Libertia grandiflora*, without losing the overall formality.

Quite often with the formal garden, especially in areas of limited space such as a courtyard, the viewer is not necessarily attracted to the most distant point. The trick is to keep the eye and interest moving around this place of order. To achieve this, central ornamentation is needed, and this can be provided by the wonder of water. Aquatic features were perfected by the Islamic garden designers, and some of their most divine manifestations can still be seen at the Alhambra in Granada, Spain. Canals with dancing water or central fountains can complete the picture and – in hot climates, where these gardens were often created – be dual-purpose, as they act as a form of air-conditioning, bringing down the prevailing heat by a few degrees. Splashing fountains or bowls of still water provide enormous delight in themselves, and often will not require planting but when they do, the plant of choice for formal water gardens has to be the water lily. Apart

from cutting down on sunlight by covering the surface of the water to the optimum of one-third and therefore helping to keep the water clean, the flowers provide such exotic delight that they are a true horticultural marvel.

Containers in formal gardens

Growing plants in containers creates enhanced focal points, as well as providing a practical way of cultivating species that may be tender or require specific soil conditions. They maximize the impact of limited spaces such as balconies and roof gardens, and are superb for injecting bright colour and seasonal interest into larger gardens, dressing up a patio and framing the entrance of a house. Pots and containers are great fun; they have infinite uses and can establish many exciting design effects.

Formal gardens have purposeful spatial arrangements that are often based on symmetrical designs, which produce restful harmonious views. A parallel row of containers can be introduced to reinforce the geometry of a scheme, guiding the eye to a focal highlight or in the direction of a stunning vista. Pots of beautifully trimmed evergreen shrubs or those brimming with cascading flowers can illuminate paved courtyards, as well as being used to enhance formal entrances or walkways. Ornate pots and those of aged stone suit a formal garden, while traditional terracotta is classic in any garden setting. Keep the different styles as limited as possible – a single style has the greatest impact.

◄ Multi-stemmed trees form a forest of spreading branches and lime-green foliage, while the planting beneath them provides a strangely contrasting chequerboard structure of coloured annuals. The planting at ground level changes the feel of the garden completely.

Large containers can become the main focal points in a formal setting. They are wonderful as structural features at the bottom of a garden, and look superb if set on a raised terrace for a feeling of grandeur, defining the boundary and ownership of the land. Architectural plants best serve this purpose. Ornate pots and terracotta look particularly beautiful when they are incorporated in the garden either set within flower borders or submerged within hedges and topiary. Matching pairs of pots can be a very effective way of defining change between different moods within the garden, while placing them in among traditional beds for height and contrast can provide a whole new perspective to the style of the border.

Although most plant species look good when grown in containers and set at regular intervals or in symmetrical positions, there are certain plants that are synonymous with a formal garden. Evergreens such as box, yew and privet create structure, shape and form, and they stand tall all year round. The symmetrical theme can be extended with topiary specimens made to look identical through skilled clipping; pyramids, spheres and columnar shapes can explode out of square-edged hedging, while organic forms morph into more outlandish shapes in a fantastic wonderland. Architectural species such as *Cordyline australis*, *Phormium tenax* and large-leaved *Fatsia japonica* also make a huge impact as large single specimens. They instil drama into a space, being robust in nature with their large distinctive leaf shapes that look striking against the decorum of the evergreen structure.

Traditionally grown container plants include aromatic rosemary (*Rosmarinus officinalis*), lavender (*Lavandula angustifolia*) and myrtle (*Myrtus communis*); pelargoniums, wallflowers and matched mixed planting can be used to inject a burst of colour. Big blowsy shrubs such as hydrangeas, roses and lilacs look wonderful in a formal garden. Grow them so they are approximately the same shape and size, and position single species in repetition in order to restore the sense of control that is easy on the eye and definitive of formal garden design.

▲ There is something overwhelmingly inviting about a stone path that has been embedded into lawn. The interrupted line is highly visual – almost like the stripes of a zebra crossing – yet the grass still manages to soften the stone. The terracotta pot makes you stop and look before reaching the final vista ahead.

▶ Strong outlines epitomize minimal-style gardens in an echo of the architecture that they surround. The painted wall serves to enclose the garden and this species of rush is carefully clipped so that the garden becomes part of the architecture completely.

◄ Architectural rushes fill the rectangular spaces in the stone patio, to form rigid blocks that are dramatic for their dense and robust nature. The straight stems of the rushes intensify the lines. The effect is calm and ordered, but the impact is immense.

► This strong and extremely simple contemporary courtyard garden makes full use of space. The wooden bench and raised beds are strongly modern in feel and are planted with evergreen shrubs and bamboos that serve to green up the space without any complication of colour.

◄ An uneventful parkland space of mature trees and grass is transformed by a snaking vertical fence that suddenly creates real drama. The uprights are aesthetically pleasing and allow users to see straight through them so that the overall view is unobstructed.

 **Minimalism in gardens**

Minimalism is a style that can be interpreted in many different crafts. It could be clothing or architecture but is mainly interiors. In gardens what exactly does the term minimalism mean? For many, the idea of a garden is abundance – of colour, of texture, of produce – and paring that down to minimal requirements is often anathema to real gardeners. Yet serenity through contemplation on simplicity and space, perhaps by appreciating one feature, one tree or one colour style of planting or a single colour or single species planting, can be appropriate.

As a style, minimal gardening is predominantly linked to the surrounding architecture, both outdoors and inside. It will complete a picture – the house doors or window may be framing a restrained view beyond. Ludwig Mies van der Rohe united interior and exterior space with these principles at his German Pavilion for the 1929 International Exposition in Barcelona, Spain. His garden there did not include a single plant. Therefore, many people questioned whether it was a garden at all.

Many gardens are minimal by default – probably the majority. The interest to cultivate simply does not exist, and my favourite gardens can often consist of a slightly unruly lawn and just an apple tree – a plot that was produced in previous generations and subsequently abandoned to the temporary tenants of the property. This is also an antidote to the Victorian idea of acquisition and excess that has unfortunately reigned long since the Victorians departed.

Whether simplicity equates with minimal or not is a valid question, as it is not necessary to fill your garden with hundreds of different plants or features. In a pied-à-terre, for example, it may be valid to have only a beautiful, mature, multi-stemmed shrub or specimen tree, with the stem stripped of foliage, highlighting its magnificent crown, which can be deciduous or evergreen and by day and by night creates sculptural interest.

▼ A Japanese garden designed as a sanctuary from the stresses of daily life, where gently mounding mosses carpet the ground, and natural white stones gather around an inviting seat. Boughs of larch and deep red primulas embellish the garden like brushstrokes on a painting.

▶ Soft evergreen plant mounds mingle with white rocks and beautify the ground in this sensuous garden. In Japanese gardens, plants are often used to create uneven surfaces, to prompt people to look down at certain points and, upon looking up, be surprised by something eye-catching.

▓ Oriental gardens

I love oriental gardens but I do not feel they work outside the orient. When great explorers were returning from the east after China opened up in the nineteenth century, their endeavours created a penchant for all things oriental. And so Chinese and Japanese gardens or features became the latest must-have for many great estates. Trading ships were laden with tea, Japanese lanterns and bamboo. In subsequent years, many estates went to the extent of commissioning renowned oriental garden designers to come with a team and build or supervise their patch of the orient. Authentic replicas were created. Yet original Japanese gardens have evolved over so many thousands of years and have so much spiritual and hereditary significance, that it is very difficult even to begin to try to understand any but the basic rules or reasons for their original evolvement. So what you tend to achieve is a pastiche.

In many parts of the world, pastiche works very well because the conditions of the Japanese garden can be mimicked so easily. In western Europe, there is a similar luxurious green background. Surrounded by great quantities of rock, gravel and water in so many localities, the traditional plants – the limited palette of species idolized in the east – do very well in their new homes. Magnificent acer trees, gorgeous pines and azaleas and rhododendrons abundant with flower can all be grown successfully. Varieties of grasses and moss in the right conditions work very well in cool-temperate areas. But armies of monks are not available at six o'clock in the morning to restore the gardens to their picturesque and evocative prime. There are just not the people to rake the gravel or the sand into the swirls representing tumultuous seas, lapping up against island rocks. Therefore, you can create a picture and you can represent a style; if that is what you enjoy, you should certainly do so. But, ultimately, you should understand that all you are creating is a representation of something that has real soul elsewhere.

◄ Bright green clumping mosses naturalize around a deep crack in the forest floor, to establish a striking natural feature through the trees. The result is extraordinary and manages to comprise drama, mystery and natural beauty in a single sweep.

▌ Plant selection

The planting in gardens that have been designed to create a certain mood, purpose or style should be selected to accentuate the garden's strong lines, to punctuate the drama and to add colour to the space. Traditional formal gardens are defined by evergreen hedging, with clipped topiary and controlled shrubs forming the main framework. These plants need to be slow growing, tolerant of repeated clipping and easy to maintain. Compact shrubs such as box, yew and holly meet all such requirements, and have been used in this way for centuries.

Minimal landscapes are generally reflective of the existing architecture and work in an expression and appreciation of the overall space. Accordingly, plants in these settings should be used to introduce texture and colour. They also need to fit effortlessly into the space, almost as if they are part of the bricks and mortar, and have the same sense of proportion. Strong blocks of planting in single species or colour make the greatest impact. Huge beds of grasses such as *Miscanthus sinensis* 'Gracillimus' or *Calamagrostis* x *acutiflora* 'Karl Foerster' are robust and upstanding, with long seasons of interest and striking grassy blooms.

Ferns are the ultimate plants for forming textural ground-hugging carpets in a formal garden. Most species such as *Asplenium scolopendrium*, *Dryopteris filix-mas* and *Blechnum spicant* need a certain amount of shade and constantly moist soil; *Polystichum setiferum* and *P. munitum* thrive in free-draining soils with some shade. Plants with sturdy foliage that grow well in clumps include *Zantedeschia aethiopica* 'White Mischief', *Euphorbia characias* subsp. *wulfenii* and the spectacular *Agapanthus* Headbourne Hybrids, the stunning cultivar of the South African perennial that is blessed with robust strap leaves and huge umbels of blue flowers.

Bulbs with strong flowering stems are spectacular for colour and seasonal impact. Deep crimson *Tulipa* 'Queen of Night' and *T.* 'Spring Green', in creamy white, are wonderful when planted in vast numbers of a single species. Beds in close proximity to water can be filled with purple or white *Iris laevigata* and small ponds with *Rodgersia aesculifolia* or horsetail grass (*Equisetum hyemale*) for compact formal planting with impact.

▲ An ordered row of identical trees traverses the space in a dramatic statement that is matched in the rich compact planting filling the ground below. Alliums and irises create strong lines, and the monochrome scheme increases the impact substantially.

▶ Strong blocks of planting composed of a single species or colour produce the greatest impact. Here, towering bamboos striate the sky and are bolstered with variegated grasses and lower-growing bamboo species that share the same texture.

▼ The plants in this garden have been selected to reflect the distinctive flat surfaces of the main building and patio. A sea of evergreen ground-covering plants extends out from the patio, drawing attention to the entrance and accentuating the size of the overall space.

▲ Spiky plant forms have been positioned to focus and lead the eye around the gravel path and up towards the grand pavilion, which stands in the central part of the garden. Tall hedges partly obscure the view, instilling a sense of mystery and privacy.

Informal and Wild Gardens

Increasingly, gardeners are recognizing the need to create more ecofriendly gardens. They can do so in a variety of ways. Some prefer to copy nature quite closely and create a miniature wild environment in their backyard or small suburban garden. Others decide to create a range of ecological features. Yet other gardeners concentrate particularly on ecofriendly plants and planting schemes.

By its nature, an informal or wild garden cannot rely on the kind of show-stopping plants for which size and colour have been the major considerations in their breeding, as these tend to result in sterile plants. Much more suitable instead are species plants, which are generally smaller flowered and less strident, and they provide valuable nectar for insects, birds and butterflies (see page 50). By massing groups of these charming but more subtle plants, you can create wonderful areas of interest that satisfy all the senses. And the quieter colours and gentle harmonies make for more easily designed planting schemes.

The key elements to natural planting and landscaping are: shelter belts of trees and shrubs (essential for birds, in particular); natural areas of grasses combined with wildflowers; informal ponds and pools; paths of ecofriendly materials, such as reclaimed wood or chipped bark, and maybe rustic garden buildings, such as arches, pergolas, summer houses or fences, made from reclaimed timber.

⫸ Shelter belts

For an informal garden, opt where possible for naturalistic fencing or hedges. If you have existing dry-stone walls, then you could plant small alpines or other fine-rooted, small perennials such as aubrieta or *Erigeron karvinskianus* into the gaps between the stones. Make rustic wooden fencing from coppiced wood, using young timber for the uprights, and split poles for the actual fences, for example. Mixed tapestry hedges are better suited to wild or informal gardens than neatly clipped evergreens because hedges should never be cut at nesting times. They also provide

◀ A living willow arbour surrounds a sunken mosaic-and-pebble patio. Contrasting informal structures with formal surfaces, such as here, is an excellent way to bring life to the design while also staying in touch with nature.

▲ An informal planting of silvery and greyish-green foliage softens a flight of steps. Small plants that self-seed, like *Erigeron karvinskianus*, with its little pink and white daisies, make a good choice for this kind of situation.

◀ Although decking is often chosen in formal gardens, it also makes a great combination when used with informal drifts of tall perennials such as rudbeckias and echinaceas. The flowers provide a great screen through which to watch foraging bees and butterflies.

▼ Informal planting styles are suitable at any elevation, as this roof terrace in the heart of a city landscape demonstrates. The drifts of flowering and foliage plants turn it into a miniature wildlife paradise.

shelter for birds, plus a wide range of nectar-producing flowers followed by berries in autumn and winter.

Rather than formally clipped hedges or geometric-looking pergolas, why not try out living screens or arbours created from planted and woven willow? They will provide attractive places to sit or can be used to compartmentalize the garden, perhaps screening a wildflower meadow from a more formal area of the garden.

To plant a willow screen or arbour, mark out the places for the willow rods, and then insert them into well-prepared planting holes in late winter or early spring (provided the ground is workable). Then bend the rods and weave them into the desired shape (such as criss-crossing them into diamond-shaped latticework for fences and screens, or bending them over and twisting them together at the top for arches or screens). To maintain the living willow structure, cut back or weave in new shoots at least once a year, as well as pruning the original rods in spring to keep the design framework visible.

▲ This amazing sea of flowers in a Swedish garden closely resembles a pointillist painting, with its vibrant golds, oranges and deep bluish purples.

◀ Echnicaceas again abound in this informal meadow planting, but this time they form part of a softer, dreamier colour scheme. Occasional spires of mulleins punctuate the lower-level planting in its pink, white and gold colour scheme.

◄ Wildflower meadows can take many forms, and the colours will change with the seasons and the different flowers that grow. Bulbs and early spring flowers take pride of place at the start of the season and are often followed by deeper colours as the year progresses.

▼ An exquisite free-flowering mix of daisy-like flowers fills this meadow with summer colour and offers a terrific banquet for the local insect population, with its splendidly varied planting.

Wildflower meadows

The furthest area of a large lawn could be turned into a natural wildflower meadow, in which the grass is left largely uncut, except for two cuts a year, one in early summer and the other in early autumn. A more frequently mown path through it allows you to reach other parts of the garden. The benefit of not making the first grass cut until early summer is that it allows all the spring-flowering plants to set and disperse seed to continue the annual show.

Wildflower seed merchants can supply mixtures of wildflowers and grasses suitable for various soil types and situations, and you should be careful to choose one that suits your local conditions. When preparing the ground for a wildflower meadow, do not incorporate manure or fertilizer, as it will encourage the growth of tough weeds that will probably crowd out wildflowers.

Sow during early or mid-spring or in early autumn, depending on soil conditions. On lighter soils, autumn-sown seeds generally germinate and establish quickly. On heavy soils, it is advisable to wait until spring, as waterlogging may cause the seed and seedlings to rot during winter. When sowing , mix the seed with silver sand, to make it easier to handle. To further ensure that the seed is scattered evenly, sow half of the area lengthways and the remaining half widthways. Rake in lightly, water thoroughly and leave the seed to grow naturally. However, be prepared to protect it from birds.

To convert an existing lawn to a wildflower meadow, stop feeding and using weedkiller in the first year. In the second year, mow once a week to weaken the grass so that, once planted up, the wildflowers will establish and thrive. You can introduce some plants as one- to two-year-old pot-grown plants. Many wildflower suppliers offer plug plants that are ideal for planting in an established lawn. If you plant in small groups of the same plant, it will give a more natural look.

Many plants flower within three months of sowing. Leave the plants to self-seed, clear them away in spring and rake over the ground to remove weeds and encourage seed to germinate. Additional sowings may be required in the first few years until the wildflower seed bank increases.

▼ Water plays a major part in supporting wildlife, and a large natural pond surrounded by reeds and bog plants is an ideal habitat for small mammals.

Pond and bog gardens

A natural pond, with shallow water around the edges and planted with reeds, allows wildlife to drink and provides creatures with shelter at the same time. Larger areas of water could be divided by a low bridge or stepping stones made from reclaimed timber, so that you get a chance to observe the natural flora and fauna at close quarters. Soil removed in order to dig out a pond can be used to create small raised banks, planted up with a wide range of spring bulbs; cut the grass on such banks only when the bulb foliage has died down completely.

A bog garden is well worth including in an informal garden, as it increases the range of plants you can grow. All that is required is that you dig out an area to the required size with a depth of around 45cm (18in) and then line it with black plastic. Puncture the base of the plastic to allow some water drainage. Once the soil has been replaced, you can grow those plants that flourish in damp conditions, such as rodgersias, ligularias, astilbes, candelabra primulas and the damp-loving irises, like *I. laevigata* and *I. kaempferi*.

Paths and steps

To keep the informal feel of the planting scheme, it is important to include natural-looking paths. These can be as simple as mown grass paths through wildflower areas or stepping stones cut from circles of timber. Gravel paths, or those covered with bark chippings, also look good in an informal garden. If the garden incorporates changes of level, then you can create functional steps using timber planks for the risers with supporting posts on either side.

◄ The rich moist soil around a natural pool is suitable for a wide choice of damp-loving plants, including reeds and grasses, while aquatics such as water lilies provide useful shade on the water's surface.

► Planted roofs have become increasingly popular; not only do they provide much needed insulation but they are also an extra habitat in urban areas for beneficial insects. Small rock plants are ideally suited for this purpose, as they are shallow rooted and enjoy dry conditions.

If you eschew hard surfaces in favour of more natural materials, you may need to think about the level of maintenance and upkeep that you are prepared to undertake, and the practical needs for the area close to the house. One solution is to create a gravelled terrace or patio for outdoor living, which also acts as a transition between the architecture of the house and the less formal areas of the garden.

Green roofs

In recent years, architects and gardeners have been experimenting with 'green roofs' – in other words, roofs covered with a waterproof surface, which, in turn, is covered with a medium such as capillary matting on which plants can grow. These green roofs have various benefits. Not only do they provide additional planting areas in crowded urban environments but they also offer a high degree of insulation and create a more or less constant temperature throughout the year – cool in summer, warm in winter. In addition, green roofs help to soften or disguise buildings in sensitive environments, so they blend in with the surrounding area, and they provide a habitat for insects and other wildlife. You can choose the style and type of planting, from wildflower meadows in microcosm to roofs covered with shallow-rooted alpines, such as sempervivums – a popular choice in Japan.

Naturally, there are various technical considerations, such as ensuring that the roof is strong enough to support the weight of the turf or plants (particularly when wet or covered in snow) and making sure it is watertight. Therefore anyone contemplating creating a green roof needs to get professional advice before starting.

▲ The steps to a swimming pool have been cleverly softened with bamboos, which will quickly cover the ground, and big-leaved rodgersias.

▼ On either side of a mown access path in this wild area lies an attractive jumble of vetches, geraniums and silver-leaved foliage, overlooked by the single-flowered red rose *Rosa moyesii*.

▲ Seedheads in autumn are an important part of the prairie planting style, with its informal drifts of perennials. They also offer much-needed food for birds and insects late in the year.

⫼ Prairie-style planting

The flowing prairie styles of gardening started in North America, where they were first made popular by landscape designers Wolfgang Oehme and James van Sweden in the 1980s. Their plan was to echo the natural landscape and create gardens that looked good all year round using primarily native grasses.

Easy to grow, these low-maintenance grasses produce soft drifts of fronds in a wonderful colour palette of golds, crimsons and mauve. Once established, they require little attention. Their wide-spreading but shallow roots are ideal for areas where the soil is shallow, poor or dry. But they can adapt to most conditions, although they do need full sun, and some will do well in marshy or acid conditions, which most plants cannot tolerate.

When planning a prairie-style garden, make sure that you do a bit of homework first. Check out a good book on grasses, and discover which plants are best suited to the soil that you have. Sketch out roughly the area you want, and plant in curves, instead of rows, to give a more natural look. Dot a few taller feature grasses at intervals to create interest. Try for continuous colour throughout the growing season.

Any prairie-style planting needs attention while it is being established because these grasses need time to develop their root systems. Otherwise, they risk being overrun by tougher weeds. It may be best to buy reasonably well-grown plants from a good supplier to start with. Equally important is good ground preparation

◄ Great swathes of purple moor grass (*Molinia caerulea*) are seen here in mid-summer in one of Piet Oudolf's designs in Yorkshire, UK. The light catches the flowerheads, creating a magical golden glow.

▼ In this prairie-style planting in Sweden, *Echinacea purpurea* 'White Swan' has been combined to great effect with purple spires of salvias and feathery grass seedheads.

◄ In this soft mauve-and-pink colour scheme, the tall flower spires form a mass of elegant verticals that tie in with the surrounding trees.

▲ Even larger spires – this time supplied by mullein (*Verbascum olympicum*) – rise tree-like above mounds of grasses in this informal planting on a sloping site.

before planting, with all traces of perennial weeds removed. Organic matter should be dug in during the season before planting, and heavy soils may need the addition of sand or grit. To maintain the prairie, mow and rake every spring and again in mid-summer, with the mower blades set high.

You can also use grasses successfully for ground cover in more shaded, woodland areas. Those that thrive naturally in these conditions are several species of *Carex*, including the variegated *C. morrowii* and *C. plantaginea*, *Briza media*, *Molinia caerulea* and *Hakonechloa macra*. You can also introduce some of the shade-tolerant woodland perennials, such as ferns and polygonatums.

Some of the big, bold grasses make great feature plants. *Miscanthus sinensis* is an eye-catcher and suitable for any largish garden. In some cultivars, the feathery heads arch elegantly, in others they are statuesquely upright. In smaller gardens, you could opt for *Panicum virgatum*, molinias or pennisetums.

⦀ Plants for informal gardens

Generally speaking, the umbellifer family is a great choice for an informal garden. The habit of the plants in this family is naturally loose, while also being delicate and fine-textured, so most of its members go well with grasses. As a bonus, several of them make imposing feature specimens in their own right. One of the most popular plants in this family is the giant bronze fennel (*Foeniculum vulgare* 'Giant Bronze'). It is not totally hardy but self-seeds so readily

that it will probably reappear whether you like it or not, even if cut down by frost. Other good plants with the characteristically flattish, multi-flowered heads of the umbellifer family are *Anthriscus sylvestris* 'Ravenswing' and a host of achilleas.

For a tapestry hedge, plants such as buckthorn, dog rose, hazels, spindle, hornbeam, dogwoods, hawthorn and field maples provide a great range of foliage, while the last three also offer some fantastic autumn colour with their foliage, berries and fruits.

For wildflower meadows, you will need to choose species that thrive naturally in your region because the different types of soil will naturally favour certain types of wildflower. Big perennials that go well with these kinds of grasses include many of the autumn-flowering ones, such as heleniums, helianthus, rudbeckias and the golden rods, all in the gold range, with sedums and asters in the purple–pink range. The bigger cultivars go best with the generous-shaped grasses. Grasses with good autumn colour include *Hakonechloa macra*, *Miscanthus sinensis* cultivars and molinias. It is always good to include some perennials that offer the bonus of striking autumn/winter silhouettes. Among them are achilleas, *Echinacea purpurea* cultivars, monardas, *Perovskia atriplicifolia*, *Verbena bonariensis*, veronicas and *Veronicastrum virginicum* cultivars. There are some grasses, too, that are

evergreen, including several carex, deschampsia, *Juncus effusus*, *Poa chaixii* and *Stipa gigantea*.

If you are creating a prairie-style planting, the grasses that you can use offer an amazing and diverse range of shape, colour and seedhead. If you are keen to create a striking range of colours, then include blues such as *Elymus hispidus* or *E. magellanicus* and many of the fescues. Good yellow grasses include *Milium effusum* 'Aureum' and *Carex elata* 'Aurea'. Among the variegated grasses are *Miscanthus sinensis* 'Morning Light' and *M.s.* 'Zebrinus', *Molinia caerulea* subsp. *caerulea* 'Variegata' and *Phalaris arundinacea* var. *picta*.

▲ A neat, mown path creates a boundary walkway, parallel to the rustic fence, through poppy-rich wildflower meadows. Using geometric lines as a counterpoint to the informal planting style gives the garden a satisfying structure.

▼ These simple but elegant wooden loungers are exactly the right choice for an informally planted garden, where the looseness of the planting is neatly contrasted by the formal arrangement of the rectangular beds.

◀ Autumn light catches the foliage of a pair of well-positioned trees and the seedheads of the grasses beyond. Attention to the way a space is shaped has been a key element in planting design, as the great landscape gardener Capability Brown demonstrated in England in the eighteenth century.

▼ Close to the house is a gravelled area full of self-seeding perennials such as *Stachys byzantina*, *Centranthus ruber* and *Lychnis coronaria*, which flourish in the sunny dry conditions. Gravel is a useful mulch for preserving moisture in the soil.

Soft and Sensual

The best informal gardens have a good underlying structure. Uggeshall Hall is no exception to the rule. Stevie Nicholson had a virtually blank canvas when she and her husband bought the former dairy farmhouse and its 2 hectares (5 acres) of land thirty years ago. There was little in the way of planting apart from a few trees, some vegetables, a rose bush here and there, and some daffodils.

In the intervening years, Stevie, an artist and now a garden designer, has sensitively created a garden that is very much in tune not only with nature but also with the Suffolk landscape that surrounds it. Her inspiration is a great love of native flowers and grasses. These are planted around the great swirling shapes of lawn, water and decking, which define the surface areas of the garden.

Stevie enjoys the interplay of different textures and colours, along with the seasonal variations, and one of her particular delights is the small circular lawn surrounded by pheasant's grass (*Anemanthele lessoniana*), which rustles and sways in the breeze. Linked to it is a larger circular lawn, close to the house, encircled by a weeping pear and a willow. This provides a relaxing sitting area.

The pond, almost a miniature lake, creates a major focal point in the garden and is a great place for visiting ducks and waterfowl. Large ponds are a common feature in Suffolk, says Stevie – they were originally dug out to provide mud for the wattle and daub of the old farmhouses. Hers is no exception, although not much of the original house remains. At one end of the pond, Stevie has constructed a decked promontory, from where you can observe the reflections and the changing seasonal colours, as you can also do from the long curved walkway around the pond's edge. The pond itself is planted with a mixture of water-loving pickerel weed, water buttercups, bogbean and native water lilies. At the farthest

▲ The big sweeps of foliage plants lining the banks and the willows with their shady canopies can be appreciated from the curved decked path and platform at the edge of the lake. Willows relish such damp conditions.

◄ A natural-style planting of lady's mantle (*Alchemilla mollis*) lines a gravel path. Plants that self-seed provide useful ground cover, which can be especially invaluable in large gardens.

STYLES

UGGESHALL HALL
SUFFOLK, UK

CASE STUDY #11 CONTINUED

DESIGNER
STEVIE NICHOLSON

▲ One of the grass circles at Uggeshall Hall is outlined by ornamental grasses, establishing a defining edge to this feature.

end, closest to the neighbouring fields, the pond becomes wilder and is planted with reeds.

The colour scheme at Uggeshall is naturally soft. Silver-foliaged plants such as *Stachys byzantina* and the silvery plumes of grasses create a light foil for the rich russet drifts of *Sedum* 'Herbstfreude' in autumn. Also in that season plenty of berries provide food for birds, with the orange hips of *Rosa* 'Sir Cedric Morris' and the scarlet berries of *Berberis vulgaris* among them.

Despite the huge expanse of water in one part of the garden, the area in front of the house is undeniably dry. For it, Stevie sought inspiration from Beth Chatto, whose gravel gardens in neighbouring Essex were created to showcase drought-tolerant plants, which are likely to become more popular due to climatic changes. At Uggeshall, grasses such as *Miscanthus sinensis* 'Silberfeder' and *M.s.* 'Kleine Silberspinne', molinias and stipas rub shoulders with euphorbias, phormiums and phlomis. Stevie's planting style is deliberately relaxed, and plants are allowed to go forth and multiply. In the gravelled area, this is just what the plants need, and the sisyrinchiums therefore pop up their spiky creamy yellow flowerheads at will among the softer leaves of bergenias and phlomis, little mounds of hebes and alchemillas, dotted here and there with the bright red flowers of *Centranthus ruber*.

◄ Planted in the gravelled area are bergenias, sisyrinchiums, alliums, artemisias, lavenders and centranthus. Plants such as sisyrinchiums will spread quickly in the right conditions.

▼ A decked promontory is a great place from which to view visiting water fowl on the expanse of water beyond. The boundary trees provide privacy for the garden and cover for many forms of wildlife.

► **Uggeshall Hall**

1 House
2 Barns
3 Gravel Garden
4 Lawn Circles
5 Platform and Jetty
6 Walled Garden
7 Orchard
8 Lime Walk
9 Vegetable Garden
10 Formal Terrace & Rose Arch
11 Herb Garden

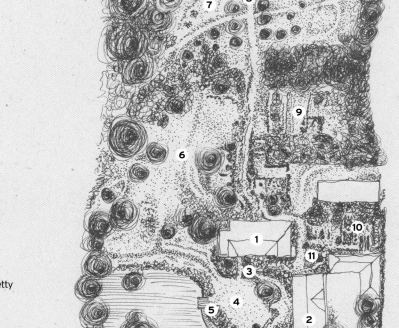

Exotic Gardens

The hot and humid growing conditions found in tropical and subtropical regions of the world have enabled an extraordinarily rich diversity of exotic plant species to thrive. Venerated as the divas of the plant world, these exotic plants combine an incomparable intensity of foliage and colour with a richness that is awe-inspiring. They produce extremes in size and form, with their gargantuan leaf sizes and flower forms that can be found alongside tiny clumping plants carpeting the ground or clinging to tree branches.

In their native habitats, exotic plants fit effortlessly into the horizon because they started life in perfect growing conditions and so look their best. In temperate regions, there is a different magic surrounding exotic plants. Like a garden that has been turned inside out, the plants that you expect to see inside the house may now be enjoying life outdoors, as a great variety of species do well in lower temperatures. Graceful ferns, bamboos and tropical trees will conjure up a jungle paradise. Plant life has the power to transport you.

The design of an exotic garden can be a simple one that depends entirely on flora for its impact. A large planting area has greater aesthetic value, allowing naturally vigorous exotics to establish a dense diversity of species with sufficient breathing space. For an exotic garden with panache, imagine a pathway that directs you around rich green swathes of exotic planting, punctuated with robust, more structural shrubs that reveal a hidden patio area all set with table and chairs for dining. This simple idea can be applied to any size of garden, with smaller ones creating a great impression when packed with luscious plants. Enclose the space with tall rustling black bamboo (*Phyllostachys nigra*) at the boundaries and dramatize it with large-leaved varieties such as *Tetrapanax papyrifer* and *Dicksonia antarctica*.

▥ Exotic suburban gardens

The average garden size has steadily decreased, particularly in built-up areas where houses in new developments are often left with very small rectangles in which to create an outdoor refuge. The best way to make the most of a small space is to have a strong focal idea or destination so as to make the whole area as useful as possible.

Creating a large patio by paving an extensive area of the garden is a bold design solution that extends the living space and creates a tropical courtyard-style garden. Set the scene by placing robust exotic species around the boundaries and soften the edges of the hard landscaping with wide beds, about 1m (3ft) across, and fill them with exotic foliage. Many smaller exotic gardens often use long rectangular pools as a central focus, within which there

is exotic planting, including gorgeous water lilies, lotus flowers or papyrus grasses. The surrounding patios are lined with large pots of lush ornamentals such as alocasias, ferns and agaves that finish the scene beautifully. Areas of ground-cover plants such as ophiopogon grass and mounding mosses can create pockets of colour within large areas of stonework.

▥ Naturalistic exotic gardens

This type of exotic garden is based on traditional landscapes such as those found within the islands of Hawaii. It incorporates natural features such as cascading waterfalls, large rocks, giant natural pools for swimming and rolling landscapes of palms and shrubs in a tropical forest scene. Apart from its strength in plant form and structure, the fundamental nature of a Hawaiian-style garden is found in its combination of wild floral colours with an essence of Japan. The coming together of people from different parts of the world has seen accent plants from the tropics placed alongside bromeliads and aloes in these gardens – gardens that will only be reproducible in their true form in hotter countries.

▲ There are a massive number of plant species that have evolved in hot and humid climates, to produce a rich diversity of forms. Foliage is found in great variations, from the huge to the very fine, but the intensity of colour is always intense and exhilarating. Here, paddle-like banana leaves rub shoulders with spiky palms and bamboos.

◄ A minimal, contemporary exotic garden has been created to reflect the architecture at this site. The walls are painted in a hot colour that is cooled by the running water. Spiky cacti and low-growing perennials are used as strong architectural forms, and the green carpets of plants do not distract from the building.

▌▌▌▌ Modern-style exotic gardens

Exotic plants do not always sit that easily in modern gardens that echo the geometry and clean lines of the modern architecture they surround. Some exotic gardens, however, have evolved a specific aesthetic through modernism, while others achieved enlightenment through the plants that filled them. Roberto Burle Marx was heavily influenced by the European Modern Art movement in his paintings and his landscapes, which, in turn, changed the face of Brazilian gardens. He incorporated organic forms that worked with the opulent curved buildings of the twentieth-century architect Oscar Niemeyer and the classic furniture of the 1950s. More recent designers have created gardens with an exotic dynamism in the form of plant life, working with the natural contrasts and textures of foliage and scale. The depth and exuberance of exotic plants were accentuated in a celebration of the architecture. In some, the influence of Zen was integrated to produce a minimalism in which bamboo and grasses were typically arranged in rows or blocks.

▌▌▌▌ Gardens under glass

A tropical paradise under glass is a world away from bringing the jungle into your own back garden. Planting opportunities are limitless in an indoor space where the conditions remain largely unaffected by the outside world. Great interior displays of exotic plants rest on emulating the growing conditions of individual plants as closely as possible; greenhouses and conservatories allow you to grow species that would struggle in temperate climates.

▼ White stone containers of citrus trees create highlights when placed within a simple bed of spiky grasses in this drought-tolerant garden. The garden could be anywhere in the world, but the distinctive plants indicate hotter climes.

◀ In this stunning contemporary garden, the principles of line and form are beautifully balanced by exotic planting. Upright yellow aloes fill great pots, which flank an attractive water feature, and mushroom-shaped cacti heighten the drama in the flower beds. The trees and shrubs create a softer background.

▼ The exotic plant world is filled with the most extraordinary shapes and textures. Varieties of sedum, euphorbia and grasses exist in very different forms from those in temperate lands, and very few species of agaves and aloes can survive in cooler places at all.

For a rich composition under glass, it is important to build up several plant layers in a gradual process. In large spaces, create a dense canopy with palms and large-leaved species, to help increase the temperature and humidity within the lower plants and to protect them from burning in the sun. Many varieties will establish themselves quickly in the tropical environment. Fast-growing plants include the *Archontophoenix cunninghamiana* palm; the tree ferns *Cyathea australis* and *Dicksonia antarctica*; the hundreds of varieties of climbers that can be found in tropical jungles; *Veitchia merrillii* (a stunning tree with a distinctive ringed trunk that is swollen at its base, and soft palm-like leaves like foxtails); and *Caryota mitis* (an eye-catching palm of fishtail-like foliage that grows well in frost-free environments). The stage is then set for a myriad of plants in contrasting forms and glamorous colours, from the spiky bromeliads and aloes to the soft ferns and calla lilies. For smaller glasshouses, there are a number of species that exude the feeling of the tropics: philodendrons and monsteras have rich, glossy, deeply cut leaves that bring an exuberance found only in exotic species. Strelitzias, bougainvilleas and hedychiums produce great flashes of colour in their brightly coloured blooms, which are equally intricate in form. The huge leaves of *Schefflera macrophylla* and the unfolding of the bright red palm leaves of *Chambeyronia macrocarpa* create tremendous impact as focal plants in an exotic garden under glass.

▲ A simple stone pond becomes a sculptural element in this garden of vibrant tropical plants. Cannas are wonderful garden plants for their fantastic foliage, which is sturdy and striking and available in many variegated cultivars. Their flowers, in colours ranging from white to yellow to orange, red and pink, live up to the foliage with ease.

▶ The shelter of the walls that enclose this courtyard raises the local temperature to produce a hot growing environment for plants and trees. Plants in pots need to be particularly drought-tolerant, having restricted water supplies and little soil to retain moisture. The garden is defined simply by the species that will survive there.

▥ Exotics in containers

Some tropical species need extra protection in their first few years, so keeping them in pots until they become established may be preferable. Pots are also extremely versatile for growing tender exotics that can be brought indoors or into the greenhouse over the winter months. They can also be shifted into sunspots or shady retreats if a plant has particular growing requirements, so it is important to consider each pot's final weight. Large planters are impractical to move, yet they still offer space to grow tender exotics as annuals – planting them outside for one great season only – and there are always short-lived plants that can be introduced for extra colour and interest around the patio. Fill the pots with an efficient water-retaining mixture of soil that is free-draining, and finish with a thick layer of mulch to help reduce evaporation (see page 250).

Containers of exuberant exotics create another level to planting and provide a stylish finishing touch to a garden design. *Alocasia* 'Calidora' is a real diva, with its massive shiny green leaves and vigorous stems that exude the tropics. Meanwhile, *Ensete ventricosum* 'Maurelii' is a stunning banana-like perennial, with huge leaves in tones of burgundy, purple, black and green, which looks amazing against a lush background of exotics. There are innumerable other beautiful exotics that grow well in containers, all of which are spectacular: for example, plant brugmansias for their magnificent trumpets; arisaemas for their unusual blooms; gardenias for fragrance; and cannas for the sheer exuberance of their colours.

◄ Containers are used as an extra opportunity to bring life and colour into spaces where there is no soil, on patio areas or in awkward spaces in the garden. This pair of containerized brugmansias exudes the exotic as the pure drama of their huge yellow trumpets directs the eye to the entrance of the house.

▼ If a garden has limited space for borders, containers are the perfect way to fill the space with flowers. Position pots in groups that display an attractive combination of plants on and around the patio, generating colour and life. Here, cannas, grasses and marigolds create an explosion of colour.

▼ In this softer-looking garden, finer foliage and pastel-coloured blooms flow in and out of striking multi-stemmed trees and shrubs. A simple path leads down to a pavilion, which is submerged in the planting of an exotic getaway.

⦀ Plant choices

Building up a vigorous tapestry of exotic flora in temperate areas is a skilled process that needs a willingness to experiment but which has great reward. A little research into individual growing conditions is required as to the degree of tenderness, but much depends on what part of the country you are in, proximity to the coast, how built-up the area is, the prevailing winds and the fact that temperatures are gradually rising. Plants from far-flung countries that were once considered to be tender have become familiar sights in cool-temperate climates. In general, colder climates that are subject to damp and frosts do not make ideal habitats for exotic plants, but in time it is possible to achieve a balance of plants that will fit into your locality and vision of a lush tropical jungle. Therefore, because there are so many plants of varying tenderness that will heighten the excitement of a scheme, you need to know the conditions of your site intimately before deciding on exact species. Some thrive only in milder areas, while others may just need to be positioned in warmer spots within the garden, with extra protection from walls or sheltering hedges.

Before making your choices, consider the minimum temperatures of your garden, if it is subject to heavy frosts, and whether any shadow is cast by the house and any neighbouring buildings. Summer temperatures and the strength of the midday sun affect the foliage of certain plants, so it is important to have some shade for this reason. Establish the prevailing winds, and remember that many large-leaved plants will not withstand strong winds.

Once armed with the relevant information, you will have endless plants to choose from, so open your mind to the more unusual, although you need to keep the number of species restricted, in order to achieve a strong tropical foil that will unify a space. *Pseudopanax ferox* is a fascinating exotic, shooting up as a thin, bare trunk crowned with stiff, dark brown juvenile leaves that are prominently toothed. Maturity occurs after 10–15 years, when the habit of the entire tree transforms into a spreading, more rounded form with wonderful stout foliage in dark green. Both forms of the tree are superb for texture and vertical accent, and the transformation it goes through will amaze everyone.

It is hard to imagine an exotic garden without palms, and there are a number that will thrive in colder temperatures. Dwarf fan palm (*Chamaerops humilis*) is a European native, fan-like palm, with dark green deeply divided leaves held rigidly on its thickened trunk. Chusan palm (*Trachycarpus fortunei*) was the palm that sparked the craze in the UK for exotic flora in the Victorian era, having survived many a severe winter. It is similar in habit to the fan palm, but has a more slender trunk covered in fibres and a much faster growth rate. Both grow well in moist, well-drained soils, the Chusan palm being much larger at maturity at 15m (50ft) than the dwarf fan palm, which reaches 2–3m (6½–10ft) and is therefore suitable for a smaller space. Canary Island date palm (*Phoenix canariensis*) has a very different habit: it produces huge arching pinnate fronds up to 6m (20ft) long, which are held on a single trunk when mature. Young plants need some protection over winter.

Tree ferns add to the texture and ambience of a garden; the hardiest tree fern, *Dicksonia antarctica*, has magnificent fronds that unfurl from stocky trunks covered with brown hair. It has a maximum height of 6m (20ft) but is extremely slow growing, so investing in a mature specimen may be worthwhile. Large-leaved plants feature strongly in any exotic garden, and there are numerous possibilities for your own: for example, *Musa basjoo* is a root-hardy banana with vast green leaves and beautifully smooth stems. With some insulation over winter, it is possible to grow a majestic banana tree that will add immeasurably to the exotica. *Schefflera* species are becoming more popular among garden enthusiasts, with *S. macrophylla* one of the most striking. Its leaves are divided into five distinct leaflets that unfold to 1m (3ft) in width and are held aloft robust stems 1m (3ft) long; it is amazing for vertical accent and drama.

Other exotic foliage plants include *Clerodendrum trichotomum*, a deciduous shrub with deep green lustrous leaves and strongly scented pink to white flowers in late summer. For contrast and height, you could try *Cordyline australis*, which has long sword-like foliage and is extremely hardy, being very wind- and salt-tolerant. *Dasylirion serratifolium* is a strongly architectural evergreen, with long spiky leaves that grow in a spherical shape and are covered in white prickles. It will eventually form a trunk and makes a fabulous focal point. An essential exotic foliage plant is *Melianthus major*, with its deeply toothed, silver-blue leaves and huge crimson flower stems later in the year. *Melianthus* and *Dasylirion* specimens will grow in temperate countries, but they benefit from the extra shade of a south-facing wall and the shelter of larger shrubs planted nearby. *Echium pininana* is another outstanding feature plant. It is biennial in nature, spending its first year as enormous spiky leaf rosettes 1m (3ft) high, and in the second season producing a massive 4m (13ft) flower spike covered in funnel-shaped flowers before it sets seed and dies.

Ferns are unbeatable ground-cover plants that quickly grow to form lush green carpets of texture and fit seamlessly into exotic gardens. *Polystichum setiferum* produces soft lance-shaped fronds and grows well in good, well-drained soils without the need for excessive moisture, and makes a good contrast to the tongue-shaped, bright green leathery leaves of *Asplenium scolopendrium*.

▶ **An incredibly ornate pavilion in wire mesh encloses a Moroccan-style courtyard space. Luscious palms add to the filigree shapes and create cool shade for refuge from the hot sun. Intricate tiles and an attractive circular pool invite you in to refresh your hands and appreciate nature's work.**

Inject flowers and colour into the scheme with exotic calla lilies in white, deep yellow and burgundy, as well as the spectacular bright blue umbels of *Agapanthus africanus*. *Eucomis bicolor* is a fascinating bulbous perennial, with mottled strap leaves and racemes of white, star-shaped flowers that are topped with a tuft of leaves. *Eucomis comosa* 'Sparkling Burgundy' is more dramatic with flowers and stems in stunning shades of burgundy; some protection with straw is required in very frost-prone areas. The ginger family is blessed with glossy leaves and sparkling blooms, and there are a few that will survive colder climates: *Hedychium densiflorum*, for example, produces dense clusters of scented flowers in yellow, while *H. greenii* steals the limelight, having stunning foliage with deep maroon undersides and flowers in a rich orange.

Climbers add to the density of an exotic planting, creating rich green foils and a scrambling jungle look. For sheer exuberance, there is nothing greater than the sight of a tropical climber or vine scaling a rock face in its natural habitat. In hot countries, a climber will quickly establish to produce a rich green covering, the perfect foil for the typically ostentatious flowers of the tropics. For hotter climes, *Bauhinia kockiana* is a vigorous woody climber that quickly reaches the crown of the trees in its native Malaysian jungles. It is a versatile garden plant, thriving in full sun or semi-shade, and it bears huge clusters of flowers almost all year round, ranging in colour from a luminous red to a golden yellow. *Thunbergia grandiflora*

is an evergreen climber that needs full sun to produce its dark and robust heart-shaped foliage, which forms a dense cover. Blue flowers with yellow throats appear in summer – and all year, if it is hot enough.

There are enough plants to provide a good number of exotic climbers that are hardy in temperate climates, some familiar and some a bit more unusual, some being root-hardy, some needing the protection of a wall. *Trachelospermum jasminoides* is hardy and one of the most beautiful evergreen climbers, being adorned with great numbers of star-shaped, white flowers and a scent that is quite simply heaven sent. It is best out of the wind against a warm sunny wall, but it will tolerate some shade. x *Fatshedera lizei* is a scrambler with real presence as an earthy jungle climber; it creates strong cover and texture with its fresh apple-green foliage. *Akebia quinata* is an elegant beauty, with a gently twining habit and attractive leaves, as well as purple to brown flowers with a spicy scent; these are followed by large pink fruits. This delicate climber will cover a pergola or a fence beautifully.

Hardy trees with a taste of the exotic include *Catalpa bignonioides*, the Indian bean tree, with its spreading crown and large deep green heart-shaped leaves and white flowers. Distinctive long beans follow the flowers and hang from the branches. This tree can be grown in a small space if it is pollarded to 3m (10ft). Another beautiful exotic tree is *Albizia julibrissin*, grown for its fine filigree foliage and pink pompom flowers, which are produced late in summer.

▼ A dense canopy of mature trees is given an extra dimension of texture and interest with exotic plant species. Deep green cycads create highlights with their finely cut leaves and spherical shapes.

◄ A magnificent flowering agave. Agaves exist as huge rosettes of fleshy water-filled leaves, but the foliage lives only long enough to produce a massive flowering stem, which bears numerous tubular flowers. The plant develops fruits and dies, but new plants are produced as suckers at the base of the stem.

► The Majorelle Garden in Marrakech was created by the French painter Jacques Majorelle in the 1920s. The planting is composed almost entirely of succulent species. Robust drought-tolerant plants include cacti, euphorbias, sedums and kalanchoes. Palms and yuccas introduce structure and contrast.

► This verdant vista is of the fountain in the Villa Taranto, in Piedmont, Italy. The immaculately striped lawn and the profusion of lotus (*Nelumbo*) in the pond in the foreground shine against the dark backdrop of trees.

Conditions

|||||| As a discipline, garden design is a unique fusion of creativity, taste and nature, where man-made materials are harmonized with plant life. Inspiration is drawn from the site itself with regard to aspect, soil and the garden's surroundings and how they are harnessed as one. A garden that is overlooked in an urban area will require an enclosed resolution with a central focus within the space.

Hardy, drought-tolerant plants will fulfil the requirements of low-maintenance gardens in cities where time is at a premium, while water has the power to change the whole ambience of a space: still pools mirror the trees, bringing blue skies into the garden, while trickling water creates sound that calms the senses.

You may be pleasantly surprised by what can be achieved in a shady bog garden with poor drainage if you use plants that have adapted to such a situation. Plants that thrive in boggy soil can be bold and bolshie; *Gunnera manicata* and *Rodgersia aesculifolia* are both stunning foliage plants that will steal the show.

Shade-loving plants are among the most beautiful, while woodland gardens are atmospheric and serene, especially with erythroniums, ferns and epimediums carpeting the ground. Plants adapt to very dry soils, and those at the coast will tolerate salt spray – by adding organic matter to the soil and planting a sheltering hedge, a beautiful garden is still possible in extreme conditions. Every site has the potential to be great. Approach every garden with a positive eye, immerse yourself in what can be achieved and set about designing something wonderful.

Urban Gardens

The demand for housing in densely populated towns and cities means that space for gardening comes at a premium. Once the housing developments and apartment blocks have been designed, planned and constructed, it is often the case that the little land that is left over is divided up into the classic rectangles that are so familiar today. Do not underestimate what can be done with your particular plot of soil; there are an amazing number of styles and design solutions that can make it unique and interesting, along with a massive variety of plants to suit and make it live.

Decide what style would suit the site and the building; mirror any shapes or colours that are characteristic of the house. If the house is Art Deco in style with rounded walls, bring that shape out in the patios and planting areas to produce a unified design. The decorative arts style was intricate and colourful, so select plants that will reflect this, but take care not to water it down with too many species. Rounded box (*Buxus sempervirens*) balls, *Echinacea purpurea* and *Knautia macedonica* would be suitable for this style of garden, being vibrant but elegant. A modern garden would be appropriate for a 'new build' type of property: wide stepping-stone paths of sandstone leading out to bold, square patio areas furnished with contemporary seating. A design such as this would need a good backbone of evergreen shrubs mixed with blocks of perennials and bulbs, to produce a low-maintenance family garden with interest all year round.

Look for species that are reasonably drought tolerant and easy to look after; urban gardens sometimes belong to people with limited free time, and many have a metred water supply, so a little forward planning will go a long way. Small evergreen shrubs that need little pruning include the almost black-leaved *Pittosporum tenuifolium*

'Tom Thumb', *P. tobira* 'Nanum' and *Euphorbia mellifera*. Beautiful perennials that thrive in dry soils include *Santolina chamaecyparis*, *Artemisia* 'Powis Castle' and *Salvia officinalis* 'Purpurascens'.

Patios

To expand your living space into the garden, design a patio. Think about how you will feel in the space and if it sits well within its locality; also identify where you are overlooked. Such an area is most comfortable when it feels like an outdoor room, with some sense of enclosure, so erect a screen, wall or fence leading from the house to provide privacy. The focus needs to be within – a beautiful wooden table, elegant lounge chairs or an ornate mosaic floor. Consider all the elements and how they will contribute to the overall effect; keep planting robust and simple. You will then automatically feel comfortable and cosy – it will be a welcoming place.

Living screens look fantastic, contributing foils of green and structure to the design as a whole. Use small trees and shrubs for the sides, while the canopy of a mature tree will create the effect of a ceiling. Single-species hedges of evergreens such as yew (*Taxus baccata*), *Viburnum tinus* or box make a great impact and will reduce strong gusts of wind to a light breeze. Densely planted shrubs will also filter out some noise and pollution, while woody deciduous plants offer structure to the landscape all year round. They can also introduce autumn colour changes.

Patio walls and fences can be softened with plants for a welcoming atmosphere. Grow fragrant climbers such as *Akebia quinata* and *Trachelospermum jasminoides* over fences and plant low box hedging at the base of a wall to finish the patio in style.

Add a sparkle with large patio pots filled with brightly coloured flowers and contrasting foliage. Containers are an easy and flexible way of introducing seasonal interest in perennials, annuals and bulbs. Set out a few permanent specimen shrubs using evergreens such as *Pittosporum tobira* 'Nanum', bay laurel (*Laurus nobilis*) or box balls that will stand tall and decorate the space all year round.

▲ A limited palette of species has been selected for a small dining area in a courtyard garden. Evergreen interest has been supplied by bamboo, which forms a backdrop on one side, and a row of *Stipa arundinacea*, which marks the foreground. Scarlet acers planted in containers bring flashes of colour, as does the *Rhus typhina*, which turns orange in autumn.

▼ This cityscape has been romanticized by a haze of soft planting – urban meets rural and cohabits harmoniously.

◄ Jungle fever has reached this contemporary courtyard, which is best viewed from above. What could be a sterile white area has been crammed full with exotics, such as giant-leaved banana plants, spiky palms and a variety of ferns, to conjure up a tropical vision.

▲ In this dining area in a contemporary courtyard garden, the warm deep red walls form a great backdrop for plants. The Perspex and metal furniture and metal grid floor are greatly softened by the relaxed planting style.

▌▌▌ **Courtyard gardens**

These are areas within the urban landscape that are carved out of or simply left over by the buildings around them; by nature, they have the same sheltered effect as a walled garden. Courtyard gardens have become precious, as they are often the only outdoor breathing spaces available to the users of the building. A particular approach to their design has therefore developed in order to maximize their potential. The design focus needs to be within the space itself because the courtyard garden may be surrounded by grey walls and air-conditioning vents. The space may be awkward and unappealing in shape, and, unlike balcony and roof gardens, it may not be possible to draw inspiration from a beautiful landscape beyond. However, by using beautiful stone flooring, furniture similar in style to that of the interior, strong planting in blocks of single species and a focal piece of sculpture, you can create a modern, luxurious and alluring courtyard garden that flows from the building, enriching the architecture and forming a usable space.

The plants in a courtyard garden will need to be drought tolerant, as the surrounding hard materials will sap the moisture out of the soil, raise local temperatures and cause a rain shadow that will ensure that plants adjacent to walls will be sheltered from incoming precipitation. The need for an irrigation system can be reduced by incorporating high amounts of organic matter and applying an annual mulch to help retain moisture

▼ The screening in and around this roof garden is almost completely composed of walls of single-species planting, creating separate definite areas.

▲ A tiny decked courtyard has been transformed by evergreen planting. Along the right-hand side is a permanent bed, while pots of lollipop *Ligustrum ovalifolium* adorn the left.

◄ Luxuriant green foliage of container plants, wall climbers and background shrubs combine to create a private garden that filters out noise and pollution.

within the soil. Very drought-tolerant species include *Sedum telephium*, lavenders, *Euphorbia characias*, *Perovskia* 'Blue Spire' and *Achillea* 'Moonshine'.

▏▏▏▏ Balconies

Balconies are often unappreciated as living space: would you waste a space this size if it were inside? The area of a balcony can easily be the same size as a store room in a house, where every inch is precious. Create a smooth transition between the indoor living area and the balcony by keeping the style and furnishings homogenous. Also, consider the views. Framing beautiful vistas draws the eye out, enlarging the space, and completely changes the way you perceive the world outside.

Introduce plants to soften the boundaries, enclose the space and create a measure of privacy. Species need to be chosen carefully, as they will be exposed to wind, periods of drought and varying degrees of sunlight, depending on the aspect. Bushy shrubs with robust foliage offer the best resistance against the elements; evergreens such as box, bay laurel and cherry laurel (*Prunus laurocerasus*) will provide structure all year round. For contrast and fragrance, introduce lavender (*Lavandula angustifolia*) and rosemary (*Rosmarinus officinalis*), while *Geranium phaeum* and *Cirsium rivulare* inject a shot of colour. Euphorbias grow in stunning blocks and, along with *Alchemilla mollis*, will quickly fill spaces. Grasses are fresh and tactile, bringing sound and movement to a composition.

Mediterranean herbs such as sage (*Salvia officinalis*), thyme (*Thymus vulgaris*) and oregano (*Origanum vulgare*) will do well on balconies with a bit of shelter from surrounding bushes, and will be close by for culinary use.

▏▏▏▏ Roof gardens

In a similar way to balconies, roof gardens are an extension of your living space, an opportunity to help towards the greening up of the cityscape, to create otherwise inaccessible places of refuge for wildlife, thereby contributing to local biodiversity. It is convenient to think that they are a backlash against the concrete jungle, which exerts so much influence on the environment, but altruistic notions are lined with the fact that roof gardens also benefit us as individuals, too. Planting on roof terraces helps to insulate buildings; it cools and cleans the air that you breathe and dampens noise pollution. Roof gardens also absorb significant amounts of rainfall, helping to prevent floods, which are more likely in heavily built-up areas. There is no downside to this type of garden: the prospect of walking outdoors onto a well-organized space on the roof is an exciting one; roof gardens give you new places to entertain, work in or take refuge.

Planting needs to be simple, stylish and lush in this heightened space. As with balconies, all species will need to be drought and wind tolerant. Deep green foliage plants such as *Fatsia japonica*, *Pittosporum tobira* and bay laurel will look fantastic. Keep the colour palette tight in one or two

◄ An aerial view of a paved plaza shows intricate yet simple ground-cover planting, beautifully patterned with contrasting foliage.

▼ A small urban garden achieves dramatic effect into the evening by illuminating the white stems and interesting foliage shapes, to form an exotic background.

shades: purple and blue; red and orange; or yellow and white. Think about fragrance within the space and introduce grasses for sound and contrast. Green roofs (see page 195) extend the idea of using every available inch of space by turning it over to the green side.

Terraces

Levelling the garden in a series of stepped terraces can produce an extremely attractive garden design, and for many sites doing so may well be the only way to manipulate the space in order to make it useful. Very sloped sites or those that are particularly uneven can be tamed by flattening out large areas to form lounge patios or places for seating, with paths and steps to connect the zones. Problems of soil erosion can be eradicated by constructing efficient draining systems within the design, the hard landscaping protecting the ground and the water being directed effectively towards the water table. Consider the aspect of the site, and build patios in sunny positions at the time of day you want to use them or in areas that will highlight beautiful views in order to transform the space.

Terracing can also be introduced along the length of a rectangular-shaped garden to create a sense of direction, and across the space to accentuate the width of a smaller site. The most magical gardens need to unfold gradually so that views or special features are hidden from view. Terraces are a chance to create separate compartments or destination points that can be enclosed with walls or hedging, secret hideaways that invite you in to investigate them. Use the walls or hedges as foils for dramatic planting, incorporating these areas as parts of the garden.

Evergreen shrubs with dense habits are the plants of choice to balance the hard materials and to maintain the structure of the garden all year round. Yew, box and Portuguese laurel (*Prunus lusitanica*) form robust partitioning hedges, with *Viburnum tinus* and *Pittosporum tobira* being wonderful flowering alternatives. For strong impact and a contemporary look, plant blocks of *Agapanthus africanus*, *Euphorbia characias* subsp. *wulfenii*, *Sedum* 'Herbstfreude', *Phlomis russeliana* and grasses such as *Miscanthus floridulus*, *Luzula sylvatica* 'Marginata' and *Anemanthele lessoniana*.

Planting choices for urban gardens

Plants create volume, texture and ambience; they have the power to excite because they are dynamic, in a state of continual change. There is always great excitement when the hard landscaping takes shape, but the plants make the garden live. In highly populated areas consideration must be given to the conditions exerted on the site by urbanization itself, as well as to the basic conditions in the form of its soil and aspect.

Large-scale construction changes land mass considerably, impacting on the environment in terms of air, water and noise pollution. Conditions become very localized, changing in accordance with the density of surrounding structures, the number of roads and industrial buildings. Concrete buildings absorb heat by day and release it by night, raising local temperatures significantly, as well as sheltering nearby planting from rainfall. Water is a precious commodity because there is less of it to go round; it is, therefore, less available for use

◄ In this show garden at the Chelsea Flower Show, wood, corten steel and block planting of single species have all been utilized to achieve a striking, contemporary effect.

▼ A small detail of a town garden illustrates how wonderful aquatics such as nymphae can happily exist in a confined space and establish a tranquil effect.

in the garden, and some people living in cities do not always have the time to water their plants anyway. Planting that is expected to survive here needs to have adapted to these environmental factors.

All these issues need consideration in an urban garden, but you can relax knowing that, within the diversity of the plant kingdom, there are many species that will fulfil these requirements. Growing a barrier of dense hedging and trees alongside a busy road can significantly reduce the noise and pollution within the garden, and there are many plants that will withstand the carbon emissions. Privet (*Ligustrum ovalifolium*), holly (*Ilex aquifolium*) and *Aucuba japonica* form thick evergreen hedges, and *Malus sylvestris*, *Sambucus nigra* and *Laburnum* x *watereri* 'Vossii' are trees resistant to pollution and coastal conditions. These species will also tolerate periods of drought and live happily in the shade of a building; they can also be combined with a range of smaller shrubs and perennials in an easily maintained scheme.

A palette of plants that will survive successfully is needed, but the aesthetic in plant relationships should not be overlooked. You need to have a strong vision of the final composition in terms of colour, volume and textural effects. The following plant combinations will work well together in urban gardens: *Achillea millefolium*, *Euphorbia amygdaloides* and *Foeniculum vulgare* with *Scabiosa caucasica*; *Hydrangea macrophylla*, *Bergenia cordifolia* and *Geum chiloense* with *Euonymus fortunei*; or *Elaeagnus* x *ebbingei*, *Cistus* x *argenteus* and *Geranium pratense* with *Buddleja davidii*. Plant all species in groups to achieve an established look with greater impact.

Water and Bog Gardens

Water supports life and it is wonderful in a garden for many reasons. Traditionally used back in the purist form of gardening, it was harnessed to cool the air of sheltered courtyards, creating refuge from the sun. There is an inherent fascination with water: it glistens in the sun and compels you to touch it; it cleans and refreshes. Ornate banisters supporting gushing streams of water feature in the gardens of the Alhambra in Granada, Spain – the water cools you instantly as you proceed on the steep walk down.

Long rectangular pools are superb as central features in more symmetrical garden designs. The use of attractive natural stone and bold blocks of planting create a clean, timeless look, which can be heightened with the use of various styles of planting. Or else introduce a still pond, which will mirror the skies, opening up the space and drawing in the light on the dullest of days. Bay trees and box topiary in large pots are popular ways to decorate a patio, but why not think about trying something different, using water? Make the pots into mini ponds and fill them with lotus plants – their leaves and flowers will enliven the space. Large water-filled square planters with arching grasses will create a very different but slick look.

Moving water features have innumerable forms, both traditional and modern. Jumping fountains offer a sense of fun. They can be incorporated into a planted bed, a lawn or within a paved area, the jets being directed into a pond or back into the plants. Gushing waterfalls and trickling streams produce a sense of calm, while fountains are the raucous sculptures of the water world, but these larger water features may look out of place in smaller gardens, so make sure that they settle within the space, not take it over.

Bright blue swimming pools are just that, so solid evergreens in pots, clean stonework and lounge furniture are the order of the day to soften their impact. Natural swimming pools are something different, almost dreamy, as if you have come out of a forest clearing to find a glistening lagoon where you can have a dip and cool off. They can become places of natural beauty; they should be designed so that you can swim in clear water with no chemicals and they should also benefit local wildlife. Plant the pool with structural rushes and naturalized water irises. For most gardens, natural pools are fantastic for introducing water-loving plants such as irises and water lilies.

Pools and ponds can be constructed in various ways and made out of different materials, including rubber water liners and a variety of preformed shapes. Preformed ponds incorporate tiered shelves that will support the growth of marginal plants as well as submerged aquatics. These shelves are also beneficial to wildlife, allowing them to pass easily in and out of the water. Water-loving plants

such as rushes, gunneras and lysichitons tend to thrive in shady areas, so position the pond away from full sun for a relaxing water garden.

Water plant choices

Water-loving plants are categorized by how much water they prefer to grow in. Marginal plants inhabit shallow water and need their tops to be dry, while floaters live on the surface of a pond gaining all their support from it. Submerged aquatics and oxygenating plants grow below the water line and, although not so decorative, they are required to help keep the water clear of algae and are therefore, healthy – they are crucial to the continued well-being of the water feature. Bog plants are slightly different in that they need a good amount of sunlight, and their roots must be in soil that is constantly moist, not waterlogged, like the conditions found along the sides of a ditch or at the edge of a pond.

Of the marginal plants, lotus plant (*Nelumbo nucifera*) thrives in the mud of shallow ponds, lagoons, marshes and flooded fields. In a garden, it is grown for its elegant disc-shaped leaves, which protrude above the water surface, and for its stunning, pink to white flowers with distinctive, yellow centres. Common bulrush (*Typha latifolia*) gives a pond a natural, established look, with large clumps of grass-like foliage, and it bears cylindrical dark brown seedheads in summer. It will establish quickly and

◄ Beth Chatto's garden in Essex is a masterclass in planting the right plant in the right place. Marginal planting by the pond in early summer includes candelabra primulas and yellow iris, while hostas enjoy the shady and damp conditions nearby.

▲ This riverbank scene is populated by species such as willow, iris and astilbe that love to have their feet in or near water. A succession of colours from spring through summer will continue to highlight different spots.

► Jinny Blom's masterpiece at the Chelsea Flower Show used *Tulipa* 'Maureen' to dramatic effect.

take over if left to its own devices. *Butomus umbellatus* is a flowering rush with wider, sword-like leaves and delicate umbels of rose-pink flowers, which are stunning in summer. Nile grass or papyrus (*Cyperus papyrus*) is long on beauty and history; the papyrus creates a striking accent, looking its best in blocks as a single species. Its requirement for space is immense, so restrict it in a pot or, for a similar look, choose the more compact *C. alternifolius*. *Caltha palustris* is an essential marginal for the colour of its luminous yellow flowers, large shiny and buttercup-shaped, and for the volume and presence of its deep green, rounded, glossy leaves. Caltha loves shallow water, but will survive relatively well in boggy soils. Japanese water iris (*Iris laevigata*) offers effortless panache with its broad sword-shaped leaves and tall, deep blue flowers painted with a narrow flash of cream. *Iris pseudacorus* is a yellow variety with purple to brown markings; it is outstanding in clumps. *Lysichiton americanus* creates impact with its dramatic paddle-shaped leaves and magnificent yellow, flame-shaped flowers that bring a pond to life in spring, while the lush foliage offers contrast to rush-like marginals such as *Equisetum ramoissimum* var. *japonicum* and *Acorus gramineus* and other flowering marginals.

Gunnera manicata, with its gargantuan leaves and robust thorny stems, provides the most impact as an architectural bog plant. The heavily textured leaves are deeply folded, creating canopies high enough to be used for shade in a garden. Massive flower spikes in burgundy-red complete the prehistoric look in the summer months. Gunnera is happiest in full sun or partial shade, with its roots in moist boggy soils. *Darmera peltata* produces large rounded leaves that grow in dense clumps, which are particularly useful for foliage cover in large expanses of water. Its stout flowering shoots are striking in spring, emerging from the soil before any foliage appears. *Ligularia dentata* 'Desdemona' is dark and moody in its mahogany-purple foliage, but lighthearted and bright when its orange daisy-like flowers appear – a wonderful plant for impact in a shady damp place.

Of the floating plants, the quintessential water lily *Nymphaea alba* is enduring in pure white and suitable for any size pond. If you do want to digress from the classic image of a water lily, try the iridescent blue *N. caerulea*. *Pistia stratiotes* is beautiful as a surface decoration, with small, furry leaves that are creased, resembling ribbed fans. This evergreen plant floats gently across the pond like a natural sculpture; it grows best in warm and sheltered ponds.

Oxygenating plants have a definite function in a water garden; therefore, with that in mind, any doubts about their aesthetics must give way to their effectiveness in keeping the pond clean. *Lagarosiphon major* is a small plant of bright green whorls that is one of the best oxygenators, but if you have a smaller pond with shallower water, there are only a few that look much more attractive. *Oenanthe fluviatilis* is known as the water carrot – it has delicate, fern-like foliage and pale purple flowering stems that stand up out of the water. *Eleocharis acicularis* is a tiny underwater grass that grows in bright green tufts. It looks gorgeous and is suitable for small ponds, while *Ceratophyllum demersum*, with its bristle-like foliage in apple-green whorls, is appropriate for much larger ponds. It thrives in very deep water and will spread extremely quickly.

Dry and Coastal Gardens

Plants have colonized practically every corner of the Earth so you can relax in the knowledge that there will be sufficient species available to create any type of garden in any situation. The residing plant life in any space is governed by the prevailing environment, and very dry sites and those directly on the coast are subject to the extremities of wind, drought and salt water, where only plants that have evolved a particular tolerance can survive.

Indigenous to hot climates, drought-loving plants are able to withstand long periods without moisture and full sun. They thrive in well-drained soil, so soils high in gravel and sand will support them, although they benefit from good soil preparation before you start planting. The addition of organic matter in the form of organic farmyard manure, homemade compost and small amounts of mushroom compost (see page 250) helps to bind the larger soil particles together and therefore improves their water-holding capacity, while providing the top-up supplies of nutrients required for strong plant growth. A yearly application of mulch will also help reduce water evaporation at ground level and minimize competition by suppressing weeds. Plants that survive in very dry gardens are robust and tolerant. Consequently, dry gardens offer low maintenance, quick establishment and bold aesthetics, which make them extremely attractive garden styles.

The foundation of a successful coastal garden lies in the efficiency of shelter from the prevailing winds that can be provided, and the garden's proximity to the sea. Leaf blackening from salt burn and damage to foliage can occur with the hardiest of plants but, with good soil preparation, appropriate sheltering and plant knowledge, a flourishing composition is possible. Hedges positioned around the site and also as subdividing internal barriers can provide invaluable shelter for plants because they filter the wind steadily, while contributing towards the environment and the aesthetic. Avoid walls; they are not effective in very windy situations because they create a solid wind block, forming local currents that can be incredibly damaging to plants.

Drought-tolerant plant choices

Successful dry garden planting lies in selecting plants that will thrive with little moisture. Silver-leaved plants reflect sunlight, reducing water evaporation, and those with fleshy leaves are efficient at retaining supplies already on board. Silver plants lend themselves to contemporary schemes: the silver spears of *Astelia chathamica* inject light and punctuation into a scheme, while the soft foliage mounds of the sedums can create a rolling ambience and volume at ground level. Other drought-tolerant, silver-leaved plant

▲ This stark, flat landscape, incorporating a rectangular pool that reflects the sky, is given a purple spherical bolt by these wonderful alliums.

▶ A combination of Mediterranean-type planting including lavender and santolina illustrates how the English colourful garden can combine successfully with an arid scene.

◀ *Euphorbia camassia* introduces a carpet of cloudy lime-green freshness to this low-level planting.

▼ *Agave parryi*, nestling among grasses in the shade of a tree, creates a naturalistic sun-drenched scene. The perennial cactus *Mammillaria elongata* is grown on supports in this original planting scheme.

choices include the Mediterranean herbs: *Salvia officinalis*, *Lavandula angustifolia* and *Rosmarinus officinalis* create ambience and fragrance around a seating area. *Eryngium bourgatii* and *Echinops ritro* are tinged with blue, quickly establishing large spiky clumps of drama. *Santolina chamaecyparissus* and *Artemisia* 'Powis Castle' contribute volume, while the towering ornamental artichoke *Cynara cardunculus* adds vertical accents and strong architectural lines, which last way into the winter months. *Thymus vulgaris* is attractive for its rounded clumps in autumn; its small leaves have evolved to reduce water loss.

Nearly all varieties of *Sorbus* thrive on dry sites, the rounded, silver-lined canopy of *S. aria* contrasting beautifully with hardy evergreen hedging and specimen shrubs. *Elaeagnus* x *ebbingei*, *Ligustrum japonicum* and *Aucuba japonica* tolerate extreme drought and look good all year round, while *Crataegus monogyna* is useful for attracting wildlife. Plant New Zealand flax (*Phormium tenax*) for focus and drama, and achieve volume at a slightly lower level with smaller shrubs such as *Hebe* 'Red Edge' and *Euonymus fortunei*. *Euphorbia characias* subsp. *wulfenii* and *Alchemilla mollis* form great blocks of texture in a dry garden, and there are many suitable perennials to decorate the scheme. Try the stunning deep pink of *Achillea millefolium* 'Cerise Queen', the intensity of Iris 'Deep Black' and the wide range of colours from varieties of aquilegia, hemerocallis, verbascum and lilies, to name but a few. Useful dry grasses include *Miscanthus sinensis*, *Festuca glauca*, *Deschampsia flexuosa* 'Tatra Gold' and *Stipa pennata* for contrasting form and foliage.

Plants on the coast have to adapt to varying amounts of sea spray as well as high winds. Fortunately, *Pinus nigra*, *Salix alba*, *Quercus ilex* and *Acer pseudoplatanus* will withstand the worst weather conditions. The full range of plants that will survive in your space can be expanded by constructing a sheltering hedge and reducing their exposure. *Ilex aquifolium* is an efficient protector; it is dark, dense and attractive as a foil for other planting. *Griselinia littoralis* and *Euonymus fortunei* brighten a coastal garden with fresh green foliage, responding well to regular pruning to keep their shape.

A few species stand out for use in very exposed sites, namely *Berberis thunbergii*, *Hippophae rhamnoides* and most species of *Elaeagnus*, all forming effective hedges or stand-alone shrubs. There are a great number of shrubs and perennials that will fill the space: flowering shrubs such as *Viburnum tinus* and *Spiraea japonica* 'Goldflame', most varieties of cytisus, hebe, kniphofia and dianthus, as well as *Cordyline australis* for ground level, and *Solanum laxum* 'Album' and *Actinidia kolomikta* for great climbing plants.

Seaside Retreat

Coastal gardens offer many challenges to the enthusiastic gardener. These include practical considerations such as wind breaks and choosing plants that withstand salt-laden gales. But there are aesthetic considerations as well – the garden needs to blend with its surroundings and do justice to its privileged setting beside the sea. The garden featured here is a perfect example of marrying good horticultural principles with a vision of beauty that uses the ocean as nature's most wonderful backdrop. It is designed and executed by renowned horticulturist and intrepid world plant explorer Dan Hinkley and his partner, architect Robert Jones. Hinkley's residence Windcliff is located on a sunny five-acre (2 hectare) site overlooking the clear blue waters of Puget Sound on the Kitsap Peninsula near Seattle in the USA. Temperatures can drop to -7°C(20°F) in the winter, add to this a sandy soil and you might think your planting options are limited. Despite this, Hinkley has produced a stunning coastal garden, packed full of exotic plants brought back from his travels around the globe. His approach is experimental – try something and if it dies, well, try something else. This way the very boundaries of what tender plants might survive are constantly being pushed, and sometimes the results are surprising. Of course, the seasons do vary from year to year, so what may survive one year, will perish the next. It is this daring and imaginative approach that has produced such a vibrant and interesting garden, which looks like it has been there forever (it was started in 2001), and the plants seem so at

▲ A simple path winds its way to a seating and dining area. Heavily planted borders spill over to soften the geometric paving, while trees in the background give necessary protection for the planting.

▶ Jeffrey Bale, an artist from Portland, Oregon, designed this sunken fire pit surrounded by a mosaic pattern of cobbles in a suitably maritime starfish pattern. A gathering at night in this sheltered place, with its magical fireplace, is truly memorable.

◄ Rock pools made using local boulders link the site with the sea beyond and provide tranquil areas and platforms for naturalistic planting.

CONDITIONS

WINDCLIFF
SEATTLE, USA

CASE STUDY #12 CONTINUED

DESIGNER
DAN HINKLEY & ROBERT JONES

▲ The creamy, drooping plumes of *Cortaderia fulvida* and the soft blonde sweep of *Stipa tenuissima* contrast beautifully with spiky yuccas and aloes, lifted with a dash of red *Lobelia tupa*, in this beautifully constructed plant tapestry.

home and flourishing that you might believe they were all indigenous.

What was once mainly lawn has now been replaced by a vast collection of herbaceous plants, shrubs and trees, with the copious use of grasses that dance gently to the off-shore breezes. Trees suitable for such an exposed site, such as eucalyptus and pines, form a shelter belt for the garden, which manages to protect without obscuring the sea views. The hard landscaping is softened by thickly planted borders, and the house itself is bedded into its surroundings with colourful and varied planting, in drifts of contrasting colours, shapes and textures. Architecture and planting are inherently connected. Pools of water created by naturalistic formations of boulders form a psychological link with the sea beyond, and a superb, slightly sunken mosaic fire pit creates a practical and attractive place to enjoy the breathtaking views. This is a joyful seaside garden, a unique celebration of its place and its creators planting enthusiasms.

▼ The main residence nestles into its surroundings, cloaked and adorned by a mass of herbaceous planting, including drifts of white agapanthus and one of Hinckley's favourites – the red plumes of *Lobelia tupa*.

▲ Tall plumes of *Stipa gigantea* in no way hinder the view of the blue water of Puget Sound, which can almost be smelt from here. Red *Lobelia tupa* softens the scene towards the boulder, providing a seating area from which to enjoy the panorama.

◀ Stunning purple-blue agapanthus provides intense colour; this plant is very happy to be beside the sea.

▶ **Windcliff**

1 Boundary fence
2 Island bed
3 Garage
4 Acer
5 House
6 Deck
7 Patio
8 Pond
9 Shelter belt of trees
10 Path
11 Boulder
12 Fire Pit
13 Large pine
14 Cliffs
15 Sea

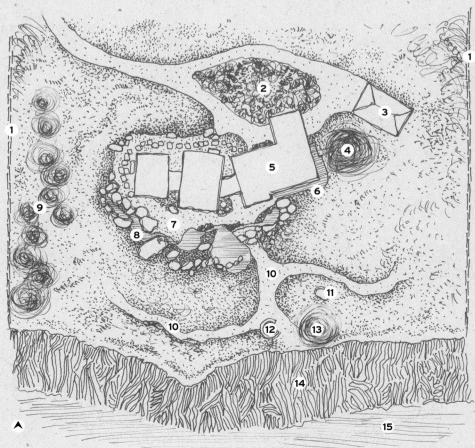

DIARMUID GAVIN & TERENCE CONRAN

Shade Gardens

There are many facets to a garden, and shade is a vital one. Shade offers refuge from the sun, a change in atmosphere and a chance to create fresh, exhilarating planting schemes. Flower borders are ablaze with colour all summer, but you will find a subtle beauty in shade planting set in a much softer light. Many urban gardens are rectangular in shape and tend to experience mixed amounts of sun and shade. Getting to know your garden intimately soon reveals the parts of the garden that are blessed with full sun, those that are lucky to gain a few odd hours of sunshine and those that remain in deep shade all day.

When planning the layout of a garden, most gardeners automatically consider surrounding buildings and adjacent trees that cast long shadows, yet gardens harbour many different levels of shade. Adding any tall structures – fences or walls, hedges and garden buildings – into a space will create shade pockets, while trees need to be chosen carefully, as the density of their canopies varies greatly with different species. A patio in a hot part of the garden will benefit from the cool, dappled shade of a silver birch (*Betula pendula*) but not the dense, heavy shade of a mature holm oak (*Quercus ilex*), which would make the area chilly. Plants also need to be sited in the correct

growing conditions, in order to carry out their function and to look their best – those used to create shade will need to tolerate the sun, while those chosen to live in it must be shade loving.

Since there are many shade-loving plants to choose from, the challenge lies in making the space look how you want it. Borders are ideally positioned in the sun, but those that are designed to soften garden boundaries tend to be shady, so the plants have to suit the conditions. Refine your plant choices to reflect different zones: dark, awkward gaps of the garden; those used to cover a garden shed or to 'green up' the cold shaded wall at the side of the house.

It may help to discuss the levels of shade that are found in a garden. Full shade occurs under low branching trees, those with large leaves and dense evergreen trees. The north side of buildings and boundaries can also have deep shade, especially if a tree is nearby. Open shade is found under small-leaved trees with higher canopies or near walls and fences. Some areas may receive shade for half of the day: for example, areas at the edge of a wooded site or beds facing the west or east side of a house or fence. Approach these individual areas as positive features, as opportunities to introduce a beautiful set of plants into the scheme.

▲ In this simple coastal scene, the relaxation area is shaded by mature trees, which have been well pruned to allow for timeless maritime views.

◄ An inviting curved path winds through shaded green borders of hostas and grasses, ultimately leading to an outdoor dining room.

Heavily shaded gardens

Buildings, boundaries and mature trees are the most common causes of deep shade in the garden. Most difficulties arise from the inability to get the lawn to grow well under trees, particularly under dense evergreen trees and old established ones. Instead of struggling with patchy grass year after year, change the scene with plant varieties that will be naturally happy in the relevant depth of shade. When making your plant selection, the availability of water also needs to be considered, as the shade under a tree canopy is quite dry. The shade of evergreen trees will be dense all year, whereas deciduous canopies will be considerably lighter for several months of the year, allowing some plant species to grow in spring.

If you are lucky enough to have the chance to build your home, consideration can be given to positioning the garden in the optimum direction for sunlight and with the best growing conditions. The unfortunate truth is that urban gardens tend to take lower priority than buildings, so that gardens are cut out from the land that remains post-construction, with no real thought given to outdoor living. Urban gardens are prone to areas of deeper shade from partition walls and high-rise buildings, as well as existing large specimen trees that can end up in odd positions within a development or street, saved by their protection orders. The position and site of your garden is permanent but, fortunately, owing to the vastness of the plant kingdom, there are species to fill all the gaps, so take charge of your space.

The majority of plants that do well in deep shade are foliage plants, so changing textures, leaf shape and tones of green come into play. Foliage plants have a much longer season of interest than those that flower for a couple of weeks each year and then proceed to set seed. With a small amount of planning, it is possible to create a composition with great depth and impact. Ferns such as *Asplenium scolopendrium* and *Athyrium niponicum* have the ability to make a dark, bare space look vibrant and lush. They are fabulous in large blocks of single species, but their elegant fronds will contrast superbly with glossy-leaved *Bergenia cordifolia* and *Asarum canadense* (a clumping ground-cover plant with heart-shaped foliage). Attractive shrubs that will dress a north-facing wall include *Elaeagnus* x *ebbingei* and *Mahonia aquifolium*, and the climber does not always have to be ivy; try delicately twining *Akebia quinata*, which is a stylish climbing species that will be happy in deep shade.

For a contemporary look, *Liriope muscari* can be planted with the black cultivar of dwarf mondo grass (*Ophiopogon planiscapus* 'Nigrescens'); this would create a robust ground cover all year round. Wild garlic (*Allium ursinium*) naturalizes beautifully to form a fine carpet of tiny white allium-like flowers and can be combined with *Symphytum grandiflorum* and the more unusual *Aralia racemosa* and *Arisaema thunbergii* for a stunning display in shade.

◄ An almost Arcadian view of an urn bathed in sunshine is the ultimate prize after climbing multiple brick steps through late summer green planting.

► An almost overgrown, naturalistic-looking scene establishes an air of escapism – the antithesis of formality.

◀ The planting in this Topher Delaney design is neatly contained behind clean lines of steel borders, producing a clear expanse of paving, while benefiting from the dramatic overhang of a beautiful specimen tree.

▼ Clipped domes of *Buxus sempervirens* in low squat pots provide an eye-catching focus in a shady part of this urban garden.

▥ Containers for shade

Casting shadows move with the sun throughout the day so that most gardens are subject to areas of partial shade, with deeper shade at the boundary edges. Permanent beds offer ideal conditions for growing plants but are not always possible to site in awkward spaces or in close proximity to the house. Containers are an extremely versatile way of embellishing such spaces and bringing in plant species that suit specific types of shade conditions throughout the seasons. A dark empty corner can be filled with colour and life in an instant display. Place containers at either side of the patio or front door for a grand entrance, to accentuate the curve of a path, at points of interest for a sense of direction, or use them as a central focus at the end of a vista, ensuring that the chosen species will be happy in the relative light intensity.

Container-grown plants must be paid a certain amount of attention in order to look their best, requiring food and water as a result of the limited amount of soil available to them. An effective water-retaining compost is essential, as is good drainage for root aeration. Containers positioned in the shade have the advantage of being sheltered from the sun and therefore receive some protection from excessive water loss. If containers are positioned under the eaves or on the lee side of a building, their watering requirements will also be affected by the rain shadow at the boundary, with little rain ever reaching the pot.

Plants with distinctive foliage work well in pots, and evergreens are specifically good for permanent displays. Species that thrive in shade include the dramatic x *Fatshedera lizei*; this wonderful cross between ivy (*Hedera hibernica*) and *Fatsia japonica* 'Moseri' bears foliage that has inherited the best of both worlds. Its large, glossy, deeply lobed leaves grow in an attractive loose habit which means that can be positioned against a wall and used as a climber if need be. *Camellia japonica* is a beautiful, shade-loving ornamental grown for its luxuriant foliage and showy flowers in shades of white through to yellow through to pink and red. It has a slow growth rate and is particularly suitable for container conditions, requiring slightly more acidic soil for optimum growth. Container-grown bushes of bay laurel (*Laurus nobilis*) are suitable for partial shade and will enjoy the protection of a boundary wall, as will *Viburnum tinus*, a species that will quickly mature into a wonderful flowering hedge.

Ferns grow naturally in the shade and will fill a planter with lush filigree foliage that will have impact alone or as a foil to reinforce a floral display. *Adiantum pedatum*, *Cyrtomium falcatum* and *Dryopteris filix-mas* will brighten up shadowy areas, their unfurling fronds creating beauty in foliage that is beyond the ordinary. *Epimedium grandiflorum* is a very elegant ground-cover plant with tiny, heart-shaped leaves, edged in bronze, and miniature orchid-like flowers in spring. It is wonderful when used to fill a container around a standard shrub or small tree, and also to contrast with the strap leaves of spring bulbs. Containers that are sited near the house or patio can be planted with more delicate species such as *Thalictrum kiusianum* and *Dicentra spectabilis*, both having finely cut foliage and dainty flowers.

Woodland gardens

There is a distinctive peace and serenity that prevails in a woodland space. The dappled shade and hazy shards of light that break through the natural tree canopy offer refuge on a hot day, a certain romance and a strong sense of tranquillity. A woodland garden is about contrasting foliage: hues of green, complementary plant associations and meandering clusters of perennials that have adapted to looking fabulous in the shade. The diversity of plant life on a woodland floor is immense, with hundreds of species competing for space and light. Spring-flowering plants grab the opportunity to shine when deciduous trees are bare, while the strongest will steal any rays of sun that reach the forest floor. There is an exuberance in plants that decorate all types of shade across the seasons, the low light intensity accentuating their detail and beauty.

Most gardens possess enough space to create a woodland garden or area. It can be as simple as a space in the shadow of one or a few mature trees at the end of the garden. Plants will be needed to fill varying depths of shade, with an evergreen canopy producing much deeper shade. Let the grass grow a lot higher in larger garden areas, to create a relaxed setting and allow lanky perennials and small bulbs to take over. A simple garden bench will make this the most popular place in the garden.

There are ample shade-loving shrubs to choose from, but the vision of a low-lying woodland carpet of plants is awe-inspiring. Huge drifts of *Epimedium* x *perralchicum* and *E.* x *youngianum* can be planted to ebb within masses of *Matteuccia struthiopteris* ferns and large clumps of *Trillium chloropetalum* and *Erythronium dens-canis*, both of which bear remarkably beautiful flowers. Slightly taller species such as *Dicentra spectabilis* 'Alba', *Euphorbia amygdaloides* var. *robbiae* and *Gillenia trifoliata* heighten the drama, the latter having wiry stalks that form a cloudy screen of fine white flowers.

The tapestry of the woodland carpet can be punctuated with great clumps of shade-loving bulbs chosen to create very different aesthetics. The arching stems of *Polygonatum* x *hybridum* and its pleated leaves are taken to another level when joined by its creamy white flowers in spring. *Fritillaria imperialis* is a beautiful giant and the ultimate bulb for vibrant colour in the shade, its robust stems reaching heights of more than 1m (3ft). *Leucojum aestivum* and the smaller *Galanthus nivalis* establish large numbers very quickly to produce a magical, snowy scene in late winter.

Plant choices

It is impossible to approach the subject of choosing the most beautiful plants for shady areas without making reference to Beth Chatto, one of the most skilful plant experts and champion of both woodland and dry gravel gardens. For practical purposes, the plants here have been selected for those that thrive in sheltered areas away from direct sunlight for part or most of the day. These species are relevant to most gardens, as they are happy in the shade of mature trees or next to walls and fences.

Among trees, *Acer palmatum* is an elegant ornamental shade-lover with lobed foliage; it is spectacular for its vibrant red autumn colour change. For partial shade, consider *Betula pendula* with its fresh apple-green leaves and white bark, bringing light and texture into the garden, or else grow the flowering dogwood *Cornus florida* for its open, spreading habit and distinctive pinkish white bracts.

Bamboos create shadowy screens and evoke a sense of the orient; *Fargesia nitida* is a graceful specimen, with fine leaves and long arching canes up to 4m (13ft) in height. If you prefer a shrub that is strongly contrasting, try *Fatsia japonica*, with its robust glossy foliage and tall stems of spherical flower clusters in autumn. It is an architectural shrub that grows equally well in a large container. Slow-growing *Camellia japonica* also enjoys some shade for its glossy green leaves and showy pink flowers in spring. For evergreen structure, *Prunus lusitanica* has a compact habit that is easily shaped into hedges, standards or topiary, and the bay laurel (*Laurus nobilis*) is a versatile shrub that enjoys the shelter of a wall. It provides evergreen interest, and its foliage is useful in cut-flower arrangements or for culinary use.

Shade-loving perennials include *Aconitum carmichaelii* 'Arendsii', a stunning border plant invaluable for its towering spires of rich blue monkshood flowers. It looks great in combination with *Aquilegia vulgaris* 'Black Barlow' (a clumping plant with lacy, lime-green foliage and fine flower spikes of purple to black flowers) and *Geranium himalayense* (an attractive cranesbill with a soft rounded shape, which creates great volume and bears many large, deep blue flowers with deep pink centres). *Digitalis ferruginea* is a shade-loving foxglove, with tall slender flower spires adorned with compact flower clusters in a distinctive copper colour that is tinged with brown.

Shady perennials for foliage include *Helleborus foetidus* and *Trachystemon orientalis*, both of which are blessed with deep green leaves in distinctive shapes. The former produces elaborate divided leaves, whereas the trachystemon's are dark green and heart-shaped, and they fill dark, awkward spaces effectively. *Liriope muscari* is a fantastic clump-forming perennial, with robust grass-like foliage all year round, as well as violet spikes of grape-like flowers late in autumn.

Grasses lift shady areas with texture and colour. Try *Hakonechloa macra* 'Aureola', a rhizomatous grass with purple stems and yellow leaves that are streaked with lime green, or *Luzula nivea*, a delicate grass with clusters of white flowers that catch the light and brighten up the shadows.

Ferns form fantastic ground cover under tree canopies or around other perennials in a border. *Asplenium scolopendrium* is a bright green fern with tongue-shaped fronds that look fabulous when contrasted with other ferns such as the dainty *Polystichum setiferum* and the very hardy *Blechnum spicant*. Other shade-loving ground-cover plants include *Muehlenbeckia complexa*, *Alchemilla erythropoda* and *Epimedium* x *youngianum* 'Niveum', all of which bear decorative foliage that lasts all year round. Add some seasonal interest with shade-loving bulbs such as *Arum italicum*, *Erythronium* 'Pagoda' and *Fritillaria persica*; they are all beautiful and guaranteed to steal the show!

▼ In this simple forest, the beautiful silver birch trees look stunning with their new leaves just unfolded after winter.

◄ This symphony of dramatic shape and background colour uses the stem of a beautiful tree to paint a romantic scene.

CONDITIONS

HERMANNSHOF
WEINHEIM, GERMANY

| CASE STUDY #13

| **DESIGNER**
| HANS LUZ & URS WALSER

▼ The gentle mounds of *Verbena rigida* f. *lilacina* and *V.r.* f. *lilacina* 'Polaris' set the background in a sea of blue, while the upright flower stems of *Verbena bonariensis* and delicate fluffy blooms of *Pennisetum villosum* create effervescence and light effects to perfection in an open, sunny area of the garden.

Diverse Conditions

The 5.5 acre (2.2 hectare) Hermannshof gardens were created just over 25 years ago as a trial ground in which to cultivate herbaceous perennials. The extraordinary result there has led to what has been labelled the New German planting style.

The garden is divided into seven distinct habitats, for which plants are chosen according to soil type and local site conditions. Each section of the garden is considered to be an individual ecological microclimate and is planted with species that would naturally thrive in these conditions. Consideration of plant relationships has been essential in the development of these various plant neighbourhoods. The result is a runaway success, as seen in the huge areas of mixed planting that look and behave as if they are in their natural surroundings and, most importantly, in places where plants have become

self-sufficient. Flower colour, heights and growth patterns have been mingled so that the whole scheme comes together in a natural undulating fusion. Now that the plants are well established, the early competition between species seems to have relaxed and plants bloom shoulder to shoulder in a symbiotic oasis.

Hermannshof is all about finding the right plants to grow in the right conditions; it is a garden where perennial drifts become huge floriferous canvases, where the plants have become all-encompassing in a landscape of their own. Narrow stone paths snake around the meadows and trees, leading the eye into the separate zones made distinct by fantastically differing combinations of plants.

Walkways pass through the North American prairie garden, which is filled with purples and yellows; hundreds of luminous yellow rudbeckia daisies are etched with tall

◀ A packed border of rudbeckia, agastache and verbena are joined by *Zinnia elegans* 'Oklahoma Scharlach', *Coreopsis verticillata* 'Grandiflora' and *Sorghastrum nutans*. All thrive well in hot and sunny conditions.

▲ This part of the North American prairie has a very different aesthetic and mood, with its cooler pinks and wheaty yellows. *Stipa tenuissima* and *Monarda punctata* create an airbrushed effect, defined by *Echinacea tennesseensis* and *E. purpurea* daisies.

▶ A grass path slices through the North American flower beds in a wonderful walkway that allows visitors to be submerged in the planting. Rolling perennial clumps are joined by larger shrubs and trees such as *Cercis siliquastrum*, which change the feel of the garden significantly.

CONDITIONS

HERMANNSHOF
WEINHEIM, GERMANY

CASE STUDY #13 CONTINUED

DESIGNER
HANS LUZ & URS WALSER

▼ Majestic *Echinacea purpurea* 'Magnus' is a wonderful cultivar with deep pink to red daisies on robust flowering stems that reach 1.5m (5ft) in height.

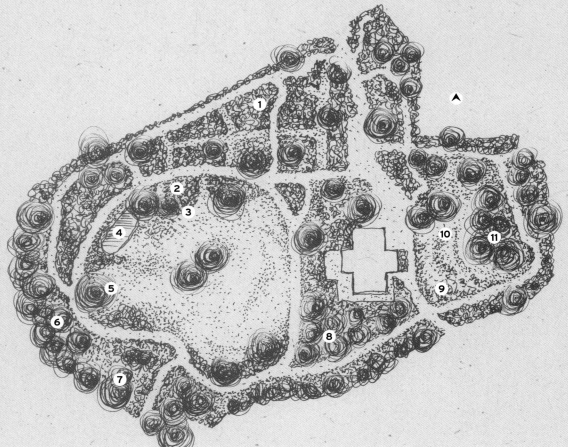

► The illuminating combination of *Zinnia elegans*, *Pennisetum setaceum* 'Kupfer', *Verbena bonariensis* and pink agastache is striking against a backdrop of soft pinks and whites in the dry, sunny borders.

◄ Hermannshof

1 North American perennials
2 Dry open ground
3 Silver summer planting
4 Pond
5 Damp open ground
6 Woodland
7 European species
8 Asian species
9 Woodland
10 Prairie garden
11 Hellebores and pulmonarias

green grasses and punctuated with *Verbena bonariensis* and fluffy headed liatris flower spikes. The blooms of *Silene regia* add riotous colour at a lower level in the brightest red. Further on, the finer yellow *Ratibida pinnata* blooms move softly into masses of upright pink *Echinacea purpurea* daisies. Then the lighter pink daisies meld into deeper pink *E. purpurea* 'Rubinstern', which are complemented beautifully by the fine foliage and spiralling flowers of *Veronicastrum virginicum*. Purple liatris pierces the composition, which fades into soft pink monarda, mauve phlox and more pink *Echinacea purpurea*. The whole space is enclosed by dogwoods and is captivating to behold.

In the beds that surround the main house is a softly mounding collection of blue and purple perennials including *Agastache rugosa*, *Verbena rigida* f. *lilacina* and *V.r.* f. *lilacina* 'Polaris', enlivened with sprays of *Verbena bonariensis* and *Pennisetum villosum*. The fluffy flowerheads look magical in the sunlight, glowing in a golden hue that beautifully picks up the soft yellow colour of the house.

At Hermannshof, the wonderful flow of colour creates excitement and a connection between the different zones. A shot of red *Lobelia* x *speciosa* 'Fan Burgundy' in the purple and blue garden hints at what is about to come; scarlet-tinged flower spikes of *Pennisetum setaceum* 'Kupfer' start to blend with deep pink agastache and sidalcea, and then suddenly you are surrounded by thousands of zinnias and penstemons in fiery red.

◄ Thousands of bluebells form a sprawling natural ground covering carpet in the deepest blue. Using a single plant species to fill a large area is a stunning way to create greater depth and impact; under trees, across lawns or in awkward shady parts of the garden.

▶ Good soil, careful planting and correct spacing, as well as an organized approach by marking rows and labelling plants, are particularly important if you want to get the best results when growing edible plants.

Practical

Stocking Your Garden

The question of what plants to purchase will be determined primarily by the style of garden you want and the conditions in which you are gardening. The latter is the key, since it will shape your choices. Although you can make minor improvements, it is nigh on impossible to completely change your soil conditions. Soil that is very acid (below pH6) will limit you to growing acid-loving plants, such as rhododendrons, azaleas and camellias; these tend to be fewer in number than plants that tolerate alkaline conditions (pH7 or above). Climate will also determine your choice of planting: if you live in an area with hard winter frosts, you will be obliged to choose hardy plants, although you can create shelter belts with hedging. These will make your garden less exposed to the elements, thereby extending the temperature range of plants you can grow.

If you take the time to discover the type of soil you have (see page 250) and the prevailing weather conditions, you will find that plants will flourish with much less effort on your part.

Some plants are more tolerant of a range of conditions than others, so if in doubt, pick those that cope in the widest range of soil types or the widest climate band. If in doubt, have a look at the gardens in your neighbourhood and make a note of what is doing well. Most plant directories will give you information on the preferred conditions of each plant, as well as a hardiness

rating (see page 262), which indicates the range of temperatures at which the plant should survive, as well as information on size, flowering time and so on.

Gardens (and the wildlife that visits them) benefit from a good mixture of plants, both in type (tree, shrub, perennial, bulb, annual), in height and shape, in foliage and flower interest and in colour and texture. With a bit of luck, your garden will offer various interesting conditions - a damp patch in a low-lying area or a dry warm spot near a wall - which will extend your planting choice and the potential interest.

Most people inherit a garden containing some elements of vertical structure such as one or two ornamental trees and some large shrubs. Others will be gardening on a virgin plot, and in this case it is important to make sure the garden has plants with varying heights, not only to create visual interest but also to provide a wider range of conditions for other smaller plants. You can grow some things in the shade or shelter of larger shrubs, for example, which might not survive in a more exposed position.

⦀ Seasonal interest

It is very important to remember that the majority of gardens are visible from the house throughout the year. Although most people want their gardens to be at a peak in summer, having something attractive to look at right through the year is uplifting to the spirits. Interest does not

depend solely on summer flowers; it can also take the form of attractively shaped or textured leaves, or bark or berries, for example. Scent is another very important consideration when planting a garden. It is rarely the first thing you think of when planning the scheme, yet it is one of the elements of planting that gives tremendous pleasure, so whenever possible choose a scented variety over an unscented one.

⦀ When to plant

When choosing plants, you need to consider the style of your planting and then select the most suitable varieties. The type of plant - tree, shrub, perennial, bulb or annual - will determine when and what you buy, and it is important that you purchase and plant at times that suit the plant, rather than you! The best times generally to plant trees and shrubs are in early autumn or spring (once the soil has started to warm up). This gives them time to acclimatize before the onset of either cold weather or hot dry conditions, neither of which is ideal for a plant that has recently been transplanted and is slightly vulnerable.

⦀ Where to buy

You can purchase seeds and plants from garden centres, which are basically retail centres supplied by specialist wholesale growers, or from individual nurseries, either by visiting them or by purchasing mail order from their catalogues. Most people buy from various sources, but the most important factor is that

they are a reputable source and look after their plants well.

Garden centres are useful for novice gardeners, as the plants are all grown in containers and usually displayed in well-signposted sections: for example, ornamental trees, fruit trees, large shrubs, small shrubs, perennials and bedding plants, with certain popular plants, such as roses, getting a section to themselves. While this is very helpful, the stock at garden centres tends to be limited to a few common plants in each genus, and once you have been gardening for a while, you may well want to choose more interesting and unusual species and varieties. These will generally be found at specialist nurseries, which concentrate on a few specific types of plant and carry a far wider range of these than the average garden centre. The staff are normally far more knowledgeable and both able and willing to offer advice. It is also worth going to flower shows, where you will probably see a more diverse and interesting selection of plants.

Most good garden centres and nurseries will label their plants with key information - the height/speed of growth, the flowering season, the sun/shade/soil preference - so do read the labels before you buy.

⦀ Checking plants

Badly cared-for young plants will often fail to thrive if, for example, they have been infrequently watered or allowed to outgrow the container in which they have been living. A plant needs a healthy root system to survive, and if the

◄ The brilliant papery flowers of ranunculus come in many colours – scarlet, gold, pink, white, yellow and orange. They are a great favourite, deservedly, with flower arrangers.

plant is not potted on at regular intervals into larger containers, the roots will become root bound, winding themselves around the rootball. Such root-bound plants are starved of oxygen and nutrients and will quickly die. Also, if the top of the compost is covered in weeds or moss, the plant has probably been in its pot for too long.

Examine any container plant you buy by turning it on its side. If the roots are extending below the pot and are matted, the plant is probably root bound and should not be purchased. If you turn the plant upside down and the compost falls

out, the plant has probably only recently been transferred from its growing position to this pot. Try to ensure that the plant you buy has a well-branched shape, no broken or misshaped branches, with leaves in good condition and, if you buy in spring, signs of healthy new growth. Avoid any plants with diseased leaves or stems.

Types of plant

Botanists have classified plants into broad groups according to their genetic make-up and their habit: for example, some retain their leaves year-round, while others are deciduous. It helps

to understand this, as the way they are grown, propagated and maintained is determined by the category into which they have been placed.

Trees are generally single-stemmed, and shrubs are multi-stemmed. The former can grow very tall, so you need to be aware of eventual size when making a choice for your garden, and also of speed of growth, as some are pretty fast and others surprisingly slow to reach their mature height. You can buy trees and shrubs as container-grown, bare-root (with the soil washed off the roots) or rootballed (with soil

around the roots, wrapped in hessian or biodegradable materials) specimens. You can buy them at various stages of development – larger trees tend to be purchased as rootballed plants. The younger ones are normally cheaper, but you may have to wait a few years for flowering or fruiting to take place. If you are planting a tree near a house or a wall, its roots could damage the foundations, so get advice on this. The same concern should be shown for underground drains or pipes being penetrated.

You may choose to buy climbing shrubs to clothe a wall or fence. They climb by different means: by tendrils, by twining, with sucker pads or using their thorns, so their planting situation will govern your choice. Container-grown climbers usually come with the branches tied to a support of some kind, either a cane or a plastic or bamboo frame. Make sure the plant has a good number of growing shoots that are healthy looking.

Perennials (also known as herbaceous perennials), as the name implies, will flower every year, usually with the foliage dying down in the autumn/ winter. These are normally sold as container-grown specimens, and the same rules apply for checking the condition of the plants (see above). Biennials, a smaller group, flower every other year. Perennials can be grown from cuttings and from seed (see pages 254–5). Those that are suitable for bedding are also available as plug plants – they are often sold in individual biodegradable pots, which you do not remove when

planting. Annuals grow, flower and die in one year. They can be sold either as plug plants or as seed for you to plant in spring.

Bulbs, corms and tubers are a group of plants that create a storage organ (mostly below ground) from which flowers emerge each year. If not, they will produce young bulbs (offsets) from the existing bulb, which will produce flowers the following year, so either way you should have a perennial display from them. They vary in type and shape. Bulbs are often sold dry, and are available shortly before the appropriate planting season. This will vary depending on the flowering time of the bulb, corm or tuber concerned. Spring-flowering bulbs are normally planted in autumn, and summer-flowering ones in early spring. Bulbs that are kept too long or stored in damp conditions are likely to rot and will not thrive.

Edible plants

Soft fruit is normally bought in the form of container-grown plants (for currants and gooseberries), bare-root plants (for raspberries) or as plants (for strawberries).

Fruiting trees can be bought as bare-root specimens or container-grown ones. Many fruit trees are grafted – in other words, one variety has been joined to the rooting stock of another, in order to provide the greatest benefit of fruiting vigour with reasonably controlled size.

Most vegetables are grown annually from seed, although a few, like rhubarb and globe artichokes, are perennial plants.

Soil

Good soil is the key to how successfully you grow your plants. Time and effort spent on knowing your soil conditions, and improving them where necessary, is never wasted. But it is the one element of gardening that most gardeners, in their enthusiasm to create a garden, tend to ignore. It is nothing like as exciting as choosing plants, unfortunately, but it is every bit as important.

Different soil types

The various soil types support different types of plant. The first lesson to learn is that the soil has a natural chemistry, which can be alkaline, acid or neutral. This chemistry, known as the pH balance, makes a big difference as to which plants do well. It is also difficult to change. Generally, particular areas of a country or region tend to belong to a particular category (owing to the underlying geology), so your neighbour's growing conditions are likely to be broadly similar to your own. If you take the time to look at the gardens in your neighbourhood, you can see that particular plants are favoured. If your neighbours' gardens are full of rhododendrons, azaleas and camellias, the soil in your part of the country is almost certainly acid. If they are successfully growing the classic border plants – delphiniums, phlox and lupins, for example – it is probably alkaline. Your planting choices will be limited to what grows well in the local conditions. If you want to be scientific, you can do a soil test, armed with a soil test kit, to find out the exact balance.

Soil test kit

You can buy a soil test kit at most garden centres. The kit will contain a test tube, or similar vessel, into which you put a sample of your soil, and shake it up with the solution contained in the kit. The solution will turn a particular colour depending on your soil's chemical balance. The kit will also contain a card with different colours, with levels of acidity or alkalinity marked against each colour. You then match the colour of the liquid in your test tube to the chart, and this will give you a rough idea of the pH balance of your soil. Under pH7 is acid, over pH7 is alkaline, and neutral is at ph7.

Soil composition

Soil can be predominantly sandy, predominantly clay, or a mixture of the two plus organic matter. This last type is known as good loam and is the best kind of soil to support plant growth. To determine which sort you have, take a handful of your garden soil and examine it.

Sandy soil is light in colour and texture, and full of small particles of grit. It will feel gritty and be difficult to roll into a ball in your hand. It is very free draining (water runs through it very quickly and the soil will also run easily through your fingers) and tends to support those plants with a shallow, fibrous root system. However, it dries out fast in hot weather, so only those plants that are drought resistant will survive unaided. To improve it, you need to add lots of organic matter (for example, well-rotted garden compost or straw), to make it more moisture-retentive.

Clay soil tends to be dark, and will form a sticky ball, which feels smooth on the fingers and does not separate easily; therefore, it does the opposite of sandy soil when rolled in a moist ball in your hand. Clay soil tends to be very moisture retentive and is prone to waterlogging in wet areas. It supports deep-rooted plants very well, but thanks to the water retention can also be very cold in winter. You need to add lots of organic matter to this soil, plus some grit, to increase its oxygen content and to make it more free draining. You will also have to start planting later in the year than with more free-draining soils.

Loam is mid-brown and crumbly in texture, and contains lots of organic matter. This is ideal garden soil. If you have it, simply keep it topped up annually with garden compost.

Improving soil

You need to improve your soil on a regular basis, particularly when growing edible crops, as plants draw the nutrients from it. This can be done by digging in various forms of organic matter, which will not only increase the nutrients but also improve the texture of the soil. Also, if the soil has been walked on, and therefore compacted, any lumps should be broken up and the soil aerated so it lets in the oxygen necessary for plant root growth. Established beds and borders, however, need only regular weeding, and the soil lightly forked over in autumn, with organic matter added at that time.

Digging is hard work, but a good spade (see page 251) helps, as does digging in the right conditions. It is best to dig in autumn (when there is less risk of disturbing emerging plants) in weather when the soil is moist but not sticky. Digging must be done systematically, to make sure you cover the whole area. To avoid treading on the soil you have just dug, work across the plot, in neat rows, a row at a time. Once the ground is well dug, and all traces of perennial weeds removed and burned, you can fork in any organic matter required.

The different forms of organic matter have their particular advantages and disadvantages, and it is important to bear these in mind when choosing what to use. Also, be aware that different kinds of plant need differing levels of key nutrients and minerals. However, if you are gardening generally, rather than trying to achieve show-quality specimens or maximum crop yields, you can be fairly general in your choices. Garden compost, provided it is fully mature, is good for most purposes, but it takes a while (around six months) before it is ready to use and it is also hard to make enough of it. Therefore, most gardeners supplement garden compost with well-rotted horse manure as their multi-purpose bulk fertilizer and soil improver (horse manure contains lots of straw, which helps to aerate the soil). Chicken pelleted manure is rich in nutrients, but does not aerate the soil as well as horse manure. Spent mushroom compost is also rich in nutrients, but is suitable only for lime-tolerant plants.

Soil drainage

Plants do best in well-drained soil, as it encourages a strong root system to form. With badly drained soil, root growth is restricted and plants cannot reach the water at lower depths in the soil during a drought. You can improve drainage by adding generous helpings of well-rotted manure or garden compost, and also by adding coarse grit. On really poorly drained soil you may need to incorporate drainage pipes, for which you will need specialist help.

To test the drainage, dig a pit about 60cm (2ft) deep or so, and leave it exposed during a period of heavy rains. Then check the water level in the hole and how long it takes to seep away. Well-drained soil will show no evidence of water in the hole a few days after the rains have stopped, but if there is still water in the hole, your soil is not draining well, so you should add organic materials to the soil. Equally, if the water all drains away within a few hours of the rain ceasing, it is probably too free draining, and you will need to add organic matter to improve absorbency.

Mulches

Plants will benefit from the soil being covered with a mulch (a layer of organic or inorganic material). This helps to prevent excessive moisture loss from the soil in warm weather and has the bonus of preventing weeds from seeding. The type of mulch you choose will depend on your soil and the kind of plants you are growing.

Organic mulches come in various forms, but they are primarily garden compost,

▼ Curly black kale is an invaluable crop: easy to grow, tasty and arresting to look at! It is grown here in a large vegetable garden, backed by beefsteak tomatoes in neat rows, supported on canes.

Tools and Equipment

well-rotted farmyard manure, bark or wood chippings, leaf mould or coir fibres. There are also some new mulches coming onto the market based on sheep's wool. Organic mulches have the benefit of adding to the nutrient content of the soil and will help to improve drainage, as they become incorporated into the upper layers of the soil through earthworm activity. However, the mulches will scatter over time and will need to be replaced annually.

Of the inorganic mulches, the most common are black plastic sheeting, horticultural fibre fleece, grit or pebbles. Plastic sheeting is not attractive, but it is useful as a membrane under organic mulches, or in the vegetable plot. Fibre fleeces help to warm up the soil for earlier planting. Coarse grit and pebbles are good for helping to conserve moisture in beds and borders.

Once you have a garden, you are involved in its upkeep, for which you need suitable tools and equipment. The speed at which any garden will revert to nature if neglected can be disturbing, so it pays to have some idea of what is required. Much depends on the style of garden and, of course, the size. A garden in which much of the surface area has been given over to hard landscaping is going to be the easiest of all to look after but possibly the least interesting in terms of planting.

If you are new to gardening, and have acquired a garden plot recently, you will need to set yourself up with some basic gardening equipment. If your space is very small – for example a roof terrace or balcony – your needs are more limited (see page 221).

▥ Basic cultivating tools

The range and style of equipment you require to maintain a garden will depend, to some degree, on the size and style of the garden, but the essentials are digging and cultivating tools, cutting and pruning tools, and watering equipment, plus a few items of carrying equipment in almost all cases. Lawn equipment, obviously, is necessary only for those with areas of grass.

A good-quality spade and fork are very important; the spade for digging the soil and the fork for general cultivation. Spades and forks come in three sizes so choose the one that feels the most comfortable and offers a decent guarantee. Cheap digging tools will not serve you well. You also need a trowel for planting small plants and a hand fork for weeding. A rake is useful for clearing up leaves as well as for removing stones and breaking up the soil into small crumbs (known as a fine tilth) for sowing seeds, while a hoe is invaluable for removing annual weeds both in the vegetable garden and in beds and borders.

▥ Other tools and equipment

You require a good-quality pair of sharp secateurs (again, no point in economizing here) for cutting small woody branches,

and also a sharp garden knife for general light cutting tasks. A pair of shears is essential for cutting soft green wood and clipping foliage on shrubs. You can buy them with telescopic handles (a useful feature when dealing with taller shrubs). A pruning saw for cutting stouter branches is invaluable, and the fold-up kind, where the blade folds into the handle, is ideal, as it will fit in a fairly capacious garden pocket.

You need a garden trug, a couple of garden carry bags and, for garden plots as opposed to patios, a wheelbarrow. A watering can, a hosepipe with a spray lance nozzle and a hand-held sprayer are also useful.

If you have a large grassed area, you will need some specialist grass-cutting equipment. A mower, which can be a hand mower or an electric or a petrol-driven version, is essential for keeping grass short, and a strimmer is useful for cutting areas of longer, rough grass. Strimmers vary a lot in effectiveness, so do some research before buying. Not all of them work as well as they should. If you have hedges, you may want to use an electric hedge trimmer rather than shears, as it will make short work of the task. For jobs such as pruning, a stout pair of gardening gloves is essential, as are goggles and ear muffs if using mechanized cutting equipment. Stout boots may also be necessary.

Planting

You do reap what you sow in any garden. But not all plants are normally grown from seed because they might take too long to reach maturity.

Seeds

Annuals and most edible plants are grown from seed, which is usually planted in spring. The seeds can vary in size from tiny round pellets to large cylindrical ones, but they all require warmth, light, moisture and nutrients to germinate (produce shoots and leaves). The seed of plants from hot countries in the world will require artificial warmth to germinate in colder climates (or if you need to get them started while the weather is still cold). These kinds of seed are usually planted about twice as deep as the seed itself in seed trays or pots filled with fine seed compost. Seed sown direct into the garden should be set in soil that has been dug over first and then raked to create a fine crumb-like texture, known as tilth. If you sow in rows, it helps to identify the emerging seedlings from weeds. Sow the seed quite thickly (hard to do otherwise with fine seed) and then thin out the rows of seedlings to the desired distance between the plants (which varies according to how large the mature plants will be). Although any seed packet will give all the necessary information, you can buck the trend and plant closer than normal if you want to harvest your plants very young – most seed companies tend to use commercial guidelines rather than catering to the needs of the small plot-holder.

Once seedlings grown in trays or pots are big enough to handle, pot them on into bigger pots to allow their roots room to develop. You need to handle all seedlings as little as possible to avoid bruising the stems, and you should also carry out any transplanting as quickly as possible. Most seedlings are potted on into 8cm (3in) diameter containers filled with fresh potting compost. Make a hole with a pencil or dibber. Holding the seedling by a leaf, insert it into the hole before replacing the compost, tamping it down and then watering well. Cover the pot with a plastic cloche (cut from an old water bottle) to retain moisture. Keep in the light but not in direct sunlight.

Plants grown in warmth indoors need to be hardened off before being transplanted into the garden. Normally, the best method is to leave the plants out during the day but bring them in at night for about a week. Plant them out in the garden either in rows at appropriate spacings (refer to your seed packet) or individually.

Planting container-grown and rootballed plants

Although this job can be done at any time of year for container-grown plants, it is best performed in spring or autumn, at the same time as rootballed plants. Any specimen will need to be planted out carefully to maximize its chances not only of surviving but also of growing well, and these are the optimum times. Growth for a badly planted specimen

will simply stop dead for quite some time, while it appears to sulk at its poor treatment.

Always ensure that the bed into which any plant is being moved is well dug and well fed, with plenty of well-rotted garden compost. Dig a hole at least three times the diameter of the plant's rootball and about twice as deep. Fork over the area to break up the soil, add bonemeal or other nutrients, and water the base of the hole. Gently tease out some of the outer roots from the rootball, then insert the plant in the hole so that the soil mark on the base of the stem will be at the same level in the soil as previously. Backfill the hole and firm around the plant by tamping down with your hands or with your boots. Water well again. Water regularly until the plant is established, or even longer if the weather is very dry.

Trees, large shrubs and climbers require appropriate and adequate support. To avoid damaging the roots, it is best to do this after you have dug the planting hole but before inserting the actual plant itself. Your support method for climbers will depend on the natural habit of the plant. Some climbers twine around a support, others cling to it with sticky pads and yet others scramble using thorns. Plant as for any container-grown plant, but make sure you have provided appropriate supports for the plant – either wires stretched horizontally along a fence or wall or suitable supports, such as a pergola or other wooden framed structure. If you are creating a framework

of wires on a wall for the plant to twine around or over, remember to allow a little space between the wires and the wall, so that the air can circulate.

To train a plant in the direction you want it to travel, you will have to tie in the new shoots as they grow, so always use ties that you can loosen or remove easily.

Planting bare-root plants

Bare-root plants are best planted in autumn or spring, having first soaked the roots in a bucket of water for a few hours. Dig a large hole that is wider than the span of the roots when spread out and is deep enough so that the new soil aligns with the soil mark on the main stem. Make sure the soil all around the hole is also well dug so that the roots will be able to penetrate the soil as they grow. Add some general-purpose fertilizer or bonemeal to the base of the hole. For single-stemmed trees, knock in a suitably stout stake. Settle the tree into the hole, spreading out the roots. Then backfill the hole with soil or garden compost, and firm it by treading it down around the stem. Secure the tree to the stake using tree ties, and water thoroughly. Thereafter, keep the plant well watered to help it establish.

Planting perennials in a border

Creating a suitable planting scheme for a bed or border is probably the most taxing element of gardening because you have to consider so many factors: the eventual height and spread of the plant, its general

◄ Neatly clipped box balls in handsome stone containers can be used to line a path or to frame a doorway. Being slow-growing with small leaves, box is an ideal plant for topiary.

Most borders have a peak season – usually early summer – but will present something of interest at other times of the year: for example, spring bulbs, which flower before the summer-flowering perennials are fully grown, or autumn-flowering plants, which take over after the summer flowers have ended. Many of the spring-flowering plants are quite small, so can be planted at the front of the border, and a lot of autumn-flowering ones are tall – heleniums, asters, echinaceas and so on – so they can provide the foliage backdrop to the summer-flowering border.

Supporting perennials and annuals

Perennials and annuals often need a simple system of support to keep the flowers more upright, but the actual type and form of support will depend on the size and growth habit of the plants. You can simply use bushy twigs pushed into the soil around each clump; these are almost invisible among the foliage. There are also neat metal supports you can buy that fulfil the same purpose and, of course, bamboo is always very reliable as a support.

You can train taller plants up and over hazel, willow or metal obelisks. Attractive ones are useful for providing structure in a border before the plants have reached their full height. Ensure that your structure is well dug in; otherwise, when it is covered with a plant, it could easily be blown over when battered by strong winds. If made of untreated wood, the support can rot at ground level.

Stop-gap planting

Almost every gardener experiences occasions when their planting fails to perform. Fortunately, annuals fill a useful function in filling these gaps, and can provide welcome colour. You should be careful, though, when using them, as many annuals are bred specifically for quite brash colours, which could look out of place in your subtle, sophisticated colour scheme! If your border has a hot colour theme and needs an injection of height, then try growing nasturtiums over a wigwam at suitably placed intervals. In a more subtly coloured border, sweet peas will make an excellent (and splendidly scented) filler grown in the same way.

Keeping plants healthy

All plants will stay healthier if they are given the right conditions. They need regular quantities of water and food to perform at their best. Not all plants need the same amounts. Plants adapted to desert conditions, for example, survive in the wild with occasional heavy downpours and have adapted leaf systems to minimize water loss or catch dew. The large-leaved plants that hail from rainforests are likely to require the most moisture. Plants are also adapted to cope with differing degrees of heat and sunlight, so, again, you need to pay attention to the plant's provenance and do the best you can to mimic these conditions.

Watering should be done when the plants are not in direct sunlight, as this can scorch the leaves. Try to water as regularly as possible to avoid stressing the plants.

Most plants will benefit from the application of an appropriate fertilizer in autumn. The kind of plant food depends on the type of plant and the purpose for which it is grown, as the nutrients contain different minerals, and leaves, shoots, flowers and fruit require varying permutations. However, unless you garden for show, most plants will benefit from the application of a multi-purpose plant food, such as a seaweed-based fertilizer which also has the benefit of being organic.

Plants also need a good flow of air around them. If there is too much wind, their leaves will burn, and they will suffer from wind-rock. If there is too little air, diseases may flourish. Some plants cope better than others with reflected heat from walls, while other plants – notably those acclimatized to tough coastal conditions – will easily tolerate whatever weather is thrown at them.

Keeping an eye on your plants and noticing any subtle changes will prevent major problems. Check that the leaves are not showing signs of stress – drooping from a lack of water or falling at times other than autumn, which may indicate poor feeding or constricted roots. Look out also for signs of pests, particularly on the undersides of leaves or on succulent new shoots, and deal with them early. Remove any pests or diseased plants as soon as you see them.

vigour, its flowering season and, of course, the colours. Do not forget, though, that the leaves and general shape of the plant play their part and will be in evidence for much longer than the flowers. First-time border designers often make the mistake of trying to include too many of their favourites. The best borders have generous groups of several plants of the same variety, and are always planted in odd numbers: three, five or seven. Remember, that you can use annuals to fill any holes or gaps and you can move plants around (ideally in their dormant season) if you have made mistakes.

When designing a bed or border, it always helps to think about the form and foliage of the plants and to try to choose plants with contrasting habits. Too many small-leaved evergreens with dark leaves will look dull. Interspersing grasses or plants with sword-shaped leaves among the clumps will add interest, as will plants with silvery foliage. Ideally, keep to one colour theme – either hot colours (yellows, oranges, reds, strong pinks) or cool colours (white, mauves, blues, pale lemons and pale pinks) to prevent an unsettling, discordant feel to the planting.

Propagation

Plants propagate themselves in the wild, but you, the gardener, can control propagation in various ways, using the seed or other parts of the plant. Seed occurs when the female parts of the flower are fertilized with male pollen, and you can gather this seed in autumn and sow it either then or the following spring. You can also create new plants by taking cuttings of a leaf, stem or root (depending on the type of plant). If you then insert these cuttings into potting compost in the right conditions, they will produce new roots from which new plants are formed. This method has the advantage that the new plant will be identical in every way to the parent plant.

⫾⫾⫾ From seed

You can harvest seeds from your own plants or buy them from seed merchants or garden centres. If you are gathering your own seed, then harvest it after a dry spell so the seed pods are dry. When collecting seed pods that contain scores of tiny seeds, it is advisable to put a plastic bag over the tip of the plant and seal it before breaking off the stem below the seed pod. Then, when the pod bursts, it scatters the seeds within the bag. If you are using bought seed, make sure the packets are not out of date. Old seed can be difficult to germinate, as can seed with a hard coating. The latter will geminate better if you can break down the seed coat first. You can either soak the seed or else chip its coating by nicking it with a sharp knife or by putting the seed in a jar lined with sand paper and then

shaking the jar (with the lid on!). Some seeds germinate only after being exposed to very low temperatures. Parsnips are a case in point. Put the seed into ice trays in the freezer overnight, and plant out the complete ice cube with its embedded seed.

The time of year at which seed is sown depends on the kind of plant. Annuals (see page 264) have their seed sown in spring (often in warmth indoors), and they then flower and set seed the same year. Perennials can be sown normally in autumn, when the seeds ripen, or early the following spring. The young plants will then take two growing seasons before they flower, so many people prefer to buy perennials as container-grown plants that will flower in the year of purchase.

When and where you sow the seed depends on the plants you are going to grow. Hardy perennials and annuals can be sown outdoors, normally in their final flowering position. The best time to do this is once there is little likelihood of spring frost. Prepare the seedbed by digging it over thoroughly in autumn and adding organic matter to the soil, as well as some grit or sand if the soil is naturally heavy. Just before sowing, dig over again lightly and rake out any stones. Bang any clumps of soil with the back of the rake until it has a fine crumbly texture. Using a garden line (two sticks joined with string) to mark out the sowing line, make a drill with the corner of a hoe in which to place the seeds. Sow the seeds thinly (usually about twice the

depth of the seed itself) and cover with a fine layer of soil. Water thoroughly with a fine rose on the watering can.

Tender plants such as some annuals and biennials, and most vegetables, need to be sown indoors or in a warm greenhouse because they require higher temperatures than you are likely to have outdoors at the time of sowing and an early start to the growing season will speed up the production of flowers or fruit in the following months. You can sow their seeds in little individual pots or in trays. Small seed is usually sown in trays, larger seed in pots. Degradable containers are useful for larger seeds, as you can then transplant them to their places in the garden without handling each plant. Broadcast very fine seed over the compost surface. Not all seed needs to be covered, so check the instructions on the seed packet. Always label your seeds with plant ID and sowing date. Nothing is more irritating than not knowing which pots contain what seeds, how long they have sulked in their pots prior to germination, or where you put the rows of seeds in your garden! Be warned: the germination time of seed varies considerably – some are very fast to produce their first leaves, others worryingly slow!

Once they have germinated, thin out the seedlings so they have room to grow unhindered. When they have outgrown their current pot or seed tray, replant them in slightly larger pots if it is still too cold to plant them outdoors. When doing this, be careful to handle the vulnerable

young seedlings as little as possible. Make a small hole in the potting compost with a dibber and drop the seedling into the hole. Firm the surrounding compost carefully. Water well.

Seedlings growing indoors or in a warm greenhouse need to be hardened off before being planted out in the garden. Gradually accustom your plants to lower temperatures by putting them outdoors during the day for a week. Then leave them out overnight for a few nights as well, before transplanting them into their final places in the garden.

◄ Many crops can be grown on a patio or terrace by using plastic growing bags full of multipurpose compost. Young sweetcorn plants are seen here, but tomatoes and salad leaves are also commonly grown in them.

Softwood and semi-ripe cuttings are normally planted in pots or trays of cuttings compost. A heated propagator will facilitate root formation by providing bottom heat. Seal the pot with a plastic bag over it (supported with a few short canes) to retain moisture. Keep at an even temperature while roots develop; cuttings that get cold or too wet will be unlikely to root, and moulds or other diseases may develop. You can plant hardwood cuttings directly into a garden bed or border, making small holes for them with a dibber or fork.

Improving rooting

• Dip the base of a cutting into hormone rooting powder to facilitate root production.
• Use a covered propagator with a heated bottom tray to provide the best possible conditions for softwood and semi-ripe cuttings.
• Make a shallow angled cut in the base of the stem to increase the area for root production.
• Including a piece of bark from the parent plant also stimulates root development.

By division

You can create new plants from many clump-forming perennials by simply splitting the rootball into two parts or by cutting portions of root and replanting them. This not only increases the number of plants but also improves the vigour of existing ones, as perennials tend to die out from the centre.

You can divide plants when they are semi-dormant, usually in spring (except for bearded irises, for example, which are left in peace until they have flowered). Splitting the rootball of a plant is not for the faint-hearted. You need to be quite brutal. For plants with a very fibrous root system, push two forks, back to back, into the centre of the clump and then lever the forks apart, splitting the clump in half. You may find this easier if you do the task with another person. Plants with fleshy roots can simply be dug up, cut into sections (each with a new shoot attached) and replanted.

Any plants that produce buds from roots can be propagated from root cuttings. Cut the roots into several short lengths about 8cm (3in) long, making a straight cut at the top end (where it was severed from its parent) and an angled cut at the bottom end, so you know which way up to plant the cuttings. Then insert the pieces into pots of cuttings compost, so the top end is level with the compost surface.

Layering

You can practise this method of propagating with any woody plant or climber whose stems will bend easily down to the soil surface. Make a diagonal cut in a stem of the current year's growth at a convenient point and then peg down the stem so that the cut end is in contact with the soil (or with a little mound of compost over it, which facilitates root formation). Once the stem has rooted and new shoots are growing (around six months later), you can sever it from the parent plant and replant it in the usual way.

From cuttings

You can create new plants by taking cuttings from shoots, leaves or roots. The shoots can be the soft tips of the current season's new shoots (softwood cuttings), woodier growth (semi-ripe cuttings) or even fully mature shoots (hardwood cuttings). Each type of cutting is propagated in a similar way but the timings are different. Softwood cuttings are normally taken in spring or early summer and need to be planted quickly (straight from plant to pot), as they wilt easily. Semi-ripe cuttings are taken in late summer; they are hardier than softwood cuttings but require longer to develop roots. They are normally protected over winter in a cold frame or cold greenhouse. Hardwood cuttings are generally taken in late autumn.

Stem cuttings are quite delicate and do not always survive, despite your best efforts, so it pays to propagate quite a few more than you are likely to need. For a softwood cutting, cut about 10cm (4in) below a fast-growing tip on a shoot of the current year's growth. Take a semi-ripe cutting as a shoot of around 10cm (4in) with a little of the main stem bark attached to it. For both types of cutting, trim away the lower leaves. For a hardwood cutting, remove a section of stem with all its current year's growth, cutting it just above a leaf node and just above the next one. You can cut a longish stem into several cuttings, each about 10cm (4in) long. It makes sense to cut the base straight across just below a leaf node, and the tip of the cutting at an angle just above a leaf node, so you can see at a glance which way up they should be planted!

▼ Blue-leaved grasses planted in swirling sinuous ribbons make an excellent choice for a strong statement in a contemporary evergreen planting or as edging for a flower border.

Pruning

What to prune and when to prune are subjects that cause most gardeners concern. The danger with inexperienced pruning is primarily that you inadvertently remove the next season's flowering shoots in your enthusiasm.

Trees

Large tree pruning, on the whole, is best left to the experts, apart from dealing with smaller fruit trees and ornamentals. As a rule of thumb, if the branch is too large to be cut with a small pruning saw, it is probably a job best tackled by experts.

You can prune a small tree after the leaves have fallen and when the sap is no longer rising. If the branch is long or heavy, cut it in sections, to avoid tearing the bark as torn bark facilitates diseases. To do this, Initially, cut the branch by a quarter of its diameter on the underside, then, slightly further along the branch away from the trunk, make a second cut from above, sawing through the branch. Finally, make a cut close to the trunk.

Trees that bear fruit need to be pruned according to type. Fruit trees can bear fruit on the tips (ends of branches) or on spurs (shoots off branches) so it is important not to cut off all the ends of the shoots on a tip-bearing tree! Apples, pears and cherries mostly bear fruit on shoots that are two years old or more, so you prune to create a balance between the new growth and the older wood that will produce fruit. The plum and damson family bears fruit on one-year-old shoots, as do figs and peaches. You should

generally prune fruit trees in autumn or winter, but stone fruit trees are best pruned in summer.

Shrubs

The reasons for pruning a shrub are: to keep the outline of the plant neat; to remove crossing branches that prevent air circulating through the plant (the lack of air will make the plant more prone to disease); to remove dead or diseased parts of the plant; and, finally, to promote the formation of fruit or flowers.

Always use a pair of sharp secateurs or loppers, to avoid tearing the stem, and make the pruning cuts just above an outward-facing bud to prevent branches crossing inwards as they grow.

If you want perfect plants, prize-winning flowers and massive yields of fruit, then you will need to make an effort to find out more about the pruning needs of the plants you are growing. As a general rule, however, most evergreens require little or no pruning compared with deciduous shrubs, although you do need to check any excessive or uneven growth; this is best done in mid-spring to reduce the risk of frost damage. Cut back the growth by about a third and thin out weak or overcrowded shoots. Most need only a light clip, to keep them neat, and the removal of the odd awkward branch.

If a shrub flowers on the current season's growth, you prune it in spring. If it flowers

on the previous season's growth, you prune it in summer. If in doubt, prune any plant immediately after flowering, cutting back by no more than a third. Plants such as roses benefit from being hard pruned in the early spring (take back the shoots to a couple of buds) and remove about a third of the older wood after the plant has flowered.

Hedges

When pruning a hedge, you need to encourage the plants to branch well and also control their vigorous growth. To do this, cut back a new hedge immediately after planting to about half its height, and in the second year cut it back by about a third. This will encourage lower branches

to form. Thereafter, you can simply trim the hedge regularly.

You must use sharp secateurs or hedge trimmers and make sure that you prune so the hedge is wider at the base than at the top, otherwise light will not reach the lower branches and they will die back. Trim upwards from the base. On a long hedge, use a brightly coloured line to provide a level cutting guide.

Topiary

The art of pruning plants into artificial shapes has become increasingly popular but be cautious: you can get awfully bored with the dog, cat and bird shapes over the years. Abstract shapes are rather more elegant. Evergreens clipped into box, cone or ball shapes make excellent sculptural additions to flower beds, providing interest and structure in the winter months.

The plants most suited to topiary are slow-growing evergreens such as box (*Buxus*) or common yew (*Taxus baccata*) but many other evergreens respond well to clipping, although they will require more work. Quick-growing topiary can also be created from a climber such as ivy, trained over a suitable frame.

You should use sharp shears or special topiary scissors for clipping. When training young plants, tie the shoots into the required shape and be tough about cutting back, to promote bushy growth. Metal frames can be bought to provide a useful cutting guide.

◄ Strong lines in a garden design can be created by hard surfaces and by careful clipping of evergreen plants, as these slabs of clipped box demonstrate. This clever design incorporates not only changes of level but also pleached trees and blocks of colours.

Container Gardening

If you have a very small outdoor space that is hard surfaced – a balcony, roof terrace or patio – you will be limited to growing plants in containers. However, limited is hardly the right word, as almost any plant that grows in the soil can be grown in a container. The plants to avoid, however, are those that are extremely vigorous, as you would then spend much of your time either potting them into ever-larger containers or having to trim their roots so as to restrict them to small spaces.

For container gardening, concentrate on just a few key tools: a good, small hand fork and trowel, a good-quality pair of sharp secateurs, a gardening knife and a watering can. Also useful is a hose and/or a drip-watering system (see right), which can be trailed around your containers so they can be watered in your absence (either on a timer or with a soil-sensitive system that switches the watering system on when the soil is dry). You will probably want to try your hand at some simple propagating, too (see page 254), so have handy a few seed trays, plant labels, a dibber and maybe a propagating unit.

▥ Types of container
You can grow plants in almost any type and style of container (except those that might leach chemicals that could destroy your plants) but aesthetics are very important in a small space close to the house. Terracotta, stone, wood and metal are the materials of choice for most people, and concrete can be effective if the chosen shape

is contemporary. If you must have plastic, which is the cheapest material, choose dark green, not white, which is far too strident in almost any setting. Of the natural materials, opt for whichever kinds suit the situation and your budget. It pays to fill the bottom of any container with a layer of broken pot shards or pebbles, to help drainage.

The form of the container will be determined largely by the size of the space available and the kind of planting you are choosing. If you want high-level planting, suspended from your walls, then light metalwork or wickerwork containers are probably the best bet. If you want to grow quite large trees or shrubs, then suitably deep pots will be needed to give the roots adequate space.

Big containers make an attractive statement of their own, and do not necessarily have to be planted with enormous plants. Huge plants, however, can never thrive in tiny containers!

For plants on windowsills, you need to choose containers that fit onto a narrow ledge, and you must also anchor the containers safely if they are on first-floor levels or above. Do this either by creating a restraining lip on the outer edge of the sill or by fixing brackets and chains to the window boxes themselves.

A container-grown climber requires not only a container shape that will suit the wall or fence against which it is to be grown, but also an adequate support system, with either trellising or stretched wires, nailed to the wall or fence.

It is certainly a good idea to recycle containers where you can. A surprising number of pieces of what might be classed as junk can be turned into effective containers, from old metal buckets to old glazed sinks, cut-down beer barrels or rusty old farmyard equipment – pig troughs are good. Much depends on the setting and the style of the plant as to whether this looks chic or, sadly, resembles a junk yard. If you do make new containers from old, remember to drill drainage holes in the base. Without them, the compost will waterlog and the plants will die.

▥ Container compost
Your containers must be filled with potting compost. Although the soil-less types are more environmentally friendly if they do not contain peat, they lose nutrients faster, so are not ideal for plants permanently in containers. Potting composts come in different formulations and mixes, but multi-purpose potting compost does well for most things, except those plants such as rhododendrons and azaleas that demand a mix with a high acid content (known as ericaceous compost). Of the special compost mixes, John Innes formulations are the best known. There are three different strengths based on their nutrient content: No. 1 is the least strong and is used for fine-rooted plants and seedlings; No. 2 is the standard strength and is suitable for most plants; No. 3 is best for fast-growing plants such as tomatoes or sweet peas.

You can buy special growing bags, filled with compost, and

these are ideal for fast-maturing crops such as lettuces or tomatoes that have fairly shallow roots. You simply cut a cross in the top of the plastic covering and insert the plants through these holes.

▥ Watering
You need to make sure containers are watered for long enough for the moisture to reach the very bottom of the compost. How much water they require depends on the type of plants (lettuces and tomatoes need copious quantities; Mediterranean herbs need very little). Try to water in the early morning or late evening in hot climates. You can revive underwatered plants by soaking them in a bowl of shallow tepid water for a few hours. The compost will absorb the water through capillary action.

Drip-watering systems can be used if you are away often, and some of them have sensors that can be placed in the compost; these activate the system, dripping water through a series of fine nozzles, as soon as the compost becomes too dry. The fine nozzles tend to clog very easily so, while helpful, automatic systems are not always foolproof.

▥ Feeding plants
You have to pay attention to feeding because container-grown plants are especially dependent on you. Plants need different nutrients for different purposes: they require nitrogen for leaf development; phosphates for root development; and potash (potassium) for hardiness and disease resistance, as well as

grown in confined spaces. Finally, the type of container must be suitable for the type of crop. Deep-rooted vegetables such as carrots and parsnips need sufficiently deep containers.

You can buy specially constructed containers, such as strawberry barrels, that have multiple planting holes in the sides and so allow you to get a good crop from one container. However, these also demand that you water well and long, otherwise those plants at the bottom will suffer from drought.

Potatoes do really well in big barrels or even an old dustbin with drainage holes inserted. Leave the seed potatoes in a warm place until they start to develop shoots. Then place the potatoes in a container half filled with potting compost. As the potatoes develop, keep topping up with compost. The main aim is to make sure all the potatoes are well covered with compost, otherwise they will turn green and become inedible. In this way, you can grow early, second early and maincrop potatoes, which mature at different periods. Harvest the early ones as the plants flower, the second earlies just after flowering, and the main crop once the leaves die down in autumn.

▥ Looking after containerized plants

As they develop, plants in containers need supporting, just as they would if growing in a flower bed. However, as the supports are more visible for container-grown plants, try to make these as aesthetically pleasing as possible. There are

some very attractive iron supports to be found, or you can use twigs, bamboo or sticks in attractive wigwam shapes for plants to grow through.

Regular deadheading of container-grown plants is vital, not only for plant health but also because the dead and dying flowers look unsightly. Removing old flowers will foster the growth of more replacement ones, too, and if the main flower spike is cut off promptly smaller subsidiary spikes will form and bloom. However, if you want fruit, berries or seeds, do not deadhead the last growth of the season.

For propagating and pruning container-grown plants, you should follow the guidelines outlined on pages 254–256. The principles are just the same and apply here, too.

▥ Miniature pools

You can even have your own mini pond with water-loving plants in a container. It should have a minimum depth of 30cm (12in) – or 45cm (18in). You could use an old glazed sink or a wooden container, such as a half barrel, provided it is lined with plastic.

If you want to have plants at the edge of the water, such as some irises, reeds or marsh marigolds, you need a ledge 23cm (9in) deep at the sides. Plant marginal and aquatic plants in special compost/grit in mesh-sided baskets. If possible, position the miniature pool out of direct sunlight and avoid areas under trees. If you include the odd water snail, they will happily eat any rotting vegetation.

good fruiting capabilities. Minerals – iron, magnesium, manganese, sulphur and calcium – are also needed but in very minute quantities. In the old days, gardeners mixed their own fertilizers. Nowadays, most people tend to buy them ready made, either as dry pellets or as liquids. Most fertilizers indicate on the packet or bottle which principal nutrients they offer, so, if you are growing tomatoes,

for example, look for a fertilizer with a higher concentration of potash (potassium).

Most proprietary composts and potting mixes contain an initial reserve of nutrients. You then bolster these by using quick-acting fertilizers when the plants are in active growth. Fertilizer should be applied to moist compost – never to a dry potting mix – and be careful not to spray it on the leaves,

which will scorch. Do not be tempted to overfeed!

▥ Growing edible plants

Crops can be grown very easily in containers, as long as you remember some key points. First, all produce requires frequent and often copious watering, so you must do this on a regular basis in drier weather. Second, edible plants need regular feeding, too, when

Maintenance

Anyone who has even the smallest plot will quickly find out that some time and attention are needed to keep it looking good and the plants performing well. A neglected garden is an unattractive sight. If you do not have the time to give your garden the maintenance it deserves, consider redesigning it so that you have more in the way of hard surfaces and rather less in the way of planting. The hard surfaces will require some upkeep but considerably less than most plants.

Lawns and ground cover

Planted surfaces, such as lawns, are time-consuming if they are to look good. A lawn is often laid without proper preparation – say, on a new-build plot – which makes maintenance more difficult.

The main enemies of lawns are poor drainage, lack of sunlight and extreme weather conditions. They respond particularly badly to be being tramped over when wet, which compacts the soil and reduces its ability to breathe. Grass roots are shallow and need oxygen, so your aim as a gardener is to increase the oxygen, to maintain even watering and to cut your grass and rake off the clippings regularly, to keep it in good health. If you leave any clippings, except very small scattered ones, these will gradually choke the grass and it will turn yellow.

You should reseed patches of grass that are worn; mark out the area so you do not walk on it until the grass is well established. It will also pay to rake and aerate the grass a couple of times a season. Walking over it in spiked golf shoes will do this very successfully. Lawns in damp areas may develop moss, and this can be treated with moss killer in autumn.

Cut the grass once a month in the growing season, using whatever mower is suitable for your size of plot. Put the clippings on the compost heap but intersperse the layers of clippings with other plant waste, as thick layers of grass clippings tend to overheat the heap, as well as form an impenetrable layer that is slow to decompose. Feed the lawn in spring and autumn.

Unlike grass, ground-cover plants require very little maintenance. You may need to remove any fallen leaves from trees above, and cut off runners or suckers in early autumn.

Beds and borders

As the new season's growth increases in height, you should stake taller, slender-stemmed or large-flowered perennials. Once the plants are flowering, it is well worthwhile taking the trouble to remove any spent flowers (known as deadheading). Not only do these look unsightly, but by removing them, you encourage the formation of more flowers. You also need to weed beds and borders, particularly in the late spring and summer months. Although annual weeds can be hoed off, perennial weeds such as couch grass and ground elder must be carefully dug up and burned. Never make the mistake of composting perennial weeds because they can grow again from small sections of root.

In late autumn, after flowering has finished, cut back clumps of deciduous perennials to around 8cm (3in) from the crown. Clear up any fallen leaves, and bag them up to use later as leaf mould. Tie up the bag and aerate it in several places with a garden fork. If you leave foliage lying in beds or borders, it might foster diseases. Apply a top-dressing of well-rotted manure or compost to beds and borders, and fork it lightly into the soil. Also in autumn, divide any overgrown clumps of perennials (see page 255).

Trees and shrubs

Check your trees and shrubs for diseased or broken branches in autumn, and remove any by pruning them close to the main trunk or stem (see page 256). Tidy up shrubs to improve their overall shape, cutting off wayward branches. Remove any suckers that have appeared below the graft line of a tree, to prevent these shoots from the rootstock eventually dominating growth, which would be to the detriment of the upper, grafted part of the tree.

Hedges

These need to be clipped on a regular basis to keep them looking good and also to make sure the plants are healthy (see page 256). How often you do this job depends on the vigour of the plant: prune slow-growing plants such as box just twice a year, while privet will need trimming about once a month during the growing season. Once a year, in autumn,

even if you have only a small patio. You are probably best buying a purpose-made plastic compost bin, so that you can turn your kitchen waste into good garden compost in around four to six months. Feed the bin with all your raw vegetable and fruit waste, tea bags, hedge clippings and some wet newspapers. To encourage waste to break down quickly, use a proprietary compost activator sprinkled over the surface of the layers every so often.

Other garden tasks

Each year, you should repot any container-grown plants, dividing those that are outgrowing their pots. Always use special compost/grit when replanting aquatic plants.

In autumn, clean out any debris in the pond, and carry out any repairs to garden sheds and fences, replacing any rotten wood. Treat any timber with preservative. Keep the glass clean on cloches or glasshouses.

Wooden surfaces such as decks will need periodic (twice a season) scrubbing down with a wire brush and water with a little detergent added, to prevent build-up of green algae. Having removed any weeds, replace any areas of gravel that have become bare.

Once a year, arrange to have any cutting equipment sharpened, and oil the blades, too. You should oil and service any machinery such as lawn mowers. Wash out old propagation pots each year. Throw away out-of-date seeds and restock supplies of labels, string and markers.

remove any diseased or dying branches and apply a top-dressing of well-rotted manure or compost to the base of the hedge. Avoid, if you can, doing any major clipping in the nesting season.

Climbers

Check every so often that any climbing plants are securely tied to their supports, and prune back those that are growing too vigorously. Certain climbers, such as wisteria and clematis, need careful pruning if you are to avoid cutting off next year's growth, so consult a pruning handbook before doing this task.

Tender plants

In colder climates, you may need to overwinter some of your more tender plants. Lift any tender bulbs or tubers (such as dahlias) and store in a frost-free cool place before replanting the following year. Perennials that are permanently planted in the garden can have their crowns covered with leaves or sacking. Protect half-hardy plants in containers by wrapping the container in sacking. Bring more tender plants indoors into a conservatory.

Looking after the soil

You should dig over the soil every autumn and add organic matter to replace the nutrients lost in the growing season. Remove any perennial weeds by digging out all the roots, as many will regrow from just a scrap of root left in the ground. After digging over and clearing beds in autumn, it is advisable to cover them with black plastic until you are ready to plant, otherwise you may find yourself repeating your hard work a second time in spring.

Any mulches, such as bark chippings, gravel, straw or garden compost, used to suppress weeds and/or help aerate or nourish the soil, will need to be topped up once a year, usually in autumn. You can easily make your own compost, and it is worth doing

Plant Directory

Key to hardiness ratings

*** **Fully hardy plants**
Tolerant of temperatures
down to -15°C (5°F)

** **Frost-hardy plants**
Tolerant of temperatures
down to -5°C (23°F)

* **Half-hardy plants**
Tolerant of temperatures
down to 0°C (32°F)

+ **Tender plants**
May be damaged by
temperatures below 5°C (41°F)

Trees

Acer japonicum
Japanese maple
H AND S: 10M (32FT) ***
This spreading deciduous tree
has the typical large deeply
lobed hand-shaped maple
leaves, which turn bright red
in autumn. 'Aconitifolium'
has particularly deeply lobed
leaves and is smaller and less
spreading; H: 5m (16ft), S: 6m
(20ft). Acers do well in sun
or partial shade, and fertile
moist soil.

Betula pendula 'Laciniata'
Silver birch
H: 10M (32FT), **S:** 3M (10FT) ***
This particularly elegant
silver birch grows less tall and
is less spreading than the
species, so is ideal for a small
garden. It has strikingly more
pendulous branches than usual
and deeply cut leaves. The
peeling white bark becomes
more marked with age, and the
leaves turn golden yellow in
autumn. In spring, 'Laciniata'
bears attractive catkins.

Carpinus betulus
Common hornbeam
H: 25M (80FT), **S:** 20M (65FT) ***
This deciduous tree is too large
for most gardens, but makes
very good hedging by virtue
of being slow-growing and able
to withstand hard pruning.

The leaves are mid-green,
oval and toothed, and turn
orange-brown in autumn.
It bears yellow male and
greenish female catkins in
spring. Grows well in sun or
partial shade. For a specimen
tree, consider smaller,
narrower *C.b.* 'Columnaris';
H: 10m (30ft), S: 6m (20ft).

Catalpa bignonioides
Indian bean tree
H AND S: 15M (50FT) ***
A great tree for gardens that
forms a spreading shape, with
huge beautiful heart-shaped
mid-green leaves. White flowers
in mid- to late summer are
followed by its characteristic
40cm (16in) long 'beans'. 'Aurea'
has bright yellow leaves. Prefers
moist well-drained soil, full sun
and shelter from strong winds.

Hamamelis
Witch-hazel
H: 4M (13FT), **S:** 5M (16FT) ***
There are several varieties
of witch-hazel, but almost
all are grown for their frost-
resistant fragrant flowers
borne on bare branches in
winter. Their mid-green oval
leaves offer excellent autumn
colour. *H. x intermedia* has
dark yellow, orange or dark
red spidery heavily scented
flowers. *H. mollis* produces
bright yellow very fragrant
flowers. Grow in sun or partial
shade on most soils.

Magnolia stellata
Star magnolia
H: 3M (10FT), **S:** 4M (13FT) ***
Among the numerous
magnolias, many bear
traditional goblet-shaped
flowers, some of them scented.
This species is very popular,
with its abundant unusual star-
like flowers in white, slightly
pink-flushed, in early to mid-
spring. The flowers, up to
12cm (5in) across, have up
to 15 petals. *M.s.* 'Rustica Rubra'
is a dark pink variety. Grow in
sun or partial shade on neutral
to acid soil.

Malus x arnoldiana
Crab apple
H: 5M (16FT), **S:** UP TO 8M (25FT) ***
Crab apples make great
decorative garden trees, with
the bonus of fruit that is ideal
for jams and jellies. There are
many varieties to choose from.
This particular crab apple has
a low spreading habit, the usual
bright green smallish oval
leaves and fragrant pink
flowers in spring, opening from
bright red buds, followed by
medium-sized yellowish red
fruit. Grows best in full sun in
well-drained soil.

Olea europaea
Olive
H AND S: 10M (32FT) **
This half-hardy Mediterranean
tree is a slow-growing evergreen
with leathery silvery green
leaves and greyish bark. Little
fragrant white flowers are borne
in summer, followed by small
green fruit (the olives), which
ripen to black. In frost-prone
areas, grow olives in containers
and overwinter them indoors.
Keep in full sun in summer, and
water sparingly in winter.

Salix
Willow
H AND S: UP TO 25M (80FT) ***
This large genus of both trees
and shrubs includes many that
are useful for gardens. Willows
prefer moist soil and full sun,
and dislike chalky soil. They are
increasingly popular for living
screens and hedges. You can
grow them from greenwood
cuttings taken in spring.
S. caprea 'Kilmarnock' is a
small weeping tree with grey
male catkins; H and S: 2m
(6½ft). *S. daphnoides*, the violet
willow, produces purple young
shoots and dark green long
oblong leaves; S: 6m (20ft).

Taxus baccata
Yew
H: 20M (65FT), **S:** 10M (32FT) ***
A slow-growing evergreen,
yew makes one of the best
hedging plants, providing an

impenetrable thick dark green
screen, often clipped into
fantastic topiary shapes. The
small much divided leaves are
borne on horizontally spreading
branches. Its small red fruits
are highly poisonous, as indeed
are all parts of the plant.
Unfussy as to conditions, yew
will grow well even in dry soil.
Propagates readily from semi-
ripe cuttings in late summer.

Shrubs

Berberis thunbergii f.
atropurpurea 'Red Pillar'
Barberry
H: 2M (6½FT), **S:** 2.4M (8FT) ***
This compact semi-evergreen
shrub gets its varietal name
from its young dark bronze to
red leaves, which turn green as
they mature. Its bright yellow
flowers in late spring are quite
large for a barberry (2.5cm/1in
across). *B. thunbergii* f.
atropurpurea also produces
darkish purplish bronze foliage,
and this has the bonus of
turning scarlet in autumn. It
makes a very good hedging
plant. Autumn colour is better
when grown in full sun. Trim
hedging plants after flowering.

Buxus
Common box
H AND S: 5M (16FT) ***
Box is a widely used evergreen
for hedging, particularly low
hedging in formal gardens.
B. sempervirens has the small
glossy green leaves typical of
the genus. There are several
varieties, including gold- and
white-variegated ones.
B.s. 'Suffruticosa' is popular for
hedging, as it is particularly
slow-growing. The small-leaved
box (*B. microphylla*) is even
more compact and forms a
dense rounded shrub; H: 75cm
(30in), S: 1.5m (5ft). Does best
in well-drained soil in partial
shade. Needs feeding after
pruning. If growing it in a
container, remember to turn
the pot around occasionally to
keep growth even.

Cercidiphyllum magnificum
Katsura tree
H: 10M (32FT), **S:** 8M (25FT) ***
This variety of the Katsura tree,
which comes from China and
Japan, is grown for its
handsome large round leaves,
which are bronze when young,
then green before turning
yellow, orange and red in
autumn. There is also a weeping
form, *C. japonicum* f. *pendulum*;
H: 6m (20ft), S: 8m (25ft).
Cercidiphyllum colours best on
acid soils. Can also be grown as
a tree with a single stem.

Chimonanthus praecox
Wintersweet
H: 4M (13FT), **S:** 3M (10FT) ***
A great deciduous shrub with
large glossy lance-shaped mid-
green leaves and fragrant
yellow bowl-shaped waxy
flowers, which hang from the
bare branches in winter. You can
train wintersweet as a wall shrub
or grow it in a border. Grows in
any fertile soil in full sun.

Choisya ternata
Mexican orange blossom
H AND S: 2.4M (8FT) ***
This evergreen plant does well
in semi-shade as well as in sun.
It is an attractive evergreen
with glossy green aromatic
leaves arranged in whorls. It
has abundant scented white
flowers in spring. *C. x dewitteana*
'Aztec Pearl' has more finely
cut leaves. Propagate Mexican
orange blossom from semi-ripe
cuttings in summer.

Fatsia japonica
Japanese aralia
H AND S: 1.5-4M (5-13FT) **
Another good evergreen shrub
that will cope with coastal
conditions and urban pollution.
Japanese aralia also tolerates
shade, so is in demand for small
urban patios and courtyards. It
needs shelter from cold winds.
The glossy green leaves are
heavily lobed. The flowers are
small and white, ball-shaped, on
long stalks, followed by round
black fruits.

Genista aetnensis
Mount Etna broom
H AND S: 8M (25FT) **

A large shrub or small tree, the Mount Etna broom bears graceful feathery foliage. It has fragrant yellow drooping pealike flowers in summer, and is very free-flowering. In colder areas, grow against a wall or in a courtyard. Does best in light well-drained soil in full sun.

Griselinia littoralis
Broadleaf
H: 8M (25FT) **S:** 5M (16FT) ***

This handsome evergreen thrives in coastal areas, where it is often used as a windbreak. The leaves are rounded and bright green. *G.l.* 'Dixon's Cream' has leaves that are splashed creamy white in the central part, while *G.l.* 'Variegata' produces white-edged leaves. Grow in well-drained soil in full sun.

Ilex aquifolium
Common holly
H: 6M (20FT) **S:** 2.4M (8FT) **

There are many species of holly in this big genus. Common holly has the usual longish spiny-edged glossy dark green leaves and red, orange or yellow berries according to the variety. There are plenty of variegated forms of this species, including several silver- or gold-variegated ones, which are best grown in full sun. Makes a good hedge, too.

Osmanthus delavayi
H: 2-6M (6½-20FT), **S:** 4M (13FT) ***

An attractive evergreen shrub with glossy small dark green leaves and little tubular white flowers, borne profusely in spring. These are followed by small blue-black fruits. *O. x burkwoodii* has bigger leaves and even more fragrant white flowers; H and S: 3m (10ft). You can use both plants for hedging or topiary, as they respond well to hard pruning after flowering. Grow in sun or partial shade, sheltered from cold winds.

Philadelphus coronarius
Mock orange
H: 3M (10FT), **S:** 2.4M (8FT) ***

Mock orange is a deciduous shrub grown primarily for its attractive and highly scented white flowers. In this species, the green leaves are slightly toothed and oval, and the flowers are creamy white, single and very fragrant. *P.c.* 'Aureus' carries golden-yellow leaves; H: 2.4m (8ft), S: 1.5m (5ft). *P.c.* 'Variegatus' produces white-margined leaves; H: 2.4m (8ft), S: 2m (6½ft). *P.* 'Buckley's Quill' has larger green leaves and double fragrant white flowers with much divided petals; H: 2m (6½ft), S: 1.2m (4ft). Grow in full sun (except for *P.c.* 'Aureus' which tends to scorch) or partial shade.

Phyllostachys nigra
Black bamboo
H: 3-5M (10-16FT), **S:** 2-3M (6½-10FT) ***

This clump-forming big bamboo hails from China. It is a great choice for a garden screen. Black bamboo is notable for its arching canes, that turn black when they are a couple of years old. The usual slender evergreen leaves are about 12cm (5in) long. *P.n.* 'Boryana' produces yellowish green canes streaked with purple. Bamboos do best in moist soil in sun or partial shade. You can also grow them in containers. Feed regularly.

Prunus lusitanica
Portugal laurel
H AND S: TO 20M (65FT) ***

This is a dense bushy evergreen shrub, which makes an excellent screen. It has dark green leaves, 12cm (5in) long, with red stalks. The white flowers are small, cup-shaped and fragrant and droop slightly from the branches. They are followed by little red fruits, which turn black on ripening. *P.l.* 'Variegata' has white-rimmed leaves. Grow in sun or partial shade on any moist well-drained soil.

Sarcococca
Christmas box, Sweet box
H AND S: TO 2M (6½FT) ***

This scented evergreen has small white flowers. There are several species, including *S. confusa*, with its tapered oval leaves and highly scented clusters of white flowers in winter. *S. hookeriana* grows from rhizomes and will form useful thickets; its flowers, too, are borne in winter and are white and fragrant; H: 1.5m (5ft). Christmas box does well in partial or deep shade, but will cope with sun in moist conditions.

Skimmia japonica
H: UP TO 6M (20FT) ***

This evergreen shrub has many varieties, including dwarf forms that can be used as ground cover. Its dark green leaves are aromatic, and the fragrant white or pink flowers are borne in dense panicles from early to late spring. On female plants, little red fruits follow if male plants are also present. *S.j.* 'Rubella' bears dark red flowers in late winter; H and S: 1m (3ft). Skimmias cope well with shade, pollution and with dry conditions – an ideal urban shrub.

▒ Perennials

Alchemilla mollis
Lady's mantle
H: 60CM (24IN), **S:** 75CM (30IN) **

This is a popular perennial, with its pretty large pale green leaves. Clouds of tiny yellowish green flowers rise above the foliage from early summer to early autumn. It tolerates dry conditions really well. Often planted between paving stones, and makes excellent ground cover, as it self-seeds easily.

Anemone x hybrida
'Honorine Jobert'
Japanese anemone
H: 1.2-1.5M (4-5FT) ***

This big anemone has a suckering habit so tends to spread in the right conditions. It has big basal leaves, from

which rise the tall flowering stems bearing single white saucer-shaped flowers with golden yellow stamens from late summer to early autumn. The seedheads are also attractive. Prefers a lightly shaded position.

Astelia chathamica
'Silver Spear'
H: 1.2M (4FT), **S:** 1.8M (6FT) **

This is a clump-forming perennial grown mainly for its attractive arching silver-green foliage. Has panicles of yellowy green tiny flowers in mid- to late spring. Female plants bear orange berries. Does best in moist peaty soil in sun or partial shade.

Crocosmia 'Lucifer'
Montbretia
H: 1.2M (4FT), **S:** 8CM (3IN) **

A striking montbretia, taller than most, with glowing orange-red flowers on attractive arching spikes. The mid-green leaves are typically slender and pleated. Does well in sun or partial shade. Montbretia grows from corms, which can be divided in spring when they start to lose vigour.

Dahlia 'Bishop of Llandaff'
H: 1.1M (3½FT), **S:** 45CM (18IN) *

There are numerous dahlias, and their flowers are classified into ten groups according to their form. This particular variety is popular and striking, with its dark purplish foliage and single bright red flowers. Single-flowered dahlias are usually slightly smaller flowered. Pinch out the growing tips to encourage bushiness when young. In cold areas, lift and overwinter dahlia tubers; in slightly warmer ones, leave tubers in situ but apply a covering mulch. Plant tubers out once there is little danger of frost.

Echinacea purpurea
Coneflower
H: TO 1.5M (5FT), **S:** 45CM (18IN) ***

Hailing from the prairies of North America, the coneflower

is striking with its slightly reflexed daisy-like flowers in purples, pinks or white, each with a striking raised cone-shaped central disc. The leaves are basal, rough and toothed. There are many named varieties. Coneflower looks best when grown in drifts. It prefers full sun and rich soil. Deadhead to encourage more flowers.

Echinops
Globe thistle
H: TO 5M (16FT), **S:** 75CM (30IN) ***

Many species produce spiky silvery foliage and neat rounded thistle-like heads of bluish flowers. *E. ritro* is a popular one, with its big leaves and neat metallic blue flowerheads; H: 60cm (24in), S:45cm (18in). *E.r.* 'Veitch's Blue' has darker blue flowers. *E. sphaerocephalus* bears silvery grey flowerheads; H: 2m (6½ft), S: 1m (3ft). Globe thistle does well in most situations and soils. Deadhead to prevent it self-seeding too freely.

Eryngium bourgatii
Eryngo, Sea holly
H: 45CM (18IN), **S:** 30CM (12IN) ***

There are several species of sea holly, some much larger than *E. bourgatii*, which has little rounded bluish grey flowers surrounded by starry bracts in mid- to late summer. Its leaves are basal, spiny and dark green. Miss Willmott's ghost (*E. x giganteum*) is a slightly bigger species with larger steel-blue flowers and silvery bracts, all of which are prickly; H: 90cm (3ft). Naturalizes well and makes good cut flowers, too.

Euphorbia amygdaloides
var. *robbiae*
Mrs Robb's bonnet
H AND S: 60CM (24IN) ***

This is a striking euphorbia that spreads via its rhizomes, making good ground cover. The evergreen leaves are leathery dark green with reddish undersides. From mid-spring to early summer, Mrs Robb's bonnet bears terminal clusters of yellowish green flowers. If you cut the flower stems after flowering, it encourages more basal growth. Prefers moist soil and dappled shade.

Ferula communis
Giant fennel

H: 3M (10FT), **S:** 60CM (24IN) **

Giant fennel is a show-stopper in early and mid-summer, when the clouds of tiny yellow flowers in flat umbels rise on branching stems above its feathery leaves. Grow as a specimen plant in a sunny border. Mulch in winter in colder areas.

Geranium
Cranesbill

H AND S: UP TO 1.2M (4FT) *–***

There is a host of hardy geraniums to choose from, and they make great garden plants for a range of situations. Perlargoniums (see below) are erroneously called geraniums and are a different, tender, plant. Of the hardy geraniums, *G.* 'Johnson's Blue'*** is a popular hybrid. It forms dense mats of lobed and toothed mid-green leaves, with large brilliant blue saucer-shaped flowers in summer; H and S: to 60cm (24in). *G. palmatum*** is a useful evergreen that produces big clumps of finely divided leaves, above which rise reddish hairy stems bearing many bright pink flowers in summer. It self-seeds very readily. Grow in sun or partial shade in well-drained soil.

Helenium 'Moerheim Beauty'
Helen's flower

H: 1M (3FT), **S:** 60CM (24IN) ***

A popular hybrid with dark red flowers, with a brownish central disc, which last from summer through to early autumn. There are bright yellow flowered varieties, such as *H.* 'Butterpat' or *H.* 'Sonnenwunder', and orange ones such as *H.* 'Septemberfuchs'. They all look best grown in drifts. Helenium produces lance-shaped green leaves and likes full sun and well-drained soil. Divide every few years to maintain vigour. Deadheading prolongs the flowering season.

Monarda
Bergamot

H: TO 1.2M (4FT), **S:** 45CM (18IN) ***

With a long flowering season and a good range of colours, bergamot is a popular choice for the flower border. Most of those in cultivation are hybrids between bee balm (*M. didyma*) and wild bergamot (*M. fistulosa*). *M.* 'Blaustrumpf' bears violet flowers with purple bracts; *M.* 'Beauty of Cobham' has pale pink flowers. Spidery looking flowers are surrounded by bracts and are borne from mid-summer to autumn. The aromatic leaves are mid-green, oval and slightly toothed. Does well in sun or partial shade but does not like winter wet.

Perovskia 'Blue Spire'

H: 1.2M (4FT), **S:** 1M (3FT) ***

Although a subshrub rather than a perennial, 'Blue Spire' is usually grown in the perennial border. It has deeply divided silvery leaves and profuse violet flowers in long spikes in late summer and early autumn. It does well on chalky soil and tolerates coastal conditions. Grow in full sun. Propagate from semi-ripe cuttings in summer.

Veronicastrum viginicum
Culver's root

H: UP TO 2M (6½FT), **S:** 45CM (18IN) ***

This North American perennial has unusual long spires of flowers that are white to pink or mauve on unbranched erect stems. The long leaves are borne in whorls of three to seven. *V.v.* 'Album' is a white-flowered variant. Grow in clumps at the back of the border. Does well in moist soil in sun or partial shade.

▌ Bulbs, tubers and corms

Canna
Indian shot plant

H: 1.8M (6FT), **S:** 50CM (20IN) *

Handsome rhizomatous perennial with long paddle-shaped purplish green leaves, and tall dark stems with big yellow pink or red flowers from mid-summer to autumn. *C.* 'Assaut' has large orange-scarlet flowers. *C.* 'Black Knight'

produces very dark red flowers and bronze foliage. Grow in fertile soil in full sun. Lift the rhizomes in frost-prone areas. Alternatively, grow in containers, overwintered in a conservatory.

Galanthus
Snowdrop

H: UP TO 20CM (8IN), **S:** 8CM (3IN) ***

The pure white flowers and slender strap-shaped leaves of snowdrops are renowned as the harbingers of spring. They will naturalize well in humus-rich soil in partial shade. There are many different ones to choose from, including the vigorous and early-flowering honey-scented *G.* 'S. Arnott'. Plant 'in the green', that is immediately after flowering.

Hyacinthoides non-scripta
English bluebell

H: UP TO 40CM (16IN), **S:** 8CM (3IN) ***

This vigorous clump-forming bulbous perennial will colonize fast in the right conditions. It prefers moist well-drained soil in dappled shade. If you do not want it to self-seed, remove the flowers after flowering. English bluebells produce bell-shaped, scented blue or white flowers in a spire that bends to one side.

Iris

H: UP TO 1M (3FT), **S:** 30CM (12IN) OR MORE ***–+

There is an iris for every occasion, every soil type and every season. The big showy bearded irises, which grow from rhizomes, are mainly grown in borders, but there are dwarf forms for containers, as well as irises that do well as marginal plants. Of the bearded irises, try the more unusual colours, such as *I.* 'Blue Eyed Brunette'*** with its brown flowers with a mauve blaze and a gold beard on each fall, or *I.* 'Magic Man'*** with its light mauve-pink standards and deep purple blue-edged falls.

Lilium regale
Regal lily

H: 1.5M (5FT) ***

This lily has really outstandingly fragrant trumpet-shaped white flowers, streaked purple on the

outside, with prominent golden anthers and shiny green leaves. Grows well in moist soils (apart from very alkaline) in full sun. *L.r.* 'Album' bears pure white flowers and bright orange anthers. Plant the bulbs at least 15cm (6in) deep in autumn. Watch out for lily beetle, which will quickly strip the plant.

Narcissus
Daffodil

H: UP TO 45CM (18IN) ***

This is a big genus of spring-flowering bulbs, divided into 12 groups, and you can choose from those with huge trumpets to those with shallow cups and scented flowers. All have the narrow green leaves. Some can be planted in grass, to spread and naturalize. *N.* 'Actaea' has strongly scented white flowers with red-margined central tiny yellow cups in late spring. *N.* 'Dove Wings' produces slightly reflexed white flowers and creamy yellow cups. *N.* 'Tête-à-tête' is a popular dwarf daffodil, with bright yellow flowers in early spring.

Scilla siberica
Siberian squill

H: 10–20CM (4–8IN), **S:** 5CM (2IN) ***

Bulbous perennial with linear green leaves and loose racemes of four to five bright blue flowers in spring. *S.s.* 'Alba' has white flowers, while *S.s.* 'Spring Beauty' bears deep blue flowers. Grow in fertile soil in full sun or partial shade. Ideal for containers.

Tulipa
Tulip

H: UP TO 60CM (24IN), **S:** UP TO 15CM (6IN) ***

This big genus of very popular bulbous perennials has a colour range second to none and includes many streaked and striped forms, too. The waxy flowers, which appear in mid- to late spring, are showy, either single or double. They can be cup-shaped, elongated in a lily shape or frilled. There are also dwarf forms for containers. *T.* 'Queen of Night' has dark purple flowers, and *T.* 'Flaming

Parrot' produces deep yellow flowers with dark red streaks and frilled petals. Shorter *T.* 'Purissima' bears pure white flowers; H: 35cm (14in). Plant in full sun. Does well in containers.

▌ Annuals and bedding

Consolida ajacis
Larkspur

H: UP TO 1.2M (4FT), **S:** UP TO 30CM (12IN) ***

These delphinium-like spires of spurred flowers in pink, white or mauve-blue look good in a border, and are excellent for cutting, too. The leaves are fern-like and slightly downy. *C.a.* Giant Imperial Series has racemes of double flowers on straight stems; H: 90cm (36in) or more; *C.a.* Dwarf Hyacinth Series plants produce double flowers on tightly packed spires; H: to 30cm (12in). Does best in light soil in full sun. Support taller cultivars with twig supports and remove dead flowers to prolong flowering.

Eschscholzia californica
California poppy

H: UP TO 30CM (12IN), **S:** UP TO 15CM (6IN) ***

Hailing from the western side of North America, as the name suggests, these bright poppy-like flowers come in yellow, red or orange. The leaves are light green and fern-like. Does best in poor soil in full sun. *E.c.* 'Monarch Art Shades' has semi-double or double flowers with frilled petals; colours include apricot, creamy yellow and red, while smaller *E.c.* Thai Silk Series has fluted semi-double bronze-tinged flowers; H: to 25cm (10in).

Pelargonium

H: UP TO 45CM (18IN), **S:** 20CM (8IN) +

These hugely popular frost-tender perennnials are commonly (but incorrectly) known as geraniums. The leaves are mid-green on long stalks, and in some forms are aromatic. The five-petalled flowers grow in clusters. There are species pelargoniums, but different hybrids are most commonly grown. These range in colour from white through pinks to scarlets and deep mauves. Trailing forms (the ivy-leaved pelargoniums) are useful for hanging baskets. All do well in containers and are drought-tolerant. They prefer full sun but will tolerate partial shade. Deadhead regularly to lengthen the flowering period, which lasts from summer to autumn.

Petunia
H: 40CM (16IN), S: TO 90CM (36IN) *

Very popular plants for hanging baskets or containers, petunias have showy, open five-lobed single or double flowers in white, pinks, mauves, scarlets and purples, often with contrasting coloured veins. Some of the Surfinia Series of petunias are scented. Look out for them as the scent is exquisite. Surfinia 'Blue Star' bears trailing highly scented double blue flowers.

Tropaeolum majus
Nasturtium
H: UP TO 3M (10FT), S: 1.5M (5FT) **-+

This vigorous annual climber has attractive kidney-shaped waxy leaves and spurred flowers in red, orange or yellow from summer until autumn. Smaller forms such as the *T.* Alaska Series* or *T.* Gleam Series* are good for hanging baskets, with semi-double flowers in scarlet, dark red, orange or yellow, or in pastel shades between. Grows best in poor soil in full sun. The leaves and flowers are edible.

▥ Herbs

Anethum graveolens
Dill
H: 60CM (24IN), S: 30CM (12IN) ***

Grown primarily as a culinary herb, dill is pretty enough to adorn the flower border. It has very divided feathery foliage in bright green and flat umbels of bright yellow flowers in summer. The aromatic seeds and leaves are both used in cooking. Grow in full sun and water freely to prevent bolting.

Lavandula angustifolia
Lavender
H: 1M (3FT), S: 1.2M (4FT) ***

Grown for its therapeutic properties, lavender is a bushy shrub with fine grey-green leaves and spires of tiny mauve-purple highly scented flowers in summer. Grow in full sun in well-drained soil. Lavender propagates very readily from semi-ripe cuttings in summer.

Origanum vulgare
Wild marjoram
H AND S: 30-90CM (1-3FT) ***

Marjoram, which is highly aromatic, is a great draw for bees and other insects. It has smallish dark green rounded oval leaves and whorls of pinkish purple flowers from mid-summer through to early autumn. Some varieties have golden or variegated leaves. Grow in full sun. Prefers alkaline soil.

Rosmarinus officinalis
Rosemary
H AND S: 1.5M (5FT) **

An aromatic evergreen shrub with tough little grey-green leaves that are white felted on the undersides. Masses of bluish mauve little flowers appear along the lengths of the leaf shoots from mid-spring to summer. There are several named varieties, some of which are more upright and less spreading. *R.o.* 'Roseus' has pink flowers. Does well in poorish soil in full sun. Trim hedges after flowering.

Salvia officinalis
Common sage
H: 70CM (28IN), S: 1M (3FT) ***

There are hundreds of salvias, many of them decorative. This little evergreen perennial with its slightly woolly greyish green leaves is a good culinary herb. Its blue/lilac flowers are borne from early to mid-summer. *S.o.* 'Purpurascens' produces reddish purple leaves; *S.o.* 'Tricolor' has leaves flushed with cream and pinkish purple. Sage does best in full sun and does not like overly wet winter conditions.

Thymus citriodorus
Lemon-scented thyme
H: 30CM (12IN), S: 45CM (18IN) ***

Thyme is a good culinary herb but also a magnet for bees. This particular thyme makes a bushy little shrub with small mid-green leaves and masses of tiny pinkish flowers in summer. There are plenty of thyme varieties, including many variegated or golden-leaved ones. Garden thyme (*T. vulgaris*) is a smaller subshrub with purple to white flowers and is good for planting in cracks between paving stones; H: 15-30cm (6-12in). Grow in full sun in well-drained soil.

▥ Grasses and ferns

Calamagrostis x acutiflora
'Karl Foerster'
Feather reed grass
H: TO 2M (6½FT), S: TO 1.2M (4FT) ***

This is a delicate clump-forming perennial with fine mid-green slender leaves to 90cm (3ft) long. The erect unbranched stems are topped with pinkish panicles of flowers from mid-summer that fade to light buff. Grow in sun or partial shade. Does well even in quite poor soil. Cut down the stands of leaves at the end of winter.

Dryopteris filix-mas
Male fern
H AND S: TO 1.2M (4FT) ***

This deciduous fern forms large clumps of lance-shaped mid-green fronds. There are several named cultivars. *D.f.-m.* 'Barnesii' is one of the biggest, with long narrow fronds. The Linearis Group cultivars have more ethereal lighter fronds.

Festuca glauca
Blue fescue
H: 30CM (12IN), S: 25CM (10IN) ***

Handsome small evergreen grass forming neat clumps of fine blue-green leaves. Bears little panicles of purple-tinged blue-green flowers from early to mid-summer. *F.g.* 'Blaufuchs' has more markedly blue leaves. Does well even in poor soil in full sun. Divide and replant every couple of years to maintain good foliage colour.

Miscanthus sinensis
H: TO 4M (13FT), S: TO 1.2M (4FT) ***

These deciduous perennial grasses have long slender blue-green leaves with big purplish panicles. Maiden grass (*M.s.* 'Gracillimus') bears very fine curving bronzed leaves; H: to 1.3m (4½ft). *M.s.* 'Silberfeder' produces pinkish brown panicles from early autumn; H: to 2.4m (8ft). Zebra grass (*M.s.* 'Zebrinus') has leaves banded horizontally in yellow-white; H: to 1.2m (4ft). Grows best in moist soil in full sun. Cut down in spring.

Polystichum setiferum
Soft shield fern
H: 1.2M (4FT), S: 90CM (36IN) ***

This evergreen fern has dark green fronds arranged like shuttlecocks. Grow in humus-rich soil in deep or partial shade. Protect crowns from very wet weather in winter.

Stipa gigantea
Giant feather grass, Golden oats
H: TO 2.4M (8FT), S: 1.2M (4FT) ***

This evergreen or semi-evergreen big grass grows in loose clumps. The narrow mid-green leaves are up to 70cm (28in) long, while the delicate young flower panicles, which are silvery purple when young, turn golden in summer. Does best in light soils in full sun. Remove dead leaves in spring.

▥ Water and marginal plants

Butomus umbellatus
Flowering rush
H: TO 1.5M (5FT), S: 45CM (18IN) ***

This marginal aquatic has long twisted rush-like leaves, mid-green turning purple, and umbels of rose-pink scented flowers in late summer. Plant at the waterside or in water to 25cm (10in) deep. Needs full sun.

Cyperus papyrus
Papyrus, Nile grass
H: TO 2M (6½FT), S: TO 1.2M (4FT) +

A clump-forming perennial with leafless stems and big umbels of starry rays bearing little brown flowers. Needs high humidity and frost-free conditions. Grow at the pond edge just below the surface of the water.

Gunnera
H: 2.4M (8FT), S: 4M (13FT) OR MORE **

This is a truly massive perennial with huge hand-shaped toothed mid-green leaves with marked veining. In summer, it bears tiny greenish red flowers on branched stems, followed by little fruits. Needs permanently moist soil in sun or partial shade. In frost-prone areas, protect the crowns in winter with dry mulch.

Nelumbo nucifera
Sacred lotus
H: UP TO 1.5M (5FT) ABOVE WATER LEVEL, S: INDEFINITE +

This aquatic perennial has huge flat shiny mid-green leaves with wavy edges. They are borne on long stalks up to 2m (6½ft) long. Huge water-lily-like scented flowers are borne in summer, on long prickled stalks. The flowers can be white or pink. Needs very rich soil in containers and full sun. *N.n.* 'Rosea Plena' bears double dark pink flowers.

Typha
Bulrush
H: TO 1.8M (6FT), S: INDEFINITE ***

This aquatic perennial produces mid-green strap-shaped leaves and dark brown dense flower spikes. *T. latifolia* is very vigorous and suitable only for large wildlife pools. *T.l.* 'Variegata' has cream-striped leaves and is much less vigorous. Grow it in water up to 40cm (16in) deep in mud; H: to 1.2m (4ft). *T. minima* has finer leaves and flower spikes and can be grown in small pools or containers; H: to 75cm (30in). Grow in sun.

Zantedeschia aethiopica
Arum lily
H: 90CM (36IN), S: 60CM (24IN) **

A clump-forming perennial that is evergreen in mild areas. Arum lily has big handsome arrow-shaped mid-green leaves and impressive white waxy flower spathes with a creamy yellow spadix from late spring to mid-summer. Grows best in moist soil in full sun, and can also be grown as a marginal aquatic.

ACKNOWLEDGEMENTS

The publisher would like to thank the following photographers, agencies and designers for their kind permission to reproduce the following photographs:

Endpapers: Yann Monel (Designers: Bella and David Gordon, Palntagenet Plantes, Normandy, France); 1 Photolibrary.com/Botanica Botanica; 4-5 Photolibrary.com/Jose Fuste Raga; 6-7 naturepl.com/Warwick Sloss; 8 Photolibrary.com/Pernilla Bergdahl/Garden Picture Library; 10-11 Photolibrary.com/Rafael Jaurequi; 12 Alamy/South America; 15 Mark Duffy (Designer: Diarmuid Gavin); 17 Harpur Garden Images/Jerry Harpur (Designer: Ulf Nordfjell, Sweden); 18-19 Helen Fickling (Designer: Diarmuid Gavin and Sir Terence Conran, RHS Chelsea 2008); 20-21 Helen Fickling; 22-23 John Pfahl; 25 Diarmuid Gavin; 26 Gap Photos/John Glover (Designer: Alan Gardener); 28 Harpur Garden Images/Jerry Harpur (Design: Fiona Brockhoff & David Swann, Victoria, Australia); 29 Garden Photo Library/Derek St Romaine; 30 Left Roger Foley (Designer: Dean Riddle Gardens); 30-31 Rowan Isaac (Cliff House, Dorset); 31 Right Marion Brenner (Designer: Ron Lutsko, Lutsko Associates/San Francisco, CA, USA); 32-35 Marion Brenner (Designer: Ron Lutsko/Lutsko Associates/San Francisco, CA, USA); 36 Above Marianne Majerus Garden Images/Marianne Majerus (Designer: Wendy Booth, Leslie Howell); 36 Below Taverne Agency/Alexander van Berge; 37 Mainstreamimages/Paul Massey; 38 Left Taverne Agency/Nathalie Krag; 38-39 Above Harpur Garden Images/Jerry Harpur (Designer: Naila Green, Devon); 38 Below right Andrea Jones (Baja Garden, Phoenix, Ariz., USA. Designer: Steve Martino & Associates, Phoenix, Ariz., USA); 39 Right Photoflex (Urban Splash, Budenberg HAUS Projekte); 40-43 LUR PAISAJISTAK S.L. (Designers: Inigo Segurola and Juan Iriarte, Spain); 44-45 Gap Photos/Nicola Browne (Design: Paul Deroose); 46 Clive Nichols; 48 Above Clive Nichols (Designer: Charlotte Rowe); 48 Below Marianne Majerus Garden Images/Marianne Majerus; 49 Marion Brenner (Designer: Andrea Cochran, San Francisco, CA, USA); 50 Above Harpur Garden Images/Marcus Harpur (Designer: Lucy Redman, Suffolk); 50 Below Jane Sebire (Designer: Jimi Blake, Dublin, Rol); 51 Above Marianne Majerus Garden Images/Andrew Lawson; 51 Below Marianne Majerus Garden Images/Marianne Majerus (Wyken Hall, Suffolk); 52 Above Harpur Garden Images/Jerry Harpur (Desisgner: Jimi Blake, Hunting Brook Gardens, Rol); 52 Below Andrew Lawson (Designer: Piet Oudolf, Pensthorpe, Waterfowl Park, Norfolk); 53 Above Yann Monel (Louis Benech, Chateau de Pange); 53 Below Marianne Majerus Garden Images/Marianne Majerus; 54-57 JC Mayer & G le Scanff (Designers: Catherine Willis and Alain Richert, Le Moulin, Normandy, France); 58 Clive Nichols (West Green House, Hampshire); 58-59 JC Mayer & G le Scanff (Potager du chateau de Hex Belgium); 59 JC Mayer & G le Scanff (Les Jardins Fruitiers de Laquenexy, 57, France); 60 Above B & P Perdereau (Design: Francia Thauvin, France); 60-61 Below B & P Perdereau (Design F: & C Cotelle, France); 61 Above Harpur Garden Images/Jerry Harpur (Sheephouse, Painswick, Glos, UK); 61 Below right Clive Nichols; 62 Above left JC Mayer & G le Scanff (Potager du Chateau Hex, Belgique); 62 Below left Yann Monel (Designers: Eric Ossart and Arno Mauriere, Musee Angland de Salers); 62-63 Jane Sebire (Mandelmann's); 63 Above right JC Mayer & G le Scanff (Potager du Chateau de Bosmelet, 76, France); 63 Below right B & P Perdereau (Glen Chantry Garden, UK); 64 Above Marianne Majerus Garden Images/Marianne Majerus (Gardens of Gothenburg Festival, Sweden 2008 /Sam Keshavarz); 64 Below Clive Nichols (Designer: Clare Matthews); 65 Marianne Majerus Garden Images/Marianne Majerus (Gunnebo House, Gardens of Gothenburg Festival, Sweden 2008 /Joakim Seiler); 66 Left B & P Perdereau (Chidmere garden, UK); 66-67 B & P Perdereau; 67 Right Gap Photos/Graham Strong; 68-71 Marion Brenner (Designer: Nancy Heckler, Washington State, USA); 72 Above The Garden Collection/Jane Sebire (Wolfram Kircher, Germany); 72 Below B & P Perdereau (Designer: Dan Milner, Tatton Park); 73 JC Mayer & G le Scanff (Chateau de Bosmelet, 76, France); 74 Clive Nichols (Designer: Clare Matthews); 75 Clive Nichols (Designer: Clare Matthews); 76 Above Harpur Garden Images/Marcus Harpur (Designer: Lucy Redman, Suffolk); 76 Below Gap Photos/Mark Bolton; 77 The Garden Collection/Andrew Lawson; 78 Left Clive Nichols (Designer: Charlotte Rowe); 78-79 Clive Nichols (Abbotsbury Garden, Dorset); 79 Right Clive Nichols (Abbotsbury Garden, Dorset); 80 Above Clive Nichols (Designer: Charlotte Rowe, London); 80 Below Clive Nichols (Designer: Trevyn McDowell); 81 Below Marianne Majerus Garden Images/Marianne Majerus (Designer: Charlotte Rowe); 82 Below Marianne Majerus Garden Images/Marianne Majerus (Henstead Exotic Garden /Andrew Brogan, Jason Payne); 82-83 Helen Fickling (Designer: Diarmuid Gavin); 83 Right Clive Nichols (Designer: Charlotte Rowe); 84 Diarmuid Gavin; 86 Above Jane Sebire (The Long Borders at Waltham Palace. Designer: Henk Gerritsen); 86 Below Photolibrary.com/Gil Hanly; 87 Andrea Jones (Private garden Massachusetts. Designed by Reed Hilderbrand Associates Inc, Mass., USA); 88 Above Andrea Jones (Private garden, Orinda, Calif. Designed by Topher Delaney/SEAM Studios, Calif., USA); 88 Below Photolibrary.com/Joseph Shuldiner; 88-89 Harpur Garden Images/Marcus Harpur (Design: Nicky Baker); 89 Above Right Andrea Jones (Baja Garden, Phoenix, Ariz., USA. Designed by Steve Martino & Associates, Phoenix, Ariz., USA); 89 Below JC Mayer & G le Scanff (La Bambouseraie de Prafrance 30 France); 90 Above left B & P Perdereau (Les Deesses Vertes garden, Belgium); 90 Below left Marianne Majerus Garden Images/Marianne Majerus (Gardens of Gothenburg, Sweden 2008/Designer: Ulf Nordfjell); 90-91 Above B & P Perdereau (Designer: Arend Jan Van Der Horst, Netherlands); 90-91 Below B & P Perdereau (Wyken Hall, UK); 91 Above Harpur Garden Images/Marcus Harpur (Design: Jacqueline Duncan); 91 Below right B & P Perdereau (Designer: Piet Blanckaert, Belgium); 92-95 Marion Brenner (Designer: surfacedesign inc., San Francisco, CA, USA); 96 Left The Garden Collection/Stephen Wooster (Designer: Anthony Paul); 96-97 Above B & P Perdereau (In Goedeaarde Garden, Netherlands); 97 Below left JC Mayer & G le Scanff (Le Jardin Plume, France); 97 Right B & P Perdereau (Bryan's Ground Garden, UK); 98 Below Clive Nichols (Designer: Tim Rees, The Gray House, Oxfordshire); 98 Above B & P Perdereau; 99 Alamy/John Norman; 100 Left Mainstreamimages/RayMain; 100-101 B & P Perdereau (Home Farm, UK); 101 Centre JC Mayer & G le Scanff (Designer: Patrick Blanc, Pershing Hall, Paris, France); 101 Right Harpur Garden Images/Jerry Harpur(Mr and Mrs Marshall, The Old Vicarage, Whixley, Yorkshire, UK); 102 Above left Yann Monel (Jardin de la Ballue, Brittany, France); 102 Below B & P Perdereau (Designer: Andre Van Wassenhove, Belgium); 103 Above B & P Perdereau (Designer: Piet Blanckaert, Netherlands); 103 Below B & P Perdereau (Designer: Serge Delsemme, Belgium); 104 Left Photolibrary.com/Mark Turner; 104-105 B & P Perdereau (Design Andre Van Wassenhove, Belgium); 105 Above Roger Foley (Designers: Oehme, van Sweden and Associates, USA); 105 Below B & P Perdereau (Designer: Andre Van Wassenhove, Belgium); 106-107 Above B & P Perdereau; 106 Below B & P Perdereau; 107 Right Yann Monel (Designers: De Patrick and Sylvie Quibel/Jardin Plume, 76, France); 107 Below Marianne Majerus Garden Images/Marianne Majerus; 108 Left Yann Monel (Designer: le Notre, Chateau de Cordes, France); 108-109 B & P Perdereau (Designer: Casanova, France); 109 B & P Perdereau (Cambridge Botanical Garden, UK); 110 Above left B & P Perdereau; 110 Above right Yann Monel (Jardin de la Ballue, Brittany, France); 110 Below right Yann Monel (Le Parc de Duigsburg, Germany. Designer: Peter Latz); 110 Below left B & P Perdereau (De Boschhoeve, Netherlands); 111 Above right Photolibrary.com/J Cassaigne (Villandry castle, Indre et Loire, France); 112 Above B & P Perdereau (Designee: Erwan Tymen, France); 112 Below left B & P Perdereau (Designer Erwan Tymen, France); 112 Below right B & P Perdereau (Design Rose Valkaert, Belgium); 113 Andrea Jones (Private garden, Orinda, Calif. Designed by Topher Delaney/SEAM Studios, Calif., USA); 114 Left JC Mayer & G le Scanff (Domaine du Rayol, 83, France); 114 Centre B & P Perdereau; 114 B & P Perdereau (Arboretum de Balaine, France); 115 Right Gap Photos/Sarah Cuttle; 116-119 Marianne Majerus Garden Images/Marianne Majerus (Designer: Tom Stuart-Smith, UK); 120 Left Gap Photos/Jerry Harpur; 120 Right Harpur Garden Images/Jerry Harpur (Designer: Jimi Blake, Hunting Brook Gardens, Rol); 121 Photolibrary.com/Mark Bolton; 122 Photolibrary.com/Pernilla Bergdahl; 122 Left B & P Perdereau (Designer: Piet Oudolf, Pensthorpe Waterfowl Park, Norfolk); 123 Right Andrew Lawson (Designer: Piet Oudolf, Pensthorpe Waterfowl Park, Norfolk); 124 Above left Yann Monel (Designer: Patrick Blanc); 124 Below Gap Photos/Rob Whitworth (Designer: Anthea Guthrie, RHS Hampton Court Flower Show); 124-125 Above L Gap Photos/Jo Whitworth; 125 Right Gap Photos; 126-127 B & P Perdereau (Designer: Piet Blanckaert, Belgium); 128 Marianne Majerus Garden Images/Marianne Majerus (Designer: Stuart Craine); 130 Left Yann Monel (Designers: Bella and David Gordon, Plantagenet Plantes, Jardin Vittel, France); 130 Right Photolibrary.com/Christi Carter/Garden Picture Library); 131 Harpur Garden Images/Jerry Harpur (Designer: Christopher Lloyd, Great Dixter, East Sussex, UK); 132 Below right Harpur Garden Images/Jerry Harpur (Design: Christopher Lloyd. Great Dixter, East Sussex, UK); 132 Below left Harpur Garden Images/Jerry Harpur (Owner and designer: Peter Manthorpe, Devils End, Haddiscoe, Norfolk, UK); 132-133 Above Marianne Majerus Garden Images/Marianne Majerus; 133 Above right Harpur Garden Images/Marcus Harpur Design: Tom Stuart-Smith, RHS Chelsea Flower Show 2006); 133 Below Gap Photos/Christina Bollen; 134 Left Gap Photos/Lynn Keddie (Designer: Ian Dexter); 134 Above Marion Brenner (Designer: Gary Ratway, Mendocino, CA, USA); 135 B & P Perdereau (Designers: Piet Oudolf and Paul MacBride, Luxemburg); 136 Above left Yann Monel (Chateau de Pange, Louis Benech); 136 Below left Harpur Garden Images/Jerry Harpur (Designer: Piet Oudolf, Hummelo, Netherlands); 136-137 Above Marianne Majerus Garden Images/Andrew Lawson (Sticky Wicket, Dorset, UK); 136-137 Below Harpur Garden Images/Jerry Harpur (Design: Ulf Nordfjell, Sweden); 137 Above right B & P Perdereau (Designer: Chris Ghyselen, Belgium); 137 Below right Marianne Majerus Garden Images/Marianne Majerus (Sleightholmedale Lodge, Yorkshire); 138-141 Above Walter Herfst (Designer: Piet Oudolf, Hummelo, Netherlands); 142 Left Harpur Garden Images/Jerry Harpur (Designer: Christopher Lloyd, Great Dixter, East Sussex, UK); 143 Above Marianne Majerus Garden Images/Marianne Majerus (Designer: Piet Oudolf, Scampston Hall, Yorkshire); 143 Below Marianne Majerus Garden Images/Marianne Majerus (Great Dixter, UK); 144-145 Above JC Mayer & G le Scanff (Design: Agence Oxalis, Geneva, Switzerland); 144 Centre Marianne Majerus Garden Images/Marianne Majerus (Great Dixter, UK); 144 Below left Marianne Majerus Garden Images/Marianne Majerus (Designer: Joanna Crane); 145 Right Marion Brenner (Designer: Eric and Silvina Blasen, Blasen Landscape Architecture/San

Anselmo CA, USA); 145 Below left Harpur Garden Images/Jerry Harpur (Designer: Christopher Lloyd, Great Dixter, East Sussex, UK); 146 Harpur Garden Images/Jerry Harpur; 146 Above right, Below right, 147, 148 Below Harpur Garden Images/Jerry Harpur (Designer: Helen Dillon, Dublin, Rol); 146 Left, 148-149 Above, 149 Right, Below Jane Sebire (Designer: Helen Dillon, Dublin, Rol); 150 Photolibrary.com/Aaron McCoy; 152 Marianne Majerus Garden Images/Marianne Majerus (Westonbirt Arboretum); 154 Above Photolibrary.com/Chris L. Jones; 154 Left Marianne Majerus Garden Images/Marianne Majerus (Great Dixter, UK); 154 Below right Marianne Majerus Garden Images/ Andrew Lawson (Wartnaby Gardens, Leicestershire); 155 Yann Monel (Le Bois de Vincennes, Paris); 156 Left Andrew Lawson (Designer: Christopher Bradley-Hole, Bury Court, Hampshire); 156-157 B & P Perdereau; 157 Right B & P Perdereau (Designer: Piet Oudolf, Netherlands); 158-161 JC Mayer & G le Scanff (Designer: Yves Gosse de Gorre, Jardins de Sericourt, 62, France); 162 Above left B & P Perdereau (De Boschhoeve, Netherlands); 162 Below left Yann Monel (Arboretum de Sedelle); 162-163 Below centre B & P Perdereau (Design Sonja Gauron, France); 163 Above left B & P Perdereau (La Petite Rochelle, France); 163 Above right Yann Monel (Designers: Bella and David Gordon, Plantagenet Plantes, Normandy, France); 163 Below right B & P Perdereau; 164 Above The Garden Collection/Jonathan Buckley (Designer: Sarah Raven); 164 Below left Harpur Garden Images/Jerry Harpur (Designer: Christopher Lloyd, Great Dixter, East Sussex, UK); 165 Helen Fickling (Desisgners: Diarmuid Gavin and Sir Terence Conran, RHS Chelsea 2008); 166-169 Andrew Lawson (Designer: Tom Stuart-Smith, Broughton Grange, Oxfordshire, UK); 170 John Pfahl; 172 Photolibrary.com/Alfredo Venturi; 174 Above B & P Perdereau (Designer: Eric Borja, France); 174 Below JC Mayer & G le Scanff (Designer: Alexandre Thomas, Jardins Agapanthe, 76, France); 175 Above Harpur Garden Images/Jerry Harpur (Designer: Julian and Isobel Bannerman, Houghton Hall, Norfolk, UK); 175 Below Harpur Garden Images/ Jerry Harpur (Chehel Sotun Palace, Shiraz, Iran); 176 Left Photolibrary.com/Nicolas Thibaut/ Photononstop; 176 Right Harpur Garden Images/Jerry Harpur (Rashtrapati Bhavan, New Delhi,

India); 177 JC Mayer & G le Scanff (Château du Vignal 06 France); 178 Above Harpur Garden Images/ Marcus Harpur (Design: Jacqueline Duncan); 178 Below Harpur Garden Images/Jerry Harpur (Designer: Steve Martino, Tucson, Arizona); 179 Above left Harpur Garden Images/Jerry Harpur (Kiftgate Court, Glos, UK); 179 Above right Harpur Garden Images/Jerry Harpur (Designer: Philip Nixon for Anita Sansford, Fulham, UK); 179 Below left Harpur Garden Images/Jerry Harpur (Designer: Luciano Giubbilei, UK); 179 Below right Marianne Majerus Garden Images/Marianne Majerus (Designer: Penelope Hobhouse, UK); 180 Above left Harpur Garden Images/Jerry Harpur (Design: Jacqueline Duncan); 180-181 Above Harpur Garden Images/ Jerry Harpur (Design: Ulf Nordfjell, Sweden); 180-181 Below Marianne Majerus Garden Images/ Andrew Lawson (The Menagerie, Northants., UK); 181 Right Harpur Garden Images/Jerry Harpur (Mr and Mrs Hugh Johnson, Saling Hall, Essex, UK); 182 left Harpur Garden Images/Jerry Harpur (Designed: by Luciano Giubbilei, UK); 182 Right B & P Perdereau (Keukenhof Garden, Netherlands); 183 Andrea Jones (Miller House Garden, Columbus, Ind., USA. Garden designed by by Daniel Urban Kiley, building designed by Eero Saarinen. Courtesy of the Irwin-Sweeney-Miller Foundation & Indianapolis Museum of Art); 184 Above left Andrea Jones (Long Island private garden, NY, USA. Designed by Reed Hilderbrand Associates Inc., MA, USA); 184 Below left Marion Brenner (Designer: Andrea Cochran, San Francisco, CA, USA); 185 Above left Marion Brenner (Designer: Andrea Cochran, San Francisco, CA, USA); 185 Above right Harpur Garden Images/Jerry Harpur(Designer: Amir Schlezinger of MyLandscapes for Howard Sharpstone, London, UK); 185 Below left Andrea Jones (Long Island private garden, NY, USA. Designed by Reed Hilderbrand Associates Inc., MA, USA); 186 Left Andrea Jones (Neil Matteucci & Norm Kalbfleisch's, garden, Portland, Oregon, USA. Design by the owners); 186 Right Andrea Jones (Private garden, Santa Barbara, Calif., USA. Designed by Isabelle Greene & Associates, Inc., Calif., USA); 187 Marianne Majerus Garden Images/Andrew Lawson (The Abby Aldrich Rockefeller Garden, Maine, USA); 188 Left Marianne Majerus Garden Images/Andrew Lawson; 188 JC Mayer & G le

Scanff (La Bambouseraie de Prafrance, 30, France); 189 Above right Andrea Jones (Miller House Garden, Columbus, Ind., USA. Garden designed by by Daniel Urban Kiley, building designed by Eero Saarinen. Courtesy of the the Irwin-Sweeney-Miller Foundation & Indianapolis Museum of Art); 189 Below right Harpur Garden Images/Marcus Harpur (Design: Jacqueline Duncan); 190 Left Harpur Garden Images/Marcus Harpur (Designer: Lucy Redman, Suffolk); 190 Right Marion Brenner (Designer: Gary Ratway, Mendocino CA, USA); 190-191 The Garden Collection/Jane Sebire (Designers: James Hitchmough and Amanda Stokes); 191 Right Yann Monel (Designers: Eric Ossart and Arno Mauriere, Paris, France); 192 Above left Clive Nichols (Designer: Kate Frey); 192 Below The Garden Collection/Jane Sebire (Landlife Meadows); 193 Above Mainstreamimages/ RayMain/reflexangelo.com; 193 Below B & P Perdereau (Designer: Erwan Tymen, France); 194 Above left Marianne Majerus Garden Images/Marianne Majerus; 194-195 Above Marianne Majerus Garden Images/Marianne Majerus; 194 Below left Marianne Majerus Garden Images/Marianne Majerus (Designers: Wendy Booth and Leslie Howell); 195 Above right Alamy/Anne Green-Armytage Flower Pictures; 195 Below right Marianne Majerus Garden Images/ Marianne Majerus; 195 Below left Jane Sebire (Nigel Dunnett); 196-197 Above Photolibrary.com/ John Glover/Garden Picture Library; 196 Below right Richard Felber (Southampton, NY, USA, Landscpe Architects: Oehme van Sweden); 196 Above left B & P Perdereau (Design Piet Oudolf & Paul Mac Bride, Luxemburg); 197 Above right Gap Photos/Jerry Harpur(Designer: Ulf Nordfjell, Hakansson garden, The Farstorp Estate, South Sweden); 197 Below Gap Photos/Mark Bolton (Lady Farm , Somerset); 198 Above B & P Perdereau (Bijsterveld garden, Belgium); 198 Below Yann Monel (Designers: M & Mme Quibel, Jardin Plume, Normandy, France); 199 B & P Perdereau (Designers: Piet Oudolf and Paul MacBride, Luxemburg); 200-203 Marianne Majerus Garden Images/Marianne Majerus (Designer: Stevie Nicholson, Uggeshall Hall, Suffolk); 204 Harpur Garden Images/Jerry Harpur (Owner and designer: John Kelf, Norfolk, UK); 205 Harpur Garden Images/Jerry Harpur (Design: Steve Martino, Phoenix, USA); 205-206 Andrea Jones (Private garden, Orinda,

Calif., USA. Garden designed by Topher Delaney/SEAM Studios, Calif., USA); 207 Marion Brenner (Designer: Brandon Tyson, Napa, CA, USA); 206 Harpur Garden Images/Jerry Harpur (Design: Steve Martino, Phoenix, Arizona, USA); 208 Left Harpur Garden Images/Jerry Harpur (Chanticleer, Penn., USA); 208-209 Above B & P Perdereau (East Ruston Old Vicarage garden, UK); 208-209 Below Marianne Majerus Garden Images/Marianne Majerus; 209 Centre Harpur Garden Images/ Jerry Harpur (Design: Enid Munro, Connecticut USA); 209 Right B & P Perdereau (Quinta Casa Branca, Madeira); 210-211 Photolibrary.com/ Peter Baistow/Garden Picture Library; 212 JC Mayer & G le Scanff (Serre de la Madone, 06, Menton, France); 213 Alamy/ Blickwinkel; 214-215 Photolibrary.com/Julian Love/ John Warburton-Lee Photography; 216 Photolibrary.com/Ellen Rooney/Garden Picture Library; 218 Above Marianne Majerus Garden Images/Marianne Majerus (Designer: Jilayne Rickards); 218 Below Yann Monel (Designers: Eric Ossart and Arno Mauriere, Paris, France); 219 Yann Monel (Designers: Eric Ossart and Arno Mauriere, Paris, France); 220 Left The Garden Collection/ Liz Eddison (Design: Phillippa Probert - Tatton Park 06); 220 Below right Robin Matthews (Designer: Diarmuid Gavin); 220 Below right Yann Monel (Designer: Hugues Peuvergne); 221 Harpur Garden Images/Jerry Harpur (Designer: Amir Schlezinger, MyLandscapes for Howard Sharpstone, London, UK); 222 Left Photolibrary.com/ Image100; 222 Centre Harpur Garden Images/Jerry Harpur (Designer: Amir Schlezinger of MyLandscapes for Howard Sharpstone, London, UK); 222-223 Harpur Garden Images Marcus Harpur(Designer: Tom Stuart-Smith, RHS Chelsea Flower Show, 2006); 223 Right B & P Perdereau (Design: Pascal Garbe, France); 224 Left Harpur Garden Images/Jerry Harpur (Beth Chatto, Elmstead Market, Essex); 224 B & P Perdereau (Design: Pascal Garbe, France); 225 Photolibrary.com/Allan Pollack-Morris/Garden Picture Library (The Laurent Perrier Garden. Design: Jinny Blom, RHS Chelsea Flower Show, 2006); 226 Left Richard Felber (North Salem, NY, USA, Landscape Architects: Oehme van Sweden); 226 Above JC Mayer & G le Scanff; 226 Below B & P Perdereau (Herbarium des Remparts,

France); 227 Right Harpur Garden Images/Jerry Harpur (Design: William Martin, Wigandia, Victoria, Australia); 228-231 Andrea Jones (Windcliff, Washington State, USA. Garden designed by Daniel J. Hinkley & house designed by Architect, Robert L. Jones (AIA); 232 Harpur Garden Images/Jerry Harpur (Design : Connie Cross, LI., USA); 233 Harpur Garden Images/Jerry Harpur (Design: Ulf Nordfjell, Sweden); 234 Above left Andrea Jones (Private garden, Orinda, Calif.. Garden designed by Topher Delaney/SEAM Studios, Calif., USA); 234 Below Harpur Garden Images/Jerry Harpur (Cloudehill, Olinda, Victoria Australia); 235 Above Taverne Agency/John Dummer; 235 Below Marianne Majerus Garden Images/Marianne Majerus (Designer: Johan Heirman); 236 Above Andrea Jones (Private garden, Santa Barbara, Calif., USA. Designed by Isabelle Greene & Associates, Inc., Calif., USA); 236-237 Below Andrea Jones (Private garden, Santa Barbara, Calif., USA. Designed by Isabelle Greene & Associates Inc., Calif., USA); 238 Photolibrary.com/ Akira Kaede/Photodisc; 239 Richard Felber (North Salem, NY, USA, Landscape Architects: Oehme van Sweden); 240-243 Marianne Majerus Garden Images/Marianne Majerus (Hermannshof, Weinheim, Germany, Designer: Cassian Schmidt); 244-245 Marianne Majerus Garden Images/Andrew Lawson; 246 JC Mayer & G le Scanff (Domaine de St Jean de Beauregard, 91, France); 248-249 Diarmuid Gavin; 251 JC Mayer & G le Scanff (Les Jardins Fruitiers de Laquenexy, 57, France); 252-253 Diarmuid Gavin; 254-255 Marianne Majerus Garden Images/Marianne Majerus (Designer: Topher Delaney /'Shipping News', Gunnebo House, Gardens of Gothenburg Festival, Sweden); 256 Alamy/ BrazilPhotos.com; 257 Harpur Garden Images/Jerry Harpur (Designer: Luciano Giubbilei, London, UK); 258-259 Marion Brenner (Designer: Mosaic Gardens, Eugene, Oregon, USA); 260 -261 Gap Photos/Jerry Harpur (Hatfield House, Hertfordshire, UK); 272 Photolibrary.com/Japan Travel Bureau Photo

Every effort has been made to trace the copyright holders. We apologise in advance for any unintentional omissions and would be pleased to insert the appropriate acknowledgement in any subsequent publication.

Dedications

'*Dedicated to the memory of Terry Keane, a wonderful woman and friend.*
My thanks to Annette Dalton, Paula Robbins and Justine Keane who all toiled to achieve great accuracy.
My thanks to the wonderful team at Conran Octopus – Lorraine, Sybella, Claire, Jonathan – and, of course,
to Terence, who continues to be a great inspiration.' — DG

'*To Jasper, I hope this will be helpful with your passion for planting in your vast and beautiful new garden.*
And to Jonathan who, when I look out of my window, is planting away on this beautiful spring day.' — TC

First published in 2009
by Conran Octopus Limited,
2–4 Heron Quays,
London E14 4JP
part of Octopus Publishing Group
www.octopusbooks.co.uk

An Hachette Livre UK Company
www.hachettelivre.co.uk

Distributed in the US and Canada
by Octopus Books USA,
c/o Hachette Book Group USA,
237 Park Avenue, New York,
NY 10017 USA

British Library Cataloguing-in-Publication Data. A catalogue record
for this book is available from the British Library.

Consultant Editor Susan Berry

Publisher Lorraine Dickey
Managing Editor Sybella Marlow
Editor Joanna Chisholm
Proofreader Helen Ridge
Indexer Ingrid Lock

Art Direction and Design Jonathan Christie
Picture & Location Researcher Claire Hamilton

Production Manager Katherine Hockley

ISBN: 978 1 84091 529 7
Printed in China

WITHDRAWN

$60.00   12/16/09